A CLASH OF CLAWS: 1066

DARIUS MORGAN

Copyright © 2024. All rights reserved.

No part of this publication may be reproduced, distributed, or transmitted in any form or by any means, including photocopying, recording, or other electronic or mechanical methods, without the prior written permission of the author and/or publisher, except in the case of brief quotations embodied in reviews and certain other non-commercial uses permitted by copyright law.

PART ONE

THE HEIRS

WINTER

Death at Westminster

A blizzard was raging over the Westminster grounds. The fox battled through the drifting snow, his red cloak choking him as icy winds attempted to rip it from his neck. He had been gone too long. The sun had slunk into hiding in his absence and dark clouds smeared the moon's efforts to guide him back. He only realised how far off the path he'd strayed when the doors to the royal palace opened in the distance, spilling firelight into the night. A great shadow was thrown over the courtyard, though the fox could not see the creature that cast it.

"Who goes there?" the fox called as he approached, squinting through the snowstorm.

"Lord Harold, sir?" squeaked a small voice some way below him.

The fox looked down and focused on a quivering mouse.

"Mabel?" Harold asked. "What are you doing out here?"

"It's King Edward, sir," said Mabel. The diminutive mousemaid was dressed in her white nurse's apron and began rubbing her tiny paws together to quell her shivering. "He's awake."

"Awake?" Harold said breathlessly, rushing over to her side. She took a few pawsteps back and looked up at him nervously, the fire from the palace shimmering in her large black eyes. He knelt lower towards her and gave an encouraging smile. "Go on, Mabel."

"He has said many strange things, sir. But when his mind was clear, he asked for you."

Harold grappled his silver windswept whiskers, curling either end into a smile, a fashion he had maintained since they had first sprouted.

"I see. Then lead me to him right away."

Mabel nodded profusely and scampered into the warmth of the palace on all fours. Ordinarily, Harold might have scolded the mouse for her lack of decorum as he strode after her on his two back paws, as was proper. Even Harold, however, could ignore it on this occasion – the king was awake, and the future of England lay in the balance.

Harold marched after the mouse, taking care not to step on her trailing tail as he went. Her bare claws slid on the wooden floor as she soon raced ahead. The sound of Harold's steady padding followed.

"You were gone a long time, sir. I looked everywhere for you," Mabel said.

"I was praying." Harold frowned, sensing a hint of accusation. "Praying for the king."

Praying for a resolution, the fox continued silently. Had God finally answered him?

For weeks the badger king had been bound to his bedchamber in the palace, battling the daze from which the mice said he may never wake.

Edward had no cubs of his own. If he were to die, who would lead the kingdom after him?

The crown had many claimants. Too many. The fox believed there would be claws out and blood spilled before this was over.

"Please hurry, sir," called Mabel from the depths of the shadows ahead. Dim torches that adorned the walls were on their last embers. Their flames had to be at full stretch to light the palace's high ceilings.

"Yes, Mabel," replied Harold. He didn't make a habit of being ordered around by mice, but the worry in her voice was genuine and unsettling. "Do you think the king will live?"

Mabel didn't answer. Harold yanked his whiskers again and picked up the pace.

They continued the rest of the way in silence, save for the whistling of the wind as it sought for a crack in the timber walls to slip through. The structure held, the blizzard was kept at bay, and the palace's many inhabitants were kept safe from winter's clutches.

It took some minutes to navigate their way to the royal chambers. Many guests had remained in the vast palace since Edward had taken a turn for the worse on Christmas Day. Others had arrived later when news broke of his sickness. Now, the royal palace was awash with well-wishers, all of whom were no doubt wishing for an outcome that would serve them best.

In the Great Hall, two spitting fires were lit on either side, and the air was thick with smoke. Even at such a late hour, the palace was alive with bustling creatures. The king's table remained empty, but swathes of creatures were still feasting. Harold and Mabel were watched with poorly disguised interest as they came through. What was the high-ranking fox, the Earl of Wessex, doing with one of the king's personal mousemaids? Silence befell the hall as all eyes turned to them. One squirrel stared open mouthed, a pawful of food suspended in mid-air.

"Keep walking, Mabel," muttered Harold to the mouse. Mabel nodded, her nose twitching.

Harold's two youngest brothers waved their paws for him to join them, but Harold declined with a shake of the head.

"Any news from the king?" called Lord Edwin, the tall and dashingly handsome young hare. His high voice cut through the silence as he spied Mabel from the corner of his eye.

"Not yet," answered Harold with a forced smile. The news that the king was awake would soon spread like wildfire; there was no reason to light it just yet.

They left the hall to whisper and speculate and made their way to the royal chamber. An armour-clad wolf was keeping watch outside Edward's door. He had white-grey fur and stood taller than Harold. He watched the mouse and fox approach through a single blue eye. The other socket was empty and scarred, leaving him half blind and disfigured. Harold shook his paw and winced at the wolf's powerful grip.

"Harold." The wolf nodded with a deep growl. Harold had fought side by side with him in Wales two years previously, and so knew not to be offended by the wolf's intimidating nature. Mabel, meanwhile, hid behind Harold's leg, not daring to make eye contact with the formidable soldier.

"Good evening, Wulfric," Harold replied. "How is the king?"

Wulfric was the leader of the King's Wolves, an army of battle-hardened warriors and sworn protectors of the king. Harold knew of no greater soldier in England, or perhaps even Europe, and had never seen his grisly face with such a look of worry.

"They won't let me in to see him," Wulfric said, trying to keep any trace of emotion from his voice. "But from what I can hear..."

Wulfric didn't need to finish his sentence for Harold to understand. There was a moment of grave silence before Wulfric swung open the door to let Harold through. Mabel followed by darting in between the wolf's open legs.

"Lord Harold!" a voice cried the second he passed the threshold. A bumbling mole waddled over to him. The mole ran one paw along the side of the wall to help him navigate his way across the room. The burden of molesight meant Harold was nothing more than an orange blur. He stumbled his way over, crashing into and knocking down several chairs and trinkets in his path. "That is you, isn't it, Harold?"

"It is, Stigand. Follow my voice," Harold said as warmly as he could manage. The mole was the Archbishop of Canterbury, and one of the most peculiar creatures Harold had ever met. He had jet black, velvety fur, with a long snout and a pink button nose. He was drowning in a purple and gold set of ill-fitting robes with just his small head poking out from the top of them.

"There you are." Stigand beamed, grasping hold of Harold's paw. Harold squirmed a little at the mole's touch; he always found the paws of their kind unsettling. They had six fingers, each with long nails meant for digging. Most moles were comfortable in the dirt and were often employed in construction or farmwork, but Stigand wasn't like his brethren and was contrarily obsessed with cleanliness. Not for the first time, Harold marvelled at how the mole had risen to the highest office in the church against the odds.

"The king has sent for me," said Harold. He daren't ask Stigand a question, for the old mole was renowned for his long speeches and insistent preaching.

"Yes, yes, the king is quite sick; the mice tell me he will not make it through the night." Stigand shook his head.

Harold stole a glance down at Mabel but found she had already left his side. At the far end of the room Harold recognised the king's silhouette, lying on a four-poster bed. An elegant vixen dressed in white was massaging the old badger's hind paws.

"...of course, I have been praying night and day for the king to come back to his senses, but it seems his soul is already on its way to heaven."

"Stigand?" prompted Harold, though the mole didn't hear him over his own ramblings. Stigand's molesight was so bad the fox was sure he could just slip by and leave the frail mole talking to the wall.

"He clings to life now with a feeble grip, and I pray now that he lets go and follows the path God has laid out for him. It is said that-"

"Stigand?"

"My lord?" Stigand looked up at him slightly off centre.

"May I see him now?"

"Of course, of course, I merely hoped-"

"Thank you," Harold said, briskly stepping past him before Stigand could continue. He approached the bed and got a proper look at the king.

Edward had never been a warrior. He was religious and forgiving to the point of fault, but Harold had always sensed strength in him. He was large and slender, with thick, bold strokes of black and white fur running across his body. The fox hadn't always agreed with him, but had always respected him, and it hurt to see the badger reduced to the sickly creature he was now.

A dozen or so of Edward's personal mousemaids were running along the bed covers, tending to his every need. He had become thin and weak, and though he slept, his eyelids fluttered and there seemed to be a look of pain across his face. The crown that lay atop his head was lopsided and teetering on the edge of falling off.

The teary-eyed vixen who knelt beside him rose and gave Harold a hug.

"Edith." Harold embraced his sister, the queen. He stroked the top of her head, which she nuzzled into his chest.

"He's going to die," Edith said simply, her voice muffled.

Having seen the king with his own eyes, Harold knew she was not wrong. Edith and Edward's marriage had not been one of love, and he knew the king was more of a father to her than a husband. After all, there was an age difference of over twenty years.

On the bed Edward suddenly stirred, muttering a string of jumbled words.

"He keeps doing this," said Edith. "We just can't understand him. Sometimes we make out a word, a sentence, but nothing mor-"

"Doomed!" Edward croaked, his voice suddenly loud and clear. Harold shared a disturbed look with Edith.

"What's doomed, Edward?" asked Edith softly.

It didn't appear the badger heard his vixen wife's voice, though he continued to speak in a state of great distress. "The devil approaches!"

Edith gasped and pressed a paw to her mouth.

"Doom! England!" Edward yelled. "Consumed by fire and steel!"

The badger's voice faded again back into incoherent, rambling whispers.

"You see?" said Stigand, coming to stand between the two foxes. He bumped into the bed and nearly fell atop of it. The mole seemed unfazed by the badger's words. "He's quite delirious."

It hurt to see the king in such a state, but Harold could not turn away. Edward rolled around, getting tangled in his bedsheets. The mice were forced to jump off the bed to not get crushed. Mabel managed to leap to the pillow. She cupped one ear to the king's mouth, hoping to understand her master's nonsense.

"What will England do now?" speculated Stigand, heaving an exaggerated sigh. "Who shall be king in his place? Without an heir-"

"Not one more word, mole," said Harold sharply, unable to hide his irritation. "Do not discuss these matters over the king's bed whilst he still breathes and fights for this life."

"Of-of course," bumbled Stigand. Harold was grateful when the mole fell uncharacteristically silent, though he couldn't deny Stigand's worries were warranted.

"Lord Harold, sir," squeaked Mabel. "The king asks for you."

King Edward had not opened his eyes, though he seemed to have grown still.

Harold shared a look with Edith, who nodded encouragingly. He knelt beside the great badger's head. "Your Majesty, King Edward. I am with you."

A single striped paw emerged from the bedsheets. Harold took hold of it, noticing how small and weak it now seemed.

"Harold," wheezed the king. Both Edith and Stigand leaned in but could not make out the words. Only Mabel and Harold could hear him. "My time has come, my friend. God's path for me is clear. I will take it now with safe knowledge that you are here. I know you will look after Edith. I know you will look after our people, our England. You have ruled by my side, and now..." Edward paused, his breathing heavy and laboured. He managed to open one eye. "You must rule alone."

Harold felt his heart pounding so loudly he was sure it would echo down the halls of the royal palace.

"You will be a strong ruler...a strong king..." Edward's eye closed and Harold felt his paw go limp. "It is God's plan...it is..."

The last spark of life slipped from the old badger. His head rolled to one side, and his paw fell from Harold's grasp to the side of the bed. The crown slid off his head, landing with a shrill *ting!* on the floor. Mabel and the other mice scrambled across the body, but there was nothing they could do. King Edward was dead.

Behind Harold, Edith gave out a cry and began ushering the mice from Edward's body, and Stigand at once broke into prayer, "Eternal rest grant unto him, O Lord, and let perpetual light shine upon him. May he rest in peace..."

All of this motion was but a blur to Harold, who had not left his kneeling position by the bed. His thoughts were swirling faster than the blizzard that seethed outside the palace's walls, and only some minutes later did he snap out of his daze. Edith's paw took hold of his furry cheek.

"What did he say to you, brother?" she asked.

"He said..." Harold found the words get lodged in his throat. "He said I am to be king."

Edith's paw slipped from his face. Her teary eyes were suddenly wide with disbelief. "King?"

"Yes," said Harold simply.

"If this is true, King Edward has bestowed upon England one last gift," Stigand announced grandly, puffing his chest out. "Though I confess, I did not hear his words..."

"Nor I." Edith shook her head.

"I heard the king," peeped Mabel. She trembled as all eyes shifted towards her. "He said Lord Harold will be a *strong king*."

"This is most excellent news," beamed Stigand, a great smile spreading across his fuzzy face. "The king has chosen his heir; the Witan must be summoned at once!"

"The meeting can wait until morning," Harold chastised the mole.

Stigand bowed his head and nodded, as if suddenly remembering that the king's death was a sombre moment.

"The Witan will decide who is to be king..." Harold's head was still buzzing with too many thoughts, and he nearly disappeared into his mind once again. "If I might have a moment alone with the king...Mabel would you please escort the queen back to her room?"

"I am no longer queen," said Edith blankly.

"Edith-" started Harold but was cut off by his sister giving him a kiss on the whiskers. She dutifully followed Mabel and the rest of

Edward's mousemaids from the room, leaving Harold alone with the mole.

"I trust you will be able to pass on the news of the king's passing?"

"I will..." Stigand paused, searching for the right word to address Harold with. If the Witan could agree with King Edward's final wishes, then the title of "Earl of Wessex" would be replaced with the far greater "King of England". In the end, Stigand didn't take any risks, and settled with a stunted half bow before trundling out of the room.

Once the door closed, Harold let out a long breath as the weight of King Edward's words still settled. The fox had been the king's trusted companion for many years. He had carried out many of the duties Edward did not have any interest in. His family had no royal blood, and he had no right to the crown, yet there was no creature finer prepared for the role.

As a younger fox, Harold remembered having such ambitions as to be king of England, though it seemed quite ridiculous and out of reach. But now that the task was within his grasp, the thought strangled his insides with icy paws, and he wished for a moment that he was still walking alone in the snow.

As king, every creature would be Harold's to protect. England would be his to protect, and Harold knew of one creature that would surely come for it.

The lynx of Normandy across the sea was always prowling.

Harold reassembled Edward's tangled bedsheets over his body and marked the moment with a prayer for the king. In death, the badger looked smaller and insignificant, his power stripped away in an instant. Harold picked up the fallen crown from the floor and went to rest it back on Edward's head.

As he did so, Harold saw his own reflection in the crown's surface, monstrously distorted by the curve of the gold. A spark of excitement tickled him for the briefest of moments, and without thinking, he brought the crown up to sit in between his own ears.

No sooner had the gold touched his fur when the door to the chambers swung open with a crash. Harold jumped and dropped the crown, cutting his right paw on one of its jagged points.

"Harold?" called Stigand at the door as the crown landed on the floor with another *ting!*

Harold quickly grabbed the crown and stuffed it back on Edward's head before turning to the mole. Stigand's molesight meant that he hadn't seen a thing, but the young hare, Lord Edwin, stood beside him and was watching Harold with a curious expression.

"Lord Edwin has come to say a prayer for King Edward," said Stigand.

"Of course," said Harold. He strode from the room, squeezing in between the mole and the hare, his right paw bleeding a trail of red droplets all the way to his own bed chambers.

WINTER

The Witan

The weather was clear by morning. Sunlight bounced off the frozen snow, nearly blinding Harold's tired eyes. Despite the surprise appearance of the sun, the January morning maintained its chill and Harold's breath stained the air as he crossed the open courtyard.

The fox had been wandering around the grounds for many hours, replaying Edward's last words to him over and over in his head. He had never asked to be king, but now he could not put the notion away. Now his and England's fate lay in the paws of the Witan, and he could not know for sure what they would decide.

A gust of wind washed over him as a winged shadow raced across the snow. Harold looked up, squinting through the brightness. As the bird disappeared over the edge of the Westminster Cathedral, which had been newly erected under King Edward's orders, he caught a glimpse of peculiar brown feathers and a pair of yellow talons.

At the same time, Edith was also crossing the courtyard, followed by Mabel and the rest of Edward's shivering mousemaids. All the mice created a winding chain across the snow as they held paws to stop them from slipping over.

"Good morning, brother," said Edith, appearing beside him.

"Morning," said Harold, not really listening. He continued to scan the skies.

"What are you looking for?"

"That," said Harold, pointing as the large bird reappeared and began circling the courtyard some hundred feet in the air. A cloud of blackbirds dodged out of the way of its great wingspan. There was no stopping gossiping beaks discussing the death of the king, but something told Harold this creature did not come from England. "I don't trust what I don't recognise."

"Surely there's more on your mind than birds, Harold."

Harold wrested his eyes from it and smiled. "Indeed."

Edith half-heartedly returned the smile. She was dressed in black and had already spent much of the morning preparing King Edward's funeral. Harold had been so wrapped up in his own thoughts he had barely spared one for her.

"Once the Witan have made their decision, we will all be there for the burial, Edith. I promise."

"Tostig should be here," said Edith with a sad, glazed look.

Harold felt sick at the mention of his younger brother's name. Tostig and Edith had always been close, as had Tostig and King Edward himself. "You know I had no choice. After everything he had done..."

"When it's family, there's always a choice," she replied.

Harold had no response as a familiar feeling of guilt upset his stomach. Some creatures had started to name Tostig the "Stray Fox" since his exile a few months earlier, and it was Harold who'd sent him away.

"Good luck today," Edith said before trudging away, mice in tow. Harold growled to himself, annoyed at her for bringing Tostig's name up. The hard snow crunched underpaw as he stomped across the courtyard. Now was not the time to think on such things – the Witan was waiting.

The Great Hall was shaking. Harold slipped through the boisterous crowd unnoticed as paws were brandished in faces and voices raised. The fox might have been strolling through the Thames markets as creatures shouted over one another to be heard.

The tables and benches used for feasting had been dragged away. Three circles of seats had been arranged in their place, with the innermost circle being reserved for the six earls of the kingdom, and both the archbishops of Canterbury and York.

Harold managed to worm his way through creatures and take his seat in the front row, as the Earl of Wessex. The noise of the hall dropped as he sat down, with many creatures angling to get a look at him. Harold wondered how much they knew already.

Stigand was already in his seat, dressed now in shining white robes, talking cheerily with the wise old beaver, Ealdred, the Archbishop of York. Ealdred was much the opposite of Stigand in every way, preferring silence and thought to the mole's quick mouth. Harold smiled inwardly at Ealdred's bitter face - listening to Stigand was tiring work.

Of the six earls (whose power was only trumped by that of the king), four were present, and two were still missing.

Earl Waltheof, the teenage otter, sat quietly on his chair, not talking to anyone. His face was light, fluffy, clean and innocent looking, none of which helped the poor creature in asserting himself in matters of politics.

Two of Harold's brothers were earls themselves. The two foxes were engaged in a spirited debate about something. Lord Gyrth was as rigid as the chair he sat on. Accustomed to barking orders, his voice boomed throughout the hall. He had a square face with neatly clipped whiskers and sharp, slanted eyes. Harold's youngest brother, Lord Leofwine, was much thinner and smaller than Gyrth, and seemed to be cursed with an affliction that meant he could never sit still. He squirmed on his chair, laughing and teasing his brother in the way that only Leofwine seemed to be able to get away with.

The presence of his brothers calmed Harold; they would stand with him no matter what. Harold glanced at the empty chair of the "Earl of Northumbria", which until recently would have been held by Harold's other brother.

Edith was right, Harold thought. *Tostig should be here.*

"Is everyone present?" asked Stigand to the hall.

Ealdred next to him shook his head in disbelief. There were still two empty seats in the first circle.

"We are waiting on the hares," rumbled Gyrth.

"Oh, really?" wondered Stigand, looking blankly over at the empty seats.

The hare brothers still hadn't arrived twenty minutes later. Murmurs of starting without them began in the back benches. Harold felt his tail wrap itself around his leg, as it did when he was nervous. Every passing minute was more painful than the last.

Eventually, and with great dramatic effect, the doors of the Great Hall swung open to reveal their late arriving members. Everyone swivelled around to watch as Lord Edwin sauntered in with a large smile.

"Apologies, my friends," Edwin said in his grating, high voice.

Behind him came his brother, Lord Morcar, who had none of Edwin's grace. One of his hind legs twisted inwards painfully, disfigured since birth. As such, Morcar had always lacked the confident spring often found in a hare's step. His fur was unkempt and patchy, and he had a pair of flat, sideways pointing ears that sloped below his chin. His small facial features were too close together, cursing him with a sort of crumpled look of constant misery.

Lastly, a third latecomer arrived, an unexpected creature indeed.

A small, bashful badger shuffled after the two hares. Edgar wasn't yet fully grown and didn't have the commanding presence his great-uncle King Edward had been blessed with. Instead, he walked with his snout to the floor, not making eye contact with the many creatures who had turned his way.

Harold had not anticipated Edgar to be involved in the Witan. The hares must have gathered him from London.

Ealdred rose onto his hind paws.

"We were not exthpecting you," he said to the royal badger. Ealdred's two front teeth were great orange chunks that barely fit in his mouth, unfortunately condemning him to a terrible lisp that many beavers struggled with. "Pleath, thit down on my theat."

Edgar looked a little confused but eventually discerned that the beaver was generously offering up his own chair to sit on. A rat servant hastily brought up a stool for Ealdred to take in turn.

The hares also took their seats; Lord Edwin next to Stigand, and Lord Morcar next to Harold, where his brother Tostig would ordinarily have been. When the Northumbrians had rebelled against Tostig, they had demanded Morcar replace him as earl. To save lives, it was Harold who had persuaded King Edward to give in to the Northumbrians' demands.

"Now that we are all here, we thall begin," said Ealdred, making his voice heard all around the hall as he waddled around the centre of the now fully gathered Witan.

"Latht night, the good King Edward pathed away. We, the Witan, have therved him well for many yearth. Now, we have to honour hith memory by choothing our nexth king."

Harold's tail was so tightly wrapped around his leg that he felt it start to go numb. He began to tap his chest in a steady beat to calm his drum rolling heart. Lord Morcar watched him with a disguised sideways glance.

Kings don't get nervous, the fox reminded himself.

"There are many who could be chothen. Two of whom are acroth the thea..."

Harold noticed his mischievous brother, Leofwine, trying not to laugh at the elderly archbishop's struggles with his speech. Many creatures shared confused glances as they tried to understand the beaver.

"There ith King Thweyn of Denmark," said Ealdred, "and Hardrada from Norway."

There was a rumble of dissent through the Witan. Both King Sweyn and King Harald 'Hardrada' had strong claims to the English crown due to their ties with the Viking stag, King Cnut. Cnut had conquered England just fifty years earlier, and if his son, Harthacanute, had not died suddenly at a wedding, then the stags would still rule.

Despite Sweyn and Hardrada's valid rights to rule, however, the Witan were passionate in their rejection of the two foreign creatures.

"Savages!" someone called from the back benches. This was met with many claps and cheers.

"Hardrada is a fierce beast," Gyrth said seriously. "Sweyn too. They would be difficult opponents to fend off in battle."

"Have they stopped fighting each other?" Edwin laughed, leaning back confidently in his chair. The claws of Denmark and Norway had been at each other's throats for many years.

"We are England!" shouted Stigand a little too loudly. "We should be ruled by the English."

"Hardrada is a creature from the mountains. A brutal thing, who has conquered many enemies and gathered much gold. We should not dismiss him lightly," Gyrth countered.

"I will never submit to a foreign ruler," declared Edwin, looking upon Gyrth with disgust. There were roars of agreement for the hare. "If they ever land on our shores, I will lead the charge on the battlefield myself!"

"I agree with Lord Edwin," Ealdred said. "England hath to find a ruler from England. We will never again thurrender to Viking rule."

Gyrth said nothing, remaining as calm and unreadable as ever.

"It seems to me that we have the perfect candidate in front of our eyes." Lord Edwin rose to his paws and took centre stage. "King Edward fathered no cubs, it is true. But we do have a creature of England who shares the black and white stripes of Edward and Alfred the Great before him! I present Edgar to be king."

The young badger was still looking at the floor. He clasped his paws together to stop them from trembling.

"If it is the will of the Witan, I shall be honoured to be your king," Edgar mumbled.

"With the right guidance, Edgar will be a great king," said Edwin with all the confidence the badger lacked.

Harold had never liked Edwin, but could see his cunning. It seemed it wouldn't be difficult to manipulate the young Edgar. If the badger was made king, the hares would be his leading earls in the country.

"I suppose *your* guidance would be considered the 'right guidance', Lord Edwin?" Gyrth said, lip curling knowingly.

"It would." Edwin gave him a sweet smile.

"Edgar ith of the royal line..." Ealdred nodded.

"My fellow creatures, there is no finer choice. My earldom of Mercia stands with Edgar, and now I ask you to stand with us," said Edwin.

It was no surprise that his brother Morcar stood. Harold imagined the whole thing had been planned in advance.

"Northumbria stands with Edgar," said Morcar gruffly.

"Huntingdon too," said the otter, Waltheof. "I stand with Edgar."

There was much spirited support from the creatures sitting in the second and third circles. Three of the earls had sided with the badger, but would it be enough? Even with Tostig exiled, the fox brothers still held enough power to combat them.

"Edgar is indeed a good creature worthy of King Edward's family name," said Stigand. "However, the cub is not a leader, and if the king really believed him worthy, he would not have named Lord Harold as his heir last night."

Audible gasps rippled throughout the Witan. Harold's brothers were both shocked and a little affronted they had to hear the news from the mole's mouth. Stigand was beside himself, relishing being the one to make such a dramatic announcement. Lord Edwin's grin had lost its gleam.

"You have kept quiet thince the beginning, Lord Harold. Ith thith true?" asked Ealdred, raking Harold with a penetrating gaze.

The whole of the Witan held its breath before Harold spoke.

"It is."

"Then it is settled!" cried Leofwine. "We must honour the good king's wishes."

"Quite convenient, fox," snarled Edwin, his pretty face contorted in bitterness. "How do we know this to be true?"

"Lord Harold was King Edward's choice," said Stigand. "I heard him myself."

This was not, strictly speaking, true, Harold remembered. The ease with which the lie came from the Holy mole was unsettling.

"Lord Harold has been nothing but an honourable servant to England in all his years," continued Stigand. "He defeated Gruffyd the Welsh goat in battle. He supported King Edward in every possible manner, and he even exiled his brother Lord Tostig for the good of the realm."

Harold winced at Tostig's name, but many voices of the Witan were now shouting in his favour.

"There is no royal blood in his veins," Edwin argued.

"It did not matter to King Edward; it should not matter to us."

Edwin seemed out of ideas. He looked to Morcar, but the ugly hare had nothing to offer but a frown.

Waltheof the otter announced that he was retracting his vote for Edgar and placing it with Harold. The back benches began chanting his name.

"Me too," said Edgar quietly. Ealdred held a paw up for the Witan to be silent so they could hear the badger speak. "Lord Harold is a brave creature. I stand with Harold to be king."

With Edgar, the last viable opposition, conceding defeat, the deal was all but settled. Edwin and Morcar were beaten and reluctantly gave their own nods of approval.

Leofwine was fidgeting on his chair harder than ever, as if desperate to break out into ecstatic dance, and even Gyrth couldn't hold back his delight at his older brother's success. But Harold could not share in his brothers' joy just yet. There was one last thing he needed to do.

Harold stood up. Something about his stoic face broke through the excited din of the Witan. All creatures fell silent to listen to him.

"My fellow lords and friends, your support is most welcome. I am willing to accept this..." Harold searched for the right word.

Burden?

"...honour. I will do everything in my power to rule England with its noble creatures in mind. However, before we agree, I do feel obliged to tell you a story.

"Two years ago, I was caught in a storm when sailing the Channel. Cruel winds blew me south. I ended up in the cloven hooves of the boar, Count Guy of Ponthieu. A most greedy, nasty creature was he. I thought it might be my doom.

"It was Duke William of Normandy who secured my release. Afterwards, I spent a great deal of time with the lynx. I even fought with him against the Bretons. William is a ferocious ruler, who has dealt with threats and enemies and assassins since being just a kitten. When I was in his company, he told me something. He told me that he expects the crown of England to come to him."

"What folly is this?" Stigand yelped. "He has no claim!"

"Hith great-aunt Emma wath wife to two Englith kingth," Ealdred pointed out.

"This small link to the crown is not why he expects it. He expects it because...because King Edward supposedly made him his heir to the throne."

Every ear of the Witan leaned closer. Harold waited for the whispers to fade before continuing.

"King Edward had spent many years in Normandy, and no doubt liked Duke William very much. I must confess, I liked the lynx too. I never asked the king whether he had made such a promise to William. It never seemed the right time..." Harold shook his head. "With this new information, I am at the mercy of the Witan's decision. On Edward's deathbed he named me as king, but many years ago, he told William the very same thing."

The Great Hall erupted into noise as creatures discussed this new crucial piece of information. Harold retook his seat, wondering if he had done the right thing. He could have chosen to not tell the Witan anything at all about what William had told him. It would have been dishonourable not to bring William's claim to the Witan's attention, though there was one vital piece of the story that the fox did not reveal. Harold had made a simple promise to the lynx, a promise that should never have been made.

Arguments raged for several minutes as creatures debated which of King Edward's heirs was his real choice – his old friend across the waves, the one he had chosen fifteen years ago? Or his closest English advisor, who he had chosen in a daze on his deathbed the night before?

In the end, having so aggressively denied the idea of a foreign ruler earlier, even Edwin had to declare allegiance to Harold over Duke William.

"By bringing this to our attention, it has proven you are an honourable creature indeed," said Stigand to Harold. "Only a king would show such fair and humble character."

"Lord Harold, you have been chothen by the Witan. God willing, you thall be king!" Ealdred cried.

"Vivat!" the creatures of the Witan shouted in celebratory custom, cheering to long life for the new king.

The rest of the day was much of a blur to the fox, with fear and delight struggling for control of his wary mind. They buried King Edward that morning and crowned Harold in the afternoon.

One thing Harold knew for sure was that the warrior duke of Normandy had expected to be king of England for a long time and would deem it little less than robbery. Harold was so occupied with thoughts of the lynx that he didn't see that the winged shadow he had noticed that morning still circled Westminster.

Whilst birds of all kinds had excitedly flown off into the horizon with the news of King Edward's death, instinct had stayed the wings of this particular golden eagle. She was duly rewarded when she saw the fox emerge from the cathedral with the crown firmly upon his head.

Only after that did the eagle finally soar south, over the snow-capped hills of England, across the stormy, boisterous waves of the Channel towards Normandy, where her master was waiting.

WINTER

The Lynx of Normandy

Duke William loved chess. Well, most of all, he loved fighting battles, constructing clever strategies, and outsmarting his opponents. When the lynx wasn't engaged in a real war, chess was the best substitute he could find.

He examined the chessboard, stroking the white fur that drooped from his chin. Struck with sudden inspiration, he moved his knight deep into enemy territory. It was a risky move. He turned his yellow eyes away from the board and stared into the roaring fire that was burning beside him.

William was playing in his private quarters in his castle at Caen. As was typical for this time of year, William's well-groomed fur was a shade of silver-grey. When the temperature rose in the summer, this would become a red-brown. One thing that never changed was the many black spots that were all over his body. A lynx could be judged on the strength of his spots, and William's were as dark as you would ever see.

His half-brother, Odo, sat across the table and considered his move. They shared the same mother, a common wildcat known as Herleva when she was alive. Odo's father had been a bobcat, a smaller, though no less fierce, species of lynx. William's father, however, traced back to the first Duke of Normandy, the Viking predator, Rollo. William was as formidable a creature as his ancestor and almost double the stature of his brother Odo who resembled the size of an average fox.

Despite the difference in size, Odo was still a respected and feared creature in Normandy. He was a well-regarded bishop though was as much a lover of war as he was of God. Much of his fur coat had turned pure white in the harsh winter they were having, making the battle scars that covered his face stand out all the more. Odo was also the only one who could beat William at chess, and William cherished their games together.

As Bishop Odo pondered his move, William's youngest son (also called William, though they called him "Rufus") slipped free of his mother's clutches and ran away on all four paws. The little kitten had a ginger fur coat which peculiarly never made the change between the summer's red to the winter's white. William's eldest son, Robert, whose lynx spots were noticeably faint, watched the game of chess without interest, whilst Matilda, William's beloved wildcat wife, playfully chased young Rufus around the room.

"Quiet, Rufus," William barked. Little Rufus knew better than to get on his father's wrong side when he was playing chess, so allowed his mother to put him back on her lap.

"It's ok," said Bishop Odo, moving a pawn to attack William's knight.

This was exactly what William hoped he would do. He retreated his knight into the path of Odo's queen.

Odo, sensing his own victory, fell for the bait. He took William's knight with his queen.

"Ha!" William cried, moving his bishop to attack and nearly upending the board in his excitement. The bishop was aiming right for Odo's queen, and behind it the king was exposed. Odo was forbidden from moving the queen out of the way – she couldn't be saved, the game was as good as done. Odo stared at the board, his shifty eyes twitching between all of the remaining pieces, searching for a way out that wasn't there.

Eventually he sighed and extended his paw.

"I resign."

William shook it with vigour as young Rufus cheered and again slipped free of his mother. William watched him run about fondly, though he certainly wouldn't have allowed it had he been the one to lose.

"Is it over?" groaned Robert.

William ignored his oldest son. "Defeated by a bishop, Odo? How ironic..."

Odo was nearly as sore a loser as William was. "That damned knight, I should have known you were up to something. A feigned retreat...a good move, brother."

"Never trust a horse." William winked. For many there was still an age-old distrust of horses, though William had always been interested in their kind. They were magnificent beasts, wild and terrifying and beautiful. They spoke in an ancient language and kept to themselves. Only in Normandy were creatures able to tame them, a fact William was proud of. The lynx considered his horse a friend, and they had fought many battles together.

The game was over. They had started shortly after luncheon but now darkness was falling. Beyond the warmth of William's castle's walls the fields of Normandy were empty and frozen solid. Farmers counted down the days until spring when they could replant their crops. Until then they struggled for warmth in whatever primitive huts they could afford.

With the lands and meadows abandoned, Peter the English pigeon barely saw another creature whilst flying into Normandy. He had flown so fast that all his friends had decided to leave him to it, choosing to pass the news of King Edward's death to some creature not so far away.

Peter had followed the waters of the English Channel as it spilled into Caen. He was thoroughly exhausted. He had departed at dawn, but now the belly of the clouds above had turned pink from the glare of the setting sun. At long last he saw the shadow of William's castle and was given a new burst of energy at the thought of what he might receive in return for the deliverance of such speedy news.

"...and the knight, the horsey looking one, can move in an L shape," William was saying to little Rufus, showing his youngest how the chess piece moved. "And this one-"

William was interrupted by a beleaguered beating of a beak at the wooden shutters.

Odo moved over to the sound and thrust them open. The shutter knocked Peter into the air with a yelp. Robert guffawed loudly at the pigeon's misfortune.

"Bring it in," ordered William.

Odo stuck out a lethally quick paw and grabbed Peter around his brittle little neck. Some of the pigeon's loosest feathers broke free and began the slow descent to the ground as Odo dragged him inside.

"Come on, then, what have you got for me?" William asked the pigeon. "It better be good for disturbing my family time."

"Speak, bird," Odo growled when the pigeon only stared blankly.

"Erm," Peter gulped as the lynxes spoke entirely in French. "The king has died," he said in his native English.

William didn't understand a word out of Peter's beak and felt his notoriously short temper flare up.

"You had better start making sense, for your sake," he snarled.

The pigeon didn't need to speak French to sense the giant lynx's fury. He glanced at the open shutters hopefully, though would he be able to escape before the bobcat grabbed him again?

"The...king...is...dead..." Peter said very slowly.

There was a moment of deadly silence as William regarded him. Eventually, the lynx seemed to conclude that the pigeon was mocking him. He hurled one of the chess pieces at his head which Peter narrowly dodged. The piece went straight out of the shutters, only succeeding in making the duke even angrier.

"Enough!"

Peter made a show of flapping his wings, but it didn't help. Odo grabbed him around the middle with both paws.

"Who are you?" William shouted. "Tell me or I'll start taking feathers!"

"Stop it, William, you're scaring the little ones!" his wife Matilda snapped.

Little Rufus hugged his mother's leg, though the look of boredom had finally left Robert's face.

"Please, please, the king is dead. King Edward is dead!" Peter whined.

"Edward?" William said. He recognised the name at least. "Put him down."

Odo dropped him to the floor.

"Yes! Yes!" Peter shouted. "Edward is..." the pigeon said, demonstrating his words by running the tip of his wing across his neck and closing his eyes, "dead."

William understood the pigeon at last.

The badger is dead, William thought to himself. *It is time.*

"Robert, take your brother to bed."

"What? No! What's happening?" Robert said, standing up to him. Robert was far shorter than his father; he didn't have the characteristic long, graceful legs of a lynx and William always teased him for it.

"Do as I say, *Curthose*," said William, the nickname French for 'short pants'.

Robert huffed and dragged his little brother Rufus from the room.

"What is it, dearest?" asked Matilda, caressing her husband's fur. Only she had the touch to calm his most ferocious of tempers.

"It seems King Edward has at long last left us." He turned to Peter and picked him up. "*Merci*." He tossed the pigeon through the shutters and slammed them shut.

Peter was grateful to be out of the lynx's clutches, though scowled at not having received any reward for his troubles. He wondered what he would tell the rest of the flock. Pigeons had a penchant for exaggeration and rarely let the truth get in the way of a good story. Peter couldn't manage the flight home that night so had plenty of time to meddle with the facts and prepare the tale that he intended to name "My Brush With Death" or perhaps the punchier title of "Claws Out!".

He fixed his beak in the loose direction of home whilst hunting for a decent shelter and place to rest. Distracted by the search, he nearly missed the approach of an enormous pair of wings that were flapping in the other direction.

"Watch it!" Peter cried, only just managing to dive beneath them.

The golden eagle paid Peter no attention and continued thundering towards William's castle with a speed and grace that a humble pigeon could only dream of.

Inside his quarters William had the finest wines from the hills of Argences brought to him. Two ferrets and a stoat from the duke's retinue were needed to roll the barrel up the stairway. The first rat who attempted it had let the barrel slip and was subsequently flattened.

William, Odo, and Matilda raised a glass to the fallen English king.

"Edward," said William, downing his drink in one and immediately reaching for another.

"I am sorry, I know you were close," Matilda said.

"Thank you, dear," said William, kissing his diminutive wildcat wife on the top of her tabby-coloured head.

What Matilda said was true; he and the badger king had shared an understanding of each other once. But that was a long time ago, and William could not suppress the feeling of glee at the old creature's demise.

Odo led a hasty prayer in honour of the badger though William was eager to race through it.

"Whilst this news is tragic, I cannot spare any wasted time in mourning," declared William. "My preoccupation is now with my own journey. I must sail to England. I wish to be crowned at once."

Matilda gave him a hug and looked up at him, "You will be a great king."

Out of the corner of William's eye he noticed Odo shake his head.

"What is it?" William barked.

"Do you really think it will be that easy?"

"Edward made me heir, brother. Is there anything easier?" He shrugged.

"And when was the last time you spoke to the badger?"

William ground his feline fangs together. "I stayed with Edward when he had those dastardly foxes thrown from his court-"

"Edward's quarrel was with the father, not the sons. They were allowed back."

"Yes," William conceded bitterly. "Edward always was too forgiving."

"Even when Edward was alive, the foxes controlled England. Nearly all the earldoms are in the paws of one brother or another."

"What is it you are trying to say, Odo? The oldest fox has already sworn allegiance to me-"

For the second time William was interrupted by a beak at the shutters. This time Matilda reached up and opened them.

"Agnès!" William smiled at the golden eagle. He gestured his old friend inside and prepared a goblet of wine for her to drink from.

"Duke William." Agnès bowed her great head. Her voice was frictionless, intangible, and as resonant as a whale coming to the surface of the sea. The lynx offered her the goblet, but she declined. Agnès was a stickler for etiquette and formalities and would not soften until her message was delivered.

"It seems you are slowing down in your old age, *mon amie!*" William said cheerily. "An English pigeon beat you here. We already know of King Edward."

"This news is already outdated," said Agnès haughtily. The suggestion that a common pigeon could fly the Channel faster was absurd. "There is more."

"More? Was he murdered?" William's yellow eyes were wide.

"Before the English laid the badger to rest, they convened to discuss his succession.

Lord Harold of Wessex was chosen to be king. He was crowned a few hours ago."

"It-it can't be," stuttered William, disbelief suspending anger for just a moment. "Harold swore his allegiance to me!"

"*Mon amour...*" Matilda said, feeling her husband's grief.

"He's a liar then, those foxes want nothing but power." Odo scowled.

"Not just a liar but an oathbreaker!" William yelled. He hurled the chessboard across the room. It shattered against the wall and sent a volley of splinters back at him. "I had him swear on holy relics - on sacred bones! He will feel God's wrath for such a betrayal... and my own."

William collapsed on to all four paws, a position he hadn't been in since being a kitten. It was no behaviour of a duke, but he could not fight the almighty sense of loss.

"Leave me," William muttered.

"*Mon-*" Matilda started.

"LEAVE ME!" he roared.

Matilda and Odo bumbled into each other in their haste to escape the lynx's wrath. Agnès bowed once more before taking flight through the shutters.

William watched the eagle grow small in the faint shafts of moonlight that slipped through the cracks of the thick cloud ceiling. He closed his eyes and imagined what was happening in England at that very moment. He imagined the fox sipping wine, lounging over the throne he had stolen, laughing with his brothers at the success of their treachery.

Just about every creature in Normandy knew that their duke was in line for the English throne. What would they say now that it had been taken from him? If the kingdom of England could be taken from him with such impudence, what was to stop some creature taking Normandy too?

William knew he could only rule so long as the Normans feared him. The fox could not go unpunished for causing such an embarrassment. William knew what must come next. There was no other choice. He would have to take England by force.

WINTER

The Letter

Weeks had passed since King Harold's coronation. He still hadn't adjusted to the extra weight of the crown atop his head. It threw his balance off considerably and with every step he took he felt like it was about to slide right off. It had been designed to sit on King Edward's flat head and looked simply strange on Harold. The badger king had never had to contend with a fox's pointy ears (Harold could only fit one under the crown at one time with the other sticking out). He longed for nothing more than to take the damned thing off.

Harold hadn't stopped since the enthronement. His first duties as king took him north as he joined the hares, Edwin and Morcar, on the long road to York. Another meeting was summoned with northern creatures of influence, with the Northumbrians desperate to learn if the new king would be attempting to reinstall Tostig as their earl. Tostig had ruled over them with an iron paw and Harold received many dirty looks by association. After sitting through accusations of Tostig's cruelty and dishonour, not to mention claims of violence and murder, Harold was finally able to assure them that he had no intentions of bringing his brother back to power.

After much deliberation, every creature was satisfied, and Harold felt safe to stroke the threat of northern discontent off the list of his many worries for now.

Whilst it seemed the English were fully behind him as king, there was still another who Harold knew would be against him. His return trip to Westminster was overcome with dread as he fully expected some news of Duke William to have arrived in his absence. He waited. But no news came from Normandy. Harold didn't rejoice in that fact and instead spent most of his days looking out for a winged messenger. Angry or composed, threatening or peaceful, he just needed to know.

King Harold was feasting in the king-crowning Witan hall. Nearly all the nobles had left save for his two brothers Gyrth and Leofwine, his sister Edith, and the overbearing mole Archbishop Stigand. The little mousemaid Mabel was also granted to sit at the king's table too. She had been such a comfort to Edith since Edward's death that the vixen demanded she be inducted into the family somehow.

The Great Hall was an ostentatious setting to feast in and unnecessary for such a small gathering. Plates had been arranged along the length of the king's table which was designed to host great swathes of creatures. They were forced to shout to each other to be heard before Harold decreed it was ridiculous and demanded a more fitting table be found. They ended up on the smallest table (ordinarily used by the abbey monks) and crammed all the platters of food onto it. It was impossible to enjoy a pawful of cheese without knocking the arm of the creature which sat beside them. Stigand found the whole experience horrifying, but the foxes laughed and drank heartily, remembering simpler days when they were just cubs.

"A toast!" Leofwine stood up. There was the rattling of clashing cutlery as he knocked the table. Leofwine had never been able to handle his wine.

"To my brother, Harold... the most reliable... the most deserving... the most unbelievably *lucky* fox there is..."

"I say!" cried Stigand and Gyrth shook his head, embarrassed.

Edith, however, burst out into tears of laughter and Harold delighted in her cheer.

"You are too generous and kind, dear brother," said Harold. "I in turn propose a toast to Gyrth...the most loyal...most dependable...most *boring* creature I have ever met!"

Edith and Leofwine howled with laughter. Gyrth's face was like stone. Harold held his breath.

"To Edith," Gyrth boomed suddenly. "Never was a creature so fair, so kind, or fatefully dim as she."

"Excuse me!" she exclaimed playfully.

Leofwine rattled the table with his flagon in approval.

"Then I must sincerely take the chance to sing the praises of our lovely Archbishop Stigand," she sang. "Stigand, you truly are the most ridiculous, bumbling, simply infuriating fool I have had the absolute misfortune to know!"

The foxes laughed at their sister's brutal words. Stigand was smiling too, not seeming to realise that Edith truly meant everything she said.

"Don't let her speak to you like that, Stiggy!" Leofwine giggled.

"Oh, I don't mind Lord Leofwine."

"Make a toast, Stigand," smiled Harold.

"Yes, we've all made one!" said Leofwine.

"Oh, alright alright," Stigand huffed good-humouredly. "Erm...what to say..."

"Just say anything!" Leofwine groaned.

"Ok, ok." Stigand got to his paws and raised his flagon. "I toast to Lord Tostig, who has kindly given up his seat at the fox table for this old mole to join in the fun!"

Stigand laughed loudly, though his laughter echoed through the Great Hall alone. The foxes fell silent at the mention of their missing brother, the mood deflated in an instant.

Thankfully they were saved from enduring the moment for long as the Great Hall doors swung open. Wulfric, the one-eyed warrior, and Dunstan, an enormous brown bear, stood in the archway. Only the wolf approached.

"King Harold," he said. "I am sorry to disturb you. A golden eagle arrived ten minutes ago. She brought a letter. We believe it's from the one you spoke about."

"I see," said Harold, wiping residue food from the fur around his mouth and standing. "I must see to this matter at once."

"What is it?" asked Leofwine.

Leofwine's face was slack, his bright blue eyes dimmed with wine.

"Nothing to worry about, keep feasting." He turned to his other brother who had a far greater control of his drinking. "Gyrth, with me."

Gyrth nodded without question. Both Harold and Gyrth disentangled themselves awkwardly from the small table. It was a clumsy affair but even Leofwine didn't laugh, noticing Harold's graveness. Harold and Gyrth followed Wulfric out of the hall where the bear was still waiting.

The king shook its mammoth, shaggy paw. "Dunstan."

Dunstan, whose name translated into *dark stone*, was a simple but brave creature who Harold had anointed as constable of the formidable housecarls of Wessex. Every earl in the country had their own housecarls; trained troops who had proven their undying loyalty to their lord. Since his coronation Harold was now commander of both the King's Wolves and Wessex's finest soldiers. Both factions amounted to well over a thousand creatures, all ready to do Harold's bidding.

The bear had a slip of sealed parchment placed delicately between two claws. He handed it to the king.

"Walk with me, friends," said Harold.

"Us too?" Wulfric said in surprise.

"I value both of your opinions," he said simply, leading them away from eavesdropping servants.

"Where are we going?" asked Gyrth as they stepped out into the courtyard.

"I know a spot," said Harold. All of the fox's late-night walks had rendered him a master of the grounds and he took any excuse to be out in the fresh air.

The solstice snows had begun to thaw and green shoots of grass poked their way out, feeling the sun for the first time in weeks. Harold took them on a less trodden path of bramble bushes to the edge of the River Thames. Harold enjoyed darting between the thorns though he heard Dunstan merely trample over them from behind. On the other side of the river merchants were busy flogging their wares, and the keenest sighted of them pointed and gossiped about the four faceless creatures on the opposite bank.

Nothing calmed Harold like clean air and the sounds of running water, though even that wasn't enough to steady his racing heart. He noted the parchment was addressed simply to "Harold", not "*King Harold*". It wasn't a promising start.

"What's this all about?" asked Gyrth.

Harold blinked, realising he had been staring at the parchment without speaking.

"An old friend," said Harold bitterly. "Wulfric, would you read it aloud?"

"I don't read so good, Your Majesty," Wulfric said in his typical growl.

Harold knew it was pointless to ask the bear. Dunstan would have been the first to admit that his qualities were strictly limited to fighting and matters of war. He handed the parchment to Gyrth and stared into the depths of the Thames as his brother spoke.

- Harold,
I hope this letter finds you well and healthy, prosperous and content. I hope that when you respond you have recovered with haste from whatever ailment has driven your mind to madness. I hope that your actions can be explained, reversed, and forgiven, and our friendship salvaged.

To avoid war, I am still willing to accept the terms which we had already agreed upon. As king, I would still be willing to accept you as my premier earl, in keeping with our vows that were sworn over the Holy Relics.

I hope that your sanity returns to you, my friend. In the absence of this redemption, you know there is only one path left for me to take. I will be king of England as King Edward intended. The storm of Normandy will rain upon you without mercy, hesitation, or remorse.

My invasion preparations have already begun. We will crush any English rebels and burn villages to the ground. You can save lives if you will only honour God, and your word.

If you are not the creature I believed you to be, and reject this proposal of peace, then I shall end you. Your life shall be forfeit for your crimes. Until the day in which I take it, I hope your betrayal haunts your every waking moment.

- King William of England, Duke of Normandy.

"He signs off as 'King William'," finished Gyrth gravely.

"He always was dramatic," said Harold.

"Did you really swear on the relics?" asked Gyrth.

"I did." Harold sighed. "Though it was not so much an agreement but a demand on William's part. I don't believe I would have been allowed out of Normandy had I resisted. And in truth, I had not foreseen Edward selecting me as heir. I never expected to be king."

"You do not need to explain yourself to me, brother," said Gyrth, gripping Harold's shoulder. "I will stand with you against this lynx, if that is your will."

"I know." He nodded. He turned to Dunstan and Wulfric. "It is as I expected. I will be counting on you both to help lead the defence of England."

"'Til the death," growled Wulfric.

"What are your orders?" said Dunstan.

"We must be ready. Summon the southern fyrds. I need every port on the south coast armed within a month. Dunstan, I need you at Pevensey. Wulfric, at Sandwich. Gyrth, you will need to assemble your own housecarls, Leofwine too. How many do you have?"

"Another thousand between us."

"Good," said Harold. Combined with his own that brought the number of trained soldiers to roughly two and a half thousand. Further recruits could be gathered from the fyrd, the common English creatures who were pledged to serve two months a year should the king make the call. Would it be enough?

"We may need every southern creature that can swing an axe before this is done."

Wulfric and Dunstan nodded, both as brave and eager for a fight as the other. Gyrth's face was less enthused, and Harold could almost hear the many cogs whirring behind his slanted eyes.

"Do not fear." Now it was Harold's turn to assure his brother with a paw on the shoulder. "Do not doubt. England is not doomed. We will defend it with our lives if we must. The second William sets a paw on our soil he will feel the ferocity of the English and wish he never set sail."

"Yes!" roared Wulfric.

"Spit 'em back into the sea!" shouted Dunstan.

"I wish I had your faith, brother," said Gyrth.

Harold smiled. Fear and doubt had already wrapped their vines around his very soul since the day of his coronation. His dreams were plagued by a fanged lynx in a suit of armoured steel, striding against him on a crowded battlefield, sword in paw.

But Harold was king now.

Kings do not show fear.

"Believe in me, brother. Believe in our strength. Do not struggle against the winds of fate, but move with them. William will come, and William will die."

WINTER

A Prickly Return

As the last of the snow melted and seeped into the ground below, all across the village of Hooe hibernating creatures emerged from their slumber. Families who had only spoken to one another as they hid from the elements now congregated in the open, finishing conversations with neighbours that had begun months earlier. The most well-off villagers had stayed awake for much of the period, but many of the poorest had been forced to sleep their way through Christmas by way of survival.

Faye was a hedgehog that was better off than most. As thane, her father was the most important creature in the village. They were lucky enough to be able to afford candles and a wooden floor which did a good job of keeping the cold at bay, whilst other villagers were made to sleep on the freezing, muddy ground. Her father would never let any of his hoglets forget their privilege. He devised a system that allowed every family in the village to have use of a candle for at least ten days of winter.

With spring on the horizon the mood around the village was exuberant. Faye received many waves and calls to chat as she wandered through. She patiently endured the villagers' praise for her father with a weary smile.

"He'th a great hog, that Alfie!" said Tata, a very fat and well-meaning beaver.

"Thank your father for the candle, dear. We might not have made it through otherwith!" said his equally round wife, Mopps.

The coming of spring meant there was much to be positive about, but not even being freed from her squabbling brothers could brighten Faye's mood. To her, spring signalled the dawn of another year trapped in the village that she had never left, with seemingly no hope of adventure. She knew it was most ungrateful of her to be so disillusioned, especially with so many creatures thankful to be alive. But she could not help it. Faye had a will to explore which was simply absent from the rest of the village.

Hooe was a typical southern community with a little over one hundred creatures existing in unison. In such a place, every birth was celebrated by all as one of their own. Every death mourned in the same way. It was a place of crops, streams, and ponds. It was said that if you followed what cubs called "Stony Creek", you would end up in Bexhill port by the sea. Beyond that was supposedly the town of Hastings, though nobody Faye knew had ever been there. That would be far too exciting. To the north was the great Ashdown forest that townsfolk were told was full of demons and ghouls that stole and ate wandering cubs in the dark.

To the citizens of Hooe these names and places might as well be works of fiction. Creatures here simply appreciated and accepted their lot, not daring to ask for more than warm summers and mild winters. Faye's father, Alfie, was the only one that regularly left the village borders. He was away on one of his trips now. The word was that all the local thanes had been summoned for a council meeting under direct orders from the king.

Alfie was expected back that night. Eleanor, Alfie's wife and Faye's mother, was preparing a large supper for his return. Asking Faye to help with the cooking almost always ended in disaster. Eleanor had given up on teaching her teenage daughter how to be "an appropriate wife and mother" and so had sent Faye plum picking instead.

Faye had tied a length of string to her back paw and secured the other end to a basket. She trailed the basket along behind her and headed for the fruit trees at the end of the village. In her front paws she kept her treasured slingshot. Her mother would tell her girls shouldn't be playing with such things, so she always had to practise in secret. When her father had seen her playing with one the year before he had taken it from her and disappeared into the trees.

"My daughter can't be using this," he had said.

She had cried on the spot until he re-emerged holding a newly fashioned slingshot that fired doubly fast and far.

"Now *this* is more like it." He had laughed, passing it to her.

The maple wood was sturdier than the feeble twig Faye had been using and formed the perfect "Y" shape. She practised whenever she could and soon, despite being burdened with the arms of a hedgehog, Faye was a crack shot.

Upon reaching the orchard she shot half a dozen plums down without missing once. She struck the branch just above the fruit so that it fell straight to the floor. Past trips had taught her to never let the stone hit the fruit; the explosion would send chunks flying everywhere and were very difficult to clean from her spikes. She collected all the plums into her basket before wandering around the orchard to find a challenging target. As she did, she was drawn to a small *thud!*

"Crackin' shot, Dre," said a high-pitched voice.

It didn't take Faye long to find the source of the commotion. A slender, chocolate furred pine marten called Drefan was shooting arrows at a plum tree. He was accompanied by Alwin, his tiny vole friend. Alwin was too small to wield a bow so was reduced to watching his longer-limbed companion.

Drefan took the arrow from the trunk and moved back. He couldn't have been ten feet from it. With concerted effort he drew the string back to fire.

"At least step back a bit," said Faye from behind them.

Drefan let the arrow loose in shock. It skimmed the bark and landed in the grass beyond.

"Nice shot." She grinned. "You must have the eyesight of a mole."

"Hey, you put me off!" moaned Drefan.

The pine marten was a popular creature of a similar age to Faye. He had a relaxed aura about him that drew attention from the less confident creatures. Without being asked, Alwin the vole darted to retrieve the arrow for him.

"I'm actually pretty good, I'll have you know," Drefan boasted. "I can teach you if you like."

"I think I'll pass." Faye laughed, turning away. Drefan slung his bow around his neck and ran after her. Her slow gait was no match for the pine marten's agility.

"Oh, go on," he said, his black eyes shimmering. "I've missed you over winter."

"Missed me?" asked Faye, genuinely taken aback and wondering what the pine marten wanted from her.

"Yeah, not like loads, but a bit, y'know?"

"Erm, thanks?"

"I thought we could go to the feast next week."

"Well, yeah, everyone's going..."

"You know, like, together?"

"Oh," said Faye, embarrassed. "I don't think so."

"C'mon." He snatched the slingshot out of her paws. "I'll play you for it."

Alwin arrived back at his side with the arrow in his mouth. Drefan snatched it back immediately.

"One of my arrows against one of your stone things," Drefan said excitedly.

Faye shook her head, unsure whether to be irritated or amused by his persistence.

"See here." Drefan pointed to a spot that had been dug into the bark. "Closest to it wins."

"Wins what?" Faye laughed.

"Wins your love, of course!" he cried dramatically.

"You are a strange one, Dre," she said.

"That's not a no!" Drefan leapt into position. He drew the arrow back as far as he could manage. The bow string stroked the rounded ears that Faye had heard other creatures fawning over.

"For love!" Drefan released the arrow and sent it *thudding* straight into the bark, an inch or two above the target spot.

"Great shot, Dre!" clapped Alwin before looking over at Faye with a sour expression, thoroughly miffed that she was interrupting them.

"Think you can top it?" taunted Drefan.

Faye groaned at the creature's smugness. She aimed at the tree and fired. The pebble whistled as it cut the air in two.

"Where'd it go?" asked Drefan blankly.

A plum fell to the ground right in front of him, perfectly severed from the branch. Faye picked up the plum and tossed it into her basket.

"Hey, where you going?" said Drefan.

"Home," Faye called back as she trotted away.

"So we'll go to the feast together?"

"How do you figure that?"

"You missed!"

"Did I?" She laughed.

Faye took her time and walked the long route around the village, wary to never get in her mother's way whilst she was cooking. She skirted the edges of the village and enjoyed imagining what excitement may lie beyond the surrounding trees and fields. Her preoccupation for daydreaming meant that she missed the commotion that had been building at the village centre. Once she reached home her brothers Hugo and Benedict came bursting out the door and ran in the opposite direction.

"Papa's home!" they shouted together, running as fast as their little legs would carry them.

Faye's portly mother, Eleanor, appeared wheezing at the door, a dirty apron wrapped around her.

"Boys, be careful!" she shouted, so loud creatures in Bexhill could have heard her. "Faye, go with them."

"Yes, Mama," said Faye, untying her basket and running after the twins.

"Come here you two." She grabbed a paw from each of her brothers. Hugo managed to wriggle free, and Faye yelped as her paw touched his ever sharpening spikes.

"Fine, go on then."

Both hoglets cheered as they ran off. Faye traipsed after them until she saw her father appear.

Alfie wasn't the biggest of hedgehogs (in fact he was smaller than his wife which was quite peculiar), but he was striking in other ways. He had an entirely round, white furred face and an upward pointing snout. His spikes were a dark brown, all perfectly even, and topped with a translucence which gleamed in moonlight.

He was impeded on his approach, not just by Hugo and Benedict who were running around him in circles, but other creatures as well. Everyone was eager to hear about the mysterious summons to a council outside of the village.

"We will convene for a meetin' tonigh', the whole village. All will be explained then!" Faye heard him say the same thing to every creature that asked.

"Hello, dear." Alfie smiled when he saw Faye.

"How are you, Papa?"

"Aye, I'm alrigh'," said Alfie, though his eyes said differently. He touched Faye's face with a cold paw and a defeated expression on his own.

"Are you sure, Papa?"

"Yes, yes," he said. He rubbed his eyes and Faye wondered if he was brushing away tears. "I'm just 'appy to be 'ome."

Their family home was the largest of the village, though that wasn't saying a lot. They slept, ate and lived all in one room. A cauldron hung over a bountiful flame at its centre, the smoke filtering out of the rough chimney in the thatched roof.

"Just in time for food!" said Eleanor giving her husband a kiss.

"Ta', dear," said Alfie with none of his usual zest.

"What happened at the meeting, Papa?" Faye asked, a little disturbed by her father's unusual sombreness.

"No!" called Eleanor. Faye's mother had only "one rule" for her family to follow – it just happened to change every day. Today's was, *"No talking before dinner!"* so Alfie was made to be silent about his trip and Faye was deprived of asking any *"silly"* questions.

There were three separate knocks at the door during their meal. Alfie shook their paws and reiterated the time and place of the village meeting that would be happening later that night.

"Is the king really dead?" Faye heard one of them ask, making her tiny ears prick up in interest.

Whatever had happened was big, that much she knew. She had never seen her father so subdued and not even Hugo and Benedict's infectious energy could cheer him up.

Once their bellies were full Eleanor started to harangue her hoglets into helping with the cleaning up, but Alfie stopped her.

"Migh' the cleanin' wait, dearest?" he said. "I got somethin' we need to discuss."

"Oh, very well," Eleanor snapped, slumping herself back down in her chair.

"I'm gunna 'ave a meetin' with all the families tonigh', but I thought perhaps yer lot should know what I've learned first."

"Is this going to be appropriate for the little 'uns?" asked Eleanor, looking at the twins and then Faye.

"I'm not a *little 'un*!" Faye tutted.

"Nor are we!" yelled Benedict.

"Is that so?" Alfie asked, pulling Benedict into a hug.

"Uh-huh!"

Alfie kissed him on his little snout. "I think it's best they all stay. This news affects us all."

"Be quick about it then," said Eleanor, her mind clearly preoccupied by the washing up.

"Righ' yer are, love," said Alfie, who fortunately found his wife's renowned impatience endearing. "The badger king is dead."

"Oh, dear," said Eleanor facetiously.

"What's a badger?" mumbled Hugo.

"Was he killed?" asked Faye.

"No, child, he fell quite sick."

"Who's king now then?" snorted Eleanor.

"The fox, 'arold of Wessex."

"Well, good luck to him," said Eleanor, getting to her paws. "Now, Faye, grab that-"

"There's more," said Alfie. Eleanor sat again with a disgruntled *thump*. "It seems there are some who ain't 'appy with this choice of king."

Eleanor yawned pointedly though Faye jumped up in excitement. This was the most interesting news her father had ever brought.

"Who is it, Papa? Is it the Danes? Are Vikings coming?"

"No, thank the Lord." Alfie shivered. "Don't go bein' excited by that prospect, Faye. We don't want no Vikin's 'ere!"

"Then who?"

"Whoever is king makes naught a bit of difference to us now does it?" Eleanor wittered on to herself, gorging on any leftover bread. "Unless the fox intends to work our crops himself, then I couldn't care less!"

"It ain't the Vikin's 'arold's worried about, so I'm told. It's Normandy."

"Normandy?"

"Hmm." Alfie frowned. "The duke wants the crown."

"What are you saying, Alf?" Eleanor's voice was suddenly sharp.

"The duke is comin' to take it, so I'm told." There was a moment's silence and Alfie shut his eyes before continuing, mentally preparing for the impact of his next words. "The fyrd 'as been summoned."

"No!" Eleanor cried. Faye turned to her and was shaken by how vulnerable her headstrong mother suddenly looked.

"What does that mean?" mumbled Benedict.

"Well, son, it means that I'm gunna 'ave to go away for a while."

"I can't believe this," lamented Eleanor, on the verge of tears.

"As I am thane I have a duty to me country, see?" Alfie continued to explain. "If the king needs us, we are to go to his aid. I'm gunna take as many creatures from round 'ere as I can muster. Tata 'as already signed up."

"You are not a fighter, Alfie! Hedgehogs are not soldiers!" Eleanor had both paws over her face.

"A soldier?" said Faye, just as bewildered as her little brothers. "Papa?"

"Aye," said Alfie. "All over the south we are bein' summoned to figh' for 'arold – for England. I don't want any of yer to worry about me; it's me duty to serve the fyrd for two months, nothin' more. Then it will be another creature's turn. I'll be back before yer know it."

"But what if you get killed?" said Hugo in a small quiet voice that jarred with the harsh reality of his words.

"Well, I'll 'ave to make sure that don't 'appen," Alfie said. "Besides, I'm sure it's just a precaution. They'd be fools to invade us, eh?"

Nobody responded to Alfie's attempt to cheer them and eventually the family fell into a heavy silence. When Alfie left to speak to the village, all three hoglets helped their mother with the washing up without resisting.

Eleanor was telling Hugo and Benedict their favourite bedtime story when Alfie returned. He took the time to speak to Faye alone.

"'ow you feelin', Spike?" he asked her, using a name he hadn't used since she was as young as the twins.

"Jealous," Faye said with a wink. "Take me with you?"

"I don't think so." Alfie smiled.

"I'd be just as helpful as any boy! You've seen me with the *slingshot*." She mouthed the last word so Eleanor wouldn't overhear. "I want to fight."

"I know yer do. Yer a much braver creature than yer old Papa, which is why I'm relyin' on yer to look after yer mother and brothers when I'm away."

"Does that mean I'm in charge?" she teased.

"I'm bein' serious, Faye," urged Alfie, his face harrowed. "Yer remember Old Monty?"

"Of course." Faye nodded. Poor Old Monty had died the summer before. The rabbit had been an eccentric character that always spoke of wild dreams and impending doom. Creatures had begun to not take him seriously and Faye knew some young folk used to throw stones at his house and bother him.

"T'was a strange fellow, ain't no mistake," said Alfie. "But Monty was always prepared. Up by Stony Creek 'e dug a burrow deep enough to live in for quite some time, should danger come knockin'. Righ' behind that great oak that looks down the stream. The entrance is righ' there! Yer'll 'ave to 'unt through the mud for it, mind. The old codger 'id it well."

"Why are we talking about this?"

"I want yer to find it. Don't tell no one. Yer start storing food away in there in case yer ever need to use it."

"Use it for what? I don't understand."

"To 'ide."

"Hide from who? The Normans? But you're going to stop them, right Papa?"

"Just promise me yer'll remember the burrow."

"I-I promise."

"There's a good girl."

"You won't let them win though, right? You'll fight them all away?"

"O' course." A tear dripped down his face and disappeared into his fur. "O' course we will."

SPRING

Truce of God

William pulled at his goatee of fur that drooped under his chin hard enough to make his eyes water. He needed to keep his paws busy before he lost control and gave Eustace, Count of Boulogne, the punch he deserved.

The duke's private quarters had ceased to be a place of relaxation or chess and were now almost always occupied by his war council. Barons of Normandy and other invited guests from the surrounding districts congregated here to discuss William's plans of invasion.

The council table was filled with bickering creatures with only a few William could depend on so far. After weeks of conversations running in circles William had already concluded that his barons were spineless things, filled with worry and doubt. Their lack of ambition and gumption was insulting, and many of them couldn't face William's golden eyes.

Seated beside William was his half-brother Odo, who at least could be relied upon for chivalrous counsel. Roger de Beaumont the wolf was too old to fight but had promised the war effort his son and sixty ships. However, many of the others lacked interest. In particular the creature that sat at the base of the table, Count Eustace.

Eustace was a chamois. He had dark brown fur, a face of black and white stripes, and two curling horns protruding from his small head. He was a smug thing who seemed to relish in telling William that his plans could not be done. The lynx called him a "glorified goat" behind his back.

"It would be easier to become king of France!" Eustace laughed heartily. There was a murmur around the council. William wished for nothing more than to rip the chamois' horns from his head.

But he knew he couldn't. If he was going to take England he would need all the help he could get, and Eustace had ships.

"We will storm the beaches of England," stated William for what felt like the hundredth time.

"They will be waiting," said Eustace with an air of confidence that needed slapping out of him. "The English housecarls are the most fearsome creatures in Europe. Of that there is no doubt."

All around creatures were nodding in agreement.

"They fight with battle axes, a most savage weapon-"

"If you could stop complimenting the enemy that would be appreciated, Eustace," said William, cutting the chamois off.

A shrill laugh followed the duke's words. There were many frowns around the table as creatures looked around for the source of it.

"*Scusa*," said a red squirrel, leaning against a wall, masked by the shadows in the corner of the room. An immaculate robe draped over his slight body. His voice far too squeaky for a creature of his mystery. "Please continue."

Eustace gave the squirrel a scathing look before turning back to face William. "I just want everyone to understand the challenge they are facing before they join you on this foolhardy attack."

"I am disappointed in your lack of faith in me," the lynx responded with gritted fangs. "Yes, our mission is dangerous, but I believe success to be a certainty. The English *do* have a weakness. They fight with a shield wall, a patient, strong mode of defence. But they do not have the same relationship with the horses as we, and therein lies our advantage."

Eustace scoffed loudly.

"They have no mounted soldiers whatsoever," continued William.

"Yes, everyone knows of your strange connection with horses and for that I applaud you. It is not easy to tame their wild hearts," said Eustace. "But what good is your ability to ride into battle when there are no horses? I assume you do not intend to find a readymade battalion of hooves waiting for you on the beach as you arrive?"

William shared a look with his half-brother Odo. The bobcat nodded back at him – it was time to reveal their plan.

"We are taking them with us."

"What?" Eustace's shock was genuine. "It's impossible."

"Nothing is impossible, Eustace," said William proudly. The chamois' small mindedness meant he would never have any real power, William thought.

He could never be a king.

"No horse has ever crossed the Channel!"

"Exactly, it's the last thing the English will expect."

All the barons looked just as unconvinced, and even those who had tried to show their support for the invasion looked troubled.

"I am afraid you are quite mad," said Eustace. "I shall have to think long and hard on this matter. I must retire now."

As Eustace got to his hooves to leave the council, so did William. The lynx growled across the table at the chamois. Eustace didn't have the right to call an end to the meeting. It was yet another insult from the old beast. If not for Odo (who covertly held William back) he would have leapt on him right then and there.

We need his ships. We need his ships. We need his ships.

"Of course," William said with a smile no one believed. "We will continue tomorrow."

Creatures filed out of the room leaving only William and the red squirrel who was still tucked away in the corner.

"Hello, Lanfranc," grunted William, still fuming at Eustace's cheek.

"*Buonasera!*" Lanfranc the Italian squirrel strutted out of the shadows, his paws in his cloak pockets.

"You see now what I am dealing with? Perhaps you can be of more use to me than those cowards."

"Perhaps." The squirrel grinned, switching to French.

"Let's take a walk," William said. "I'll have my sword brought to me."

"You will need it, hmm?"

"English spies and assassins are everywhere, Lanfranc." William scowled. "Maybe even behind these very walls."

In the streets of Caen rain was falling steadily. Already muddy roads had been transformed into a sodden mire and every creature that stepped outside had to be wary. There was talk that a young mouse had been stuck in the bog for several hours before managing to wriggle free.

William strode through it, splashing passersby with his forceful steps. Lanfranc went slower as he held his enormous bushy tail up by his side to avoid dragging it through the swamp-like floor. Their way was hindered by Caen's peasants (mostly mice, rats, and voles) who were finishing a tiring day's work and moving slowly.

Many of the peasants seemed to recognise their tall, towering duke under his cloak and stayed clear of him. There was a silence that befell the streets as William came through. He was sure they were all whispering about him. Once he turned and saw two ravens watching him. As soon as he faced them they squawked and flew off into the skies. He began to imagine their snide voices.

Look at the fool.

He's weak.

Why did we ever think he would be king of England?

Distracted by the birds, William nearly wandered straight into a puddle that flooded the road. All creatures that passed were made to squeeze down a sliver of dry land around the side of it.

"Beware the king of England!" some creature cried sarcastically from the midst of the shuffling crowd.

"Who was that?" William shouted, immediately drawing his sword. "Reveal yourself at once!"

The peasant creatures scattered out of his way. One vole was knocked into the puddle in the chaos. She rose out of it wet as an otter, spewing dirty water everywhere. It was easier to swim away than attempt to climb free.

"Cravens!" William yelled, still brandishing his sword. The street emptied within seconds.

Little Lanfranc touched the cool steel and lowered it gently.

"Remember the Truce of God, my lord," he said patiently.

William scowled and holstered his sword. The Truce of God was a decree from the pope that had sought to end a pandemic of violence that had spread across Europe, not least the turbulent Duchy of Normandy.

For young Normans there were only two choices; become a creature of the church or become a *chevalier*, a knight. Many young souls chose the latter, and even bishops like William's brother Odo were creatures of war. Normandy as a result had become a place flooded with uneducated, battle-trained creatures that were eager for a fight and happy to sell their services to the highest bidder. William thought perhaps an invasion of England would finally provide them with a purpose, but before they set sail the Truce of God still had its uses. All fighting was forbidden from Wednesday evenings through to Monday mornings. Farmers did well to plough their fields on these safe days before hiding inside on the others.

In truth, the duke shouldn't have brought his sword with him on a day when the Truce was active, but Harold had already shown himself to be dishonourable and William didn't put it past the fox to send an assassin on a day of peace.

The lynx and the squirrel continued through busy, rain-drenched Caen streets. Creatures stayed well clear, but William still spoke to his friend in whispers.

"My barons are weak. They look to that fool, Eustace." He sighed bitterly. "I hate to say it, but I can't invade without them. I don't have the ships."

"*Si*," Lanfranc agreed. "It is a nasty conundrum, you have."

William regarded the red squirrel with a hint of amusement. He was an innocent enough looking thing with bright red fur and those cute, dark eyes. His little head was always twitching from side to side, and he seemed to have an unquenchable itch on his ear that he scratched at every couple of seconds. To an outsider he would seem quite ordinary; a devoted abbot that had dedicated his life to the church.

The lynx knew better. There weren't many as cunning as the squirrel, and William needed him now more than ever.

"What do you suggest I do?" William asked.

Lanfranc hummed broodingly. He slipped a paw into the depths of his cloak and emerged holding a shiny nut. He nibbled at the edges as he spoke.

"Creatures see this invasion as a personal vendetta of yours against the fox. *Si*, you can dazzle them with promises of money and titles should they win but why take the risk, hmm? *'The English are too strong, why should I risk my life for a creature I don't know?'* they will say."

"For justice!" William barked.

"Justice is when you chop the paw off a thief, not when you risk common creatures' lives for nothing."

"Nothing?" William bristled.

"You must distract them from your personal feud with Harold and make this invasion one they can believe in." Lanfranc stopped twitching. William had come to associate his rare stillness with the striking of inspiration. "What about if this is not an invasion at all? Not an invasion; a *crusade*."

William's ears pricked up. This is why he came to Lanfranc. "Go on."

Lanfranc puffed up his chest and raised his paws, staring off faintly into nothing. "Imagine this: A holy war against the English! Corruption is everywhere! They are a bunch of fools and frauds! That tiny island schemes and plots, hiding from the pope. Who knows what lies they spread, hmm? And now their leader turns his back on a sacred oath with impunity!"

Lanfranc looked slightly manic when he finished with both paws raised dramatically above his head.

"Is any of that true?" William asked.

Lanfranc's paws dropped to his side and the air of grandeur dissipated in an instant. "Does it matter? Now the thought is in your mind; the seed is planted. The English are traitors to the church and need to be punished, *è semplice!*"

"And you think this will convince creatures to join me? To build me ships because I say all that?"

"No." Lanfranc shook his head. "Nobody would believe you, *mio amico*. You will need Rome."

"The pope?"

"*Naturalmente!* Pope Alexander was once a student of mine at Bec. Send me to him and I will get you the support you need."

William felt a chill down his spine. It seemed Lanfranc was even more cunning than he had given him credit for. Could they really deceive the pope in such a way?

"Trust me, my lord," said Lanfranc, sensing William's doubt. "This is how you gain support. You can only offer so much money and land. Wealth may last a lifetime, but the chance of *salvation* can last an eternity. If a soldier is to die for a holy cause, the pope can promise them heaven. Maybe I will fight myself!"

"And if they live?"

"Then *fantastico!* If they live, you will provide them with a reward. It's a win-win scenario, hmm? This is what will inspire creatures to join you on this mission, and you will get your ships I have no doubt."

"This is quite a task you would be undertaking, Lanfranc. What do you seek in return for this...service?"

William knew there was no such thing as a free favour with a creature like Lanfranc, not without an expectation of a usually greater favour in return.

"Only to serve!" Lanfranc shrugged. "I hear Canterbury is a lovely spot to pray."

"I see." William nodded. So the squirrel wanted to be archbishop. That could certainly be arranged once the kingdom was his.

"If you get me the pope's support, *and* it changes my fortunes as you say it will, then Archbishop of Canterbury you will be."

Lanfranc smiled broadly. He pulled a second nut from his robes and cracked it in two with one bite.

"*Grazie, mio amico!* This is a welcome surprise! I will honour your demands and head for Rome at once."

A breeze cleared the clouds, and the sun shone on Normandy for the first time in weeks.

"God is already with us!" The squirrel smiled.

"Safe travels, my friend," said William. "How long until you return?"

"I-" Lanfranc began to respond but was distracted by two creatures who were endeavouring to walk against the strong gusts of wind with little success. The first creature was a duck; it had a bright, bottle green head on top of a squat, feathered body. The second creature was tall and slender and held itself with a grace that suggested nobility. Like William, it was draped in a dark cloak from ear to paw. Only a set of fine whiskers could be seen peeking out from the shadow of its hood.

A stinging gale knocked the duck over on its back. The taller one seemed outraged at this and aggressively pulled it back to its webbed feet. Strange, arguing voices appeared on the wind.

"What language is that?" William said.

Lanfranc looked grave. "*Inglese.*"

"English?" William stared at the two strangers. "Spies."

"*Per favore!*" Lanfranc blocked William's paw as he reached for his sword again. "Remember the Truce."

William looked down at the squirrel with a look of fury. "Release your paw."

"What are you going to do with them?"

"I haven't decided yet," said William, glaring after the two English creatures were reaching the end of the street.

"If you are going to hurt them, wait until after the Truce-"

"Goodbye, Lanfranc. I look forward to your return." William left the squirrel there and strode out after the English.

The lynx kept his distance from the strangers so as not to reveal himself. He braced himself against the wind that burned his amber eyes and brought with it scraps of the conversation ahead. William didn't understand a word but knew that the two creatures were in some sort of row.

He followed them for a long time. Once they reached a crossroads, they stopped for several minutes, gesticulating and pointing down two roads that led to two opposite directions. The pair were clearly foreigners.

William's patience was a wilting candle at the best of times. He was soon ready to seize them and bring them back to his castle for questioning. Had William spoken English, he would have known that was exactly where the two English creatures wanted to go.

"We're lost," wailed the duck. "Let's ask for directions."

"Never mind that now," whispered the cloaked creature. "We're being followed."

William lost sight of the English creatures as another group of Norman peasants were coming down the road towards them. After the peasants passed the lynx could only see the duck, now walking alone.

Cursing to himself, William swept after it. He couldn't afford to lose them both.

William remembered Lanfranc's words as he drew his sword. "Remember the Truce."

If the duck complies, there will be no need to harm him.

"Not one more waddle, duck," William said calmly, resting the tip of his blade on the duck's slender neck.

"*S'il vous plaît!*" the duck cried in perfect French. It fell to the ground with a squeak. "Do not hurt me!"

"What is your business here?" William demanded.

"I would advise you to lower your sword, sir," the duck gulped. "If you want to live, that is."

William couldn't help but laugh at the meek duck's boldness. The creature looked as helpless in a battle as a creature could be.

"You think so?" William smirked. "Where is the creature you were with?"

"We thought we were being followed," said the duck. "So he doubled back."

Behind William came the sudden sound of paws crashing through puddles.

"Here he comes," said the duck.

William spun. The tall creature was running at him, a thin needle of a sword in his paws. The stranger charged and stabbed at the lynx in a frightful blur of steel. William only just managed to swing his sword in an upwards arc to parry. The creature continued with a flurry of jabs so quick William had to be at his best to block.

The duck scrambled out of the way of the duel, staying just out of reach to watch it unfold. The tall creature was a worthy opponent and William was soon panting. The lynx was the larger creature with the stronger arm, but the stranger was too quick for William to land a serious blow.

William stood still as the stranger darted around him, attacking with forceful stabs. The lynx struggled on the wet ground and nearly lost his balance whilst the stranger seemed to be able to use the terrain to its advantage. It skidded artfully on the wet mud, ducking under William's heavy swipes and appearing behind him to jab again.

The stranger slipped around his side and feinted a jab at William's leg. William fell for it completely; as he moved to block it, the stranger redirected his sword into an uppercut movement. It sliced through his cloak and shaved one of the lynx's dark spots clean off. Another couple of inches to the right and it would have gone through his neck.

It had been too close for William's liking, but there was no time to think about it now. He began to move forward, not allowing the stranger to dictate the fight. Now William was the aggressor. He swung his sword with both paws in a powerful downwards motion and the stranger's arm couldn't handle William's strength. He blocked one strike, but it near shattered his sword. The stranger ducked and skidded out of the way, hoping that William would tire.

The lynx, however, was just beginning to enjoy himself. It had been too long since he'd met a warrior of the skill of this English creature, and he was relishing the challenge. The stranger yelped as their swords clanged together. A spasm went up the English creature's arm and William attacked, expecting to end it, but the stranger tossed his sword into his left paw and blocked again. The end was near, and William seized his opportunity. He brought three thunderous strikes down upon the stranger. On the first, it managed to stay on its paws, on the second it fell to the mud, and on the third the sword came crashing out.

William stood panting over the stranger. It was defenceless and a fourth strike would mean its death, but its cloak had fallen away, and William was forced to pause. It had bright blue eyes, a dark snout, and a pair of orange-coloured ears that William had known on a creature before.

"Harold?" he said, disbelieving. He lowered his sword in shock and pulled off his own cloak.

The stranger started laughing when he saw the lynx's face. "William?"

William squinted into the rain and saw the fox that knelt before him. A proper glance was enough to reveal that this stranger was not the king of England at all. It had a striking complexion. Its fur was predominantly black but splattered with streaks of the brightest orange flame, like scorching charcoal and burning embers piercing through the cracks.

"Who are you?" William asked.

The English duck plodded over and helped its friend to stand. The fox shooed the duck away and spoke with broken French.

"*Bonjour*, William. *Je suis* Tostig."

SPRING

The Stray Fox

Tostig wasn't used to losing duels. The fox had always been rapid with a blade, quicker than any of his brothers. His enemies only saw the blazing blur of his black and orange fur before they were engulfed. Tostig did not stab, he *poked,* and his enemies would leak to death from a thousand tiny holes. It was said the fox was impossible to beat.

But William had done it. Tostig was impressed as much as he was alarmed. As he gathered his breath he smiled; he had come to the right place.

"I have been looking for you, William, though I am not here to fight," said Tostig in English. He turned to his lieutenant and translator Copsi, the bedraggled duck who stood beside him. "Why do I always have to save you, Copsi? I nearly killed the duke."

"You're right. I'm sorry, sir."

"Now say something flattering, you know the deal."

Copsi nodded furiously and began a tirade of pompous compliments in his master's name.

"Tell him I am *Harold*'s brother." The fox felt a metallic taste run up his throat when he mentioned the name. "Tell him of my triumphs and victories. All my achievements."

"Absolutely, sir." Copsi nodded again, trying to settle himself. The duck had never seen his master bested in battle before.

Tostig studied the lynx's face as it listened to the duck's translation. There was deadly silence for some time and the fox's heart fluttered uncomfortably. The lynx was still panting from the exertion of the duel. He still had his sword clutched in his paw too.

Eventually the lynx growled an answer in French, its venomous eyes not lifting off the fox.

"Oh, ok," said Copsi.

"What did he say?" Tostig snapped. "Be quick about it."

"He says... he says the last time he trusted your kind he was undone," Copsi breathed. The giant lynx looked like it had the strength to carve him in two with a single strike if it so wished. "He says you must give him a reason he should let you live."

"Tell him Harold did not send me," said Tostig. "He is no king of mine. I hope to join forces and end his treacherous rule."

Copsi nodded and did as he was told. This time there was an even longer silence before the lynx responded.

"Maybe you are telling the truth...maybe not." William lifted his sword and casually pointed the tip between Tostig's eyes. "Why should I take the risk?"

"Now listen," blustered Tostig, who could see William's threat without Copsi's frantic translation. "I know you are planning to invade my home country. The rumours are all over Europe. I have sixty ships at my disposal, ready to sail. One hundred rats per ship. They are not big, but they can fight. Let us combine and we can knock Harold off the perch he stole."

William leaned back and twisted his fur goatee, letting his sword sag in the other paw. The blade lolled in front of Copsi's face who cowered behind Tostig's leg. The fox scowled and nudged the duck loose.

"You are a creature of England, no?" said William. "Why do you find me here? Ready to turn on your brother? Why do you hate him so?"

"It's a long story - perhaps we can discuss over ale at your castle?" Tostig smiled hopefully.

The lynx's eyes were empty. His grip on his sword tightened once more.

"Or perhaps I can tell you here, even better..." Tostig cleared his throat, all too aware that if William didn't like his story, he would be struck down and left in the mud right here in this nameless Normandy alley. Tostig saw his sword on the floor and instinctively reached down for it.

"I wouldn't do that, sir," Copsi whined.

"I'm only – I'm not trying to–"

"He says put it back."

William glared, and the fox nodded. He dropped the sword back in the mud and stood up, his blood boiling.

"Duke William, what exactly do you know of Northumbria?" Tostig waited for Copsi to translate a response, but when it became clear the lynx had no interest in answering, he launched into his tale.

"Northumbria needs a strong ruler. Naturally, I was chosen for the job. If you wander through the marshes and woods of Northumbria in a group of twenty or less, it is likely you will be dead. The land is ripe with bandits, thieves, and traitors, and the savages from Scotland are always raiding. To succeed I had to be...*tough*. Some would say I was *cruel*. Pah! Is cruelty to evildoers wrong at all? Or is it merely righteous?

"All I ever did was attempt to bring peace and justice to the north. There were incidents, yes...unfortunate things. The old House of Bamburgh resisted my rule, but I swiftly dealt with them..."

Tostig felt Copsi stiffen behind him. There was no need to tell the duke all about that; how Tostig had invited them into his home as guests and had them murdered in secret behind his walls.

"Some of the natives – the Northumbrian creatures that is – considered me to be too harsh, too demanding. I know you know that sometimes a leader must be so. They gathered together." Tostig snarled now, remembering the sudden rebel attack. "My treasury was broken into. They killed all my soldiers. Only myself and Copsi here survived. The rebels demanded the *hare*," Tostig spat the word, "replace me! Pah!"

Tostig looked away down the street. Sunshine was pouring in from a break in the clouds and the light bounced off every puddle.

"The rebels forced me out of York. They marched on London. The king had to decide." Tostig laughed derisively. "Which really meant Harold had to decide."

The fox stared into a glossy puddle, his eyes burning. His reflection sneered back at him as he remembered the night of his older brother's betrayal...

A dark corridor. A one-eyed wolf standing guard outside the Great Hall.

"Why are they taking so long?" said Tostig. He kicked the duck that was sitting patiently outside the door. "Hey, I'm talking to you."

"I don't know, sir." Copsi winced before patting down his ruffled feathers.

"There's nothing to discuss!" Tostig shouted, knowing his voice would be heard inside the hall.

Almost at once the doors opened. A mole in luxurious robes shuffled out.

"Hello, Lord Tostig." Stigand beamed. "A pleasure to see you again."

Tostig stormed past the mole without responding. He stomped into the centre of the hall with Copsi flapping to keep up behind him. There were a little over two dozen creatures in the hall. None of them could meet his eye.

"Your Majesty." Tostig bowed.

King Edward was slumped in his chair, his eyes so close to shut Tostig thought for a moment the badger was asleep. The colours of his stripes were fading with old age, and he coughed raspily every few seconds.

Beside the badger was Harold. The fox showed no emotion as Tostig stood before him. His face was blank, and only his whiskers were smiling.

"Lord Tostig." Harold nodded.

"Harold." Tostig nodded back. He looked around at the rest of the Witan. He saw his brothers, Gyrth and Leofwine, the archbishops Stigand and Ealdred. There were other bishops and nobles, and over there in the corner...

"You!" Tostig snarled, pointing at the two hares. "What are they doing here, Harold?"

Edwin laughed in his slimy high-pitched way. Morcar's grin somehow managed to make him look even uglier.

"The Northumbrians have demanded Morcar be made earl," said Harold.

"Pah! Preposterous!"

"If we do not give in to their wishes, there will be a civil war."

"Then war it is!" Tostig stamped his paw.

"The Witan have already voted on the matter, Tostig," said Harold.

"And?" Tostig shouted. Still, no other creature would make eye contact with him. Gyrth and Leofwine were staring pointedly at the ground.

Harold looked at King Edward. The badger grumbled something, but nobody could hear him. Harold cleared his throat and spoke for him.

"We will not have war. Morcar will be Earl of Northumbria."

Tostig blinked.

"No!" Copsi breathed.

"You must go into exile," said Harold. His lip trembled slightly. "I'm sorry. It has been agreed."

"You can't be serious?"

"You have a week to leave the country-"

"Harold, I'm warning you-"

"Word will be sent to your wife and cubs-"

"Is this you? Did you have a paw in this?"

"We are sorry it came to this-"

"YOU ARE IN LEAGUE WITH THEM!" Tostig pointed at the hares. They were both smirking. Many of the other creatures were muttering at Tostig's outburst. King Edward was being helped out of his chair. "Your Majesty, please! I can control the north! Just give me one more chance!"

The badger gave him a weary smile but said nothing. A stream of mice followed him out of the room.

"Brothers?" Tostig turned to Gyrth and Leofwine. The latter looked on the verge of tears. "What am I supposed to do? Where am I supposed to go?"

"Do not blame them," Harold said quietly. "You left us no choice. It is the only way."

Tostig went for him. Wulfric the one-eyed wolf intervened before his claws made contact. There was pandemonium in the hall as Tostig was dragged away from the Witan and his brothers. Copsi followed, weeping all the way.

"It was Harold," said Tostig, shaking his head clear of the memory and looking up at the lynx of Normandy. "King Edward was already dying. It was Harold that banished me. Harold that was whispering lies into Edward's ear. These acts must not go...unpunished."

William did not react to Tostig's tale. He picked at a bit of dirt stuck underneath his claws and waited.

"I am on a mission," declared Tostig, raising his voice now. Copsi's translations struggled to convey the same sense of grandeur. "Harold cannot be king! I suggest we come together, lynx and fox, to bring him down."

William stopped picking at his claw. His yellow eyes burrowed into Tostig's and the fox felt his mind being dissected and probed for treachery.

"The time to strike is now - hard and fast! We mustn't let Harold assemble his armies. I have fought alongside them in the past; no English creature is easy to kill. Let's take my sixty ships, and whatever you have, and end this war before it can begin!"

William nodded slowly, a snide smile appearing on his lips.

"You want to be king?" said the lynx.

Tostig hesitated for half a beat. "No."

William began a low, rumbling laugh. Tostig and Copsi shared a disturbed look.

"No," Tostig repeated. "I only want Northumbria. I want my lands and titles restored. I want my life back. I will serve you as king."

Tostig knelt in the mud. Copsi, who was already flat on the ground, lowered his head into his belly of feathers. William strolled closer before squatting in front of them.

"I can get you more soldiers when we land," said Tostig. "The true creatures of Northumbria want and need me back! They raise secret toasts for me in the dark; they live in fear of Harold and the hare! I must return home and free-"

"Shhh," said William. He ran a claw down Tostig's cheek before standing and turning away. He began to walk down the street.

"Well?" Tostig called after him. He flattened the fur which William had touched. "Do you accept?"

The lynx stopped. He didn't even bother to turn around.

"*Non.*"

"What?" bleated Tostig.

"It means, 'no'," whispered Copsi.

"I know what it means, fool!" snapped the fox.

William continued to walk away. Tostig scuttled after him.

"Hey! We're not done here-"

William spun, his fangs bared. Tostig nearly slipped over in the mud as he tried to stop. The lynx burst into a hissing speech which covered the fox in spittle.

"He says he does not want to join us," said Copsi.

"Tell me everything he says, Copsi! Do not miss a single word!"

"He says...he says you are deluded. You allowed your own creatures to conspire and work against you, you allowed them to take over your capital, you allowed them to banish you from your own lands. He says you inspire no love, no fear, and no other reason why creatures should follow you. He says your own brother sees no reason to be loyal to you, no reason to support you in your darkest hour. You are a failure, a coward, and a liar. He says he is in desperate need of ships, and yet he still does not want your help. He says only a devil's creature would consider turning on a brother. There is a dark aura about you; he sees nothing but pain, regret and death in the journey that lies before you.

He says leave now, and don't come back. If he sees you again, it better not be with a sword in your paw. Next time he will finish the job."

Tostig's paw twitched, automatically circling around his hip where his sword should be.

"Tell the *mighty* duke," Tostig said, his voice laced with malice and sarcasm, "that I will simply have to take England by myself. If he comes to his senses, he can join us when we set sail tomorrow."

"*Non,*" said William again, his grisly face upturned in disgust.

"If that is the case, then tell him…once Harold is defeated, and England is mine… I will be forced to defend my country against any creature who wishes to take it."

The lynx growled, his paw tightening on his sword. He might have struck the fox down then had the sky not suddenly been set ablaze with light.

Tostig and William saw it at the same time. They gazed up as a ball of white fire streaked across the sky, leaving a winding trail of clouds in its wake. Screams echoed through the backstreets of Normandy as creatures looked up in panic and wonder.

"What is it?" Copsi croaked.

"I don't know," said Tostig.

"It's a sword," William mumbled in French, tracing the comet's movement with a paw. "It points to England."

"Maybe it's a sign, Copsi," said Tostig. "God is showing His support for me."

"It is a wonderful sign from Heaven," said William to himself, now raising both paws in the sky as if to touch it. "God stands with me."

"It is directing us home, Copsi," said Tostig.

"It scares me, sir."

"Don't be scared – rejoice! We are going home!"

The fox and duck hurried away, heading for their rat fleet that would take them to England. William did not even see them leave as he continued to stare at the skies.

"Thank you, God." William crossed his chest and said a small prayer. Tears streamed openly and fell from his goatee in drips. "I will not let you down."

SPRING

The Enemy

On one foggy morning in May, small families of rabbits and moles poked their snouts out of their burrows as the drums of marching paws came their way. The youngest creatures weren't frightened in the slightest, and raced up to the open air to see what was coming. The older creatures could still remember how the ground shook when Vikings paraded through their lands. They began to tunnel their burrows deeper and pull their younglings away from the surface.

"Ge' down from 'der, Willa!" said young Willa's mother, but the rabbit would not listen. She stared as the first creature emerged from the mist. Dressed in a swirling red cloak and steel armoured plates, with a glinting sword at his hip, came a thin but sturdy looking fox with smiling whiskers, and a golden crown sat upon its head.

"It's the king!" Willa breathed. At once her brothers and sisters, who had been held back admirably well by both parents, wriggled free of their paws and scrambled to the surface.

"Wow!" they chorused together.

The king looked around to find the source of their little voices. He spotted their ears poking out through the tall grass. All the rabbits' jaws dropped open as they saw the gracious king.

"Good morning," Harold said with a wink.

"Mornin'!" shouted Willa, whilst her siblings were too awestruck to speak.

"Say hello, Mabel," said the king. A delicate-looking mouse poked her head over Harold's crown.

"Hello, dears," she squeaked, looking a little queasy at being so unnaturally high up.

Out of the fog came two wolves marching in perfect unison, their steps squelching on the wet grass in a satisfying steadfast beat. They were kitted out with helmets and chainmail dresses. Only their tails and eyes weren't covered in steel, and in their front paws they carried long battle axes with curled blades larger than Harry. Behind the two wolves came another pair. Then another. Then again. Harry counted one hundred and fifty-six wolves but his sister was closer with her guess of three hundred.

Harold had levied a battalion of crack wolves, all of whom had been specifically chosen to accompany the king at all times. Their leader Wulfric, one-eyed yet seeing more than most with pairs, selected these killers as his most dependable soldiers. Harold was happy to have them, but thought they'd be better served stationed along the southern coast than following him across the country. Wulfric said otherwise. The one-eyed captain was hard to argue with and even harder to not be persuaded by.

Harold had assembled all his top creatures at several southern ports as there was no way of knowing where exactly William would attack. His brothers Gyrth and Leofwine, as well as Dunstan the bear and Wulfric, were all defending England with a mixture of trained housecarls and the ordinary farmer creatures of the fyrd. It was impossible to cover every stretch of land and the fox didn't sleep easy with such strained defences. He had a new plan, and there was no time to waste.

The only reason Harold wasn't on the front lines himself was because of his new kingly duties. Archbishop Stigand had insisted he attend the Easter Witan meeting to keep everybody informed.

"Tell us how your heroic defence of England is coming, Your Highness?" the mole had asked cheerfully at the meeting. It was clear Stigand didn't take the threat of William particularly seriously. There were many others who shared his scepticism – bringing an army across the English Channel was no easy feat.

"It's hard to say when I'm not there with my soldiers," Harold had responded a little testily. "I'm going to manoeuvre the fleet to the Isle of Wight; I believe it is the strongest military standpoint for many reasons..."

Harold had paused then, assuming some creature might ask him to elaborate, but nobody did. The Easter Witan had less than half of the members present as the previous one, and they were quite uninterested in the whole affair. Neither of the hares, Earls Edwin and Morcar, were there. The most notable creatures were Waltheof the otter and Edgar the badger, but both were young creatures and had little more to offer than nods and claps.

Most of the creatures that were there spent their time gossiping about the astonishing light that had appeared in the sky. Stigand assured everyone that it was God promising Harold a long reign as king and England a bountiful summer harvest. The fox was not so convinced. More than once he had dreamed of the light. Turning in his sleep, he had imagined it brighter than the sun, blinding him and everything he had ever loved. When awoken, appalled at what he had seen, he would find nothing but emptiness in the room. It often took minutes to pry his leg loose from the grip of his quivering tail.

Harold had managed to see his sister, Edith, before he headed back south to join his armies. She had bestowed the services of Mabel upon him the morning he left. The mousemaid and the vixen had become close since the death of the badger king.

"There is not a kinder, more dedicated mouse alive," Edith had said. "Please keep each other safe."

"We will," Harold told her. The foxes embraced each other and did not pull away for a long time.

Mabel had indeed proved an enjoyable companion as Harold led the wolves across the Kent Downs, an expanse of hills and rolling fields that spread from Surrey down towards the white cliffs of Dover. At the beginning she still spoke to him with the trepidation and respect creatures reserved for their king, but Harold insisted she speak to him like anyone else.

"All this *Your Majesty* this and *Your Highness* that! Nothing would ever get done if we all had to waste time with such nonsense!"

On the morning when Harold and his housecarls crossed beside young Willa and the rest of the litter's burrow, the fox had invited Mabel up to sit atop his head as her little legs could not keep up with the march. Harold walked with long strides and could go for hours on end without needing to stop.

"Maud is a mousemaid for Lord Edwin, though I'm not sure she enjoys it much, sir. Poor Martin passed away last year-" Mabel was explaining about her many relatives when a raven suddenly dropped from the foggy sky, skidding to a halt mid-air in a frantic waving of wings. It squawked and collapsed on the grass.

"Easy, easy," said Harold, kneeling down. "Take it slow."

The raven was young and ambitious. This was his first big flight and he was keen to show his credentials to the king.

"*Your Highness*, it is such an honour to serve you, *Your Majesty*," the raven bowed its beak so that it scraped the grass.

"You see?" Harold said quietly, making Mabel giggle. "What have you seen, raven?"

"Ships, sir, lots of ships! I come from Dover; I saw them with mine own eyes! The skies are full of rumours, sir! Every beak says the same thing! Attacks at Folkestone and other ports too, sir! Every story is the same; ships comin' 'n stealin' everything they gets their pawses on, sir! They be stealin' food 'n then sailin' off again, Your Majesty!"

Harold growled and twirled his whiskers, thinking frantically.

"Lieutenant!"

"Yes, sir," Ceej leapt to attention.

"We will have to move quickly. William will not rest, and neither can we. Raven, I'm afraid you will have to take to the skies once more. Alert as many ports as you can that the lynx is heading for Sandwich-"

"I ought tell you one more thing, sir," said the raven.

"Yes?"

"It's just that, at Dover sir, the figurehead of the lead ship had..." The raven hesitated. He looked unsettled, almost embarrassed.

"We don't have much time, lad."

"It's just it weren't a lynx, sir, like what we was told to look out for."

Harold felt a chill go down his back and shivered so much that Mabel tipped onto her back. Somehow he knew what the raven was going to say before he said it.

"It was a *fox*."

"It's Tostig," stated the king.

Harold felt Mabel freeze. What was the etiquette when the king's own brother was raiding England's shores? She stayed silent as the king thought.

You were never going to stay in exile for long, were you Tostig? But why now? When the lynx is prowling my shores?

"What shall we do, Your Majesty?" whispered Mabel eventually.

North or south? Tostig or William? Two enemies, but which threat was greater?

"Raven, you must fly north at once. Find the hares, Morcar and Edwin. Warn them that Tostig is coming for them. I must stay focused on William. If they want the north so badly, they can be the ones to defend it."

SPRING

The Earls of Northumbria

Sixty ships rowed unopposed through the murky Humber river, the strip of water where the lands of Mercia and Northumbria met. Innocent creatures spied them from the cover of trees on either bank, listening out for the splashing of oars and grunts of rats. Tostig stood on the prow of the *Vindicta,* the arrowhead of the fleet. Carved into the wood at the bow was a fox, its teeth bared. Tostig draped a paw around its neck and hung off it.

"Get up here, Copsi," he called, his whiskers blowing in the wind.

"I am quite happy here, sir," Copsi moaned. The duck was lying flat on the quarterdeck on the verge of being sick as the ship skipped forward.

"You're an embarrassment to your species!" Tostig laughed.

"We prefer to stick to canals usually, sir!"

Tostig dug his claws deep into the wood. He swung around the curved front of the ship, his lower paws sweeping the top of the water, before landing expertly next to Copsi on the deck.

"You see that?" said Tostig.

"Please be careful, sir," groaned Copsi.

"Don't patronise me, Copsi."

"Yes, sir."

Tostig turned away from the duck and looked out over the prow once more. For the first time since his exile he was at peace; he was going to war. He took a deep, contented breath and immediately regretted it. The one hundred rats working the oars had built up a sweat and the ship stunk.

The Stray Fox had not spent his exile moping about his misfortune. He had sourced a pirate platoon of rats in Flanders. Tostig conceded they were not exactly the sort of well-trained creatures that Harold would have at his disposal, but what they lacked in organisation they made up for in viciousness. One-on-one, his rats would be no match for the King's Wolves, but a whole family of the vermin working in unison was another prospect altogether. They fought with short knives and were not afraid to use their teeth to gnaw at their enemies. It was the general etiquette of war for creatures to use their weapons and not their teeth and claws, but Tostig had always thought that ridiculous, and intended on telling every creature that fought for him to use whatever was necessary to win.

Whether the rats were an elite fighting force or not, Tostig knew they were just the beginning. The fox had rounded up their support with promises of plunder and titles, but he would secure most of his allies in England. There would be outrage at his exile and many creatures would join him in righting this grievous wrong. Tostig was sure of it.

The fox had already moved on from the disappointment in Normandy, deciding that he didn't want to answer to the lynx anyway. He had directed his rats across the Channel and landed in Norfolk and Lincolnshire. They were met with resistance wherever they landed and so Tostig had allowed his rats to raid and pillage like the Vikings of old.

After scavenging as much food and treasures as they could, the fleet took the Humber river and headed inland. They were delayed somewhat as many ports were dammed by do-gooding otters and beavers. They had lost a lot of time and Tostig was beginning to get restless. He could not relax until they had taken York, the capital of Northumbria.

"Faster! Faster! Are you rats or mice?" Tostig shouted. The hundred muscular sea-rats had spent a lifetime on the deck of one ship or another. They scowled up at the fox. Tostig didn't much care; he had promised the rats far more wealth than they deserved – he would make them earn it.

"Tails! Tails!" called the rats. The rats simultaneously wrapped their tails around their oars for extra power and speed.

"Better!" said Tostig.

"Hrrr," Copsi whined. He retched but it was dry, his stomach was already empty several times over.

"I'm close, Copsi, so close I can almost taste it," Tostig grinned. "This will all be over soon," he looked down at the pitiful duck and yanked him to his feet.

"Thank you, sir."

"I will have us back in York in no time, Copsi. Just wait."

"I believe in you, sir."

Tostig closed his eyes, imagining taking back Northumbria and leaving the hares full of bloody holes.

Then what? Tostig dreamt. *Then maybe we go south, and greet our new king...*

He imagined the look of fear on Harold's face before he drove his sword into his heart.

"Just wait," he smiled to himself.

At the first free opportunity Tostig's sixty ships made port. Thousands of rats poured on land, slithering silently through the wet grass. The small fishing village nearby was seized and all the local creatures summoned to the centre. The smaller creatures submitted at once, but the village had a rabble of beavers and otters who needed more coercing. It needed one otter to be swarmed by a clump of rats to restore order.

Tostig entered later, enjoying the theatrics. He pulled back his black cloak and delighted in the gasps from the cowering crowd.

"The Earl of Northumbria has returned!" Copsi announced.

The news wasn't followed by the cheers Tostig would have expected. He blamed the stench of the rats.

"Do not fear!" Tostig smiled. "I am not here to harm you, I am here to save you!"

Again there was silence from the villagers. Most were too busy looking at the circle of rats that enclosed them. The vermin relished being back on land and could not stay still. Instead they slunk around the villagers, their excitable whispers merging into a sinister hiss.

"Save us from what?" a creature shouted from the crowd. There were a few mutterings of support.

"Join my quest for justice!" Tostig said, ignoring the outburst. "I have been ruler of Northumbria for ten years - the hare Morcar is a common thief! Join me as I march on York and take back what is mine!"

This was greeted with more silence and then, *laughter?*

"We don' wan' yeh 'ere!" cried an ageing mole at the front.

"What don' you understan'?" laughed an otter.

"I welcome any of you strong enough to wield a blade!" continued Tostig.

"Yeh a southerner!"

"Go back to Wessex!"

"Together we can defeat Morcar!" Tostig roared.

The crowd began to boo. A brown and sticky lump slapped him across the face.

"Who did that? I hope that was mud!" the fox yelled.

There was more laughter from the Northumbrians and Tostig's anger flared. He whipped out his sword in a silver flash. That got their attention.

"Now," Tostig raised his sword above his head and saw every pair of eyes follow it. "Who's with me?"

The Northumbrian mole limped forward. Every inch of its fuzzy black fur was coated with a lifetime of dried mud. It looked around blindly for the fox.

"Yeh ain't our earl no more. Yeh ain't nobody no more. Earl Morcar is twice the creature yeh'll ever-"

Tostig slashed him over the chest with his sword. The old mole collapsed, his ugly pink paws scrambling over his wound. The villagers roared and surged forward. Thrice as many rats swarmed them, wielding their stubby knives and forcing them back with a series of nasty jabs.

Tostig turned his back on the ensuing chaos, wiping his sword clean of mole blood. Copsi blinked up at him.

"What?" Tostig snapped.

"Nothing," Copsi shook his head.

The fox glowered and grabbed a nearby rat.

"Burn it all," he growled. "Take whatever you want."

His rats gladly obliged the order. They flooded into houses and turfed out any hiding creatures. Any prize possessions were collected and hoarded in great piles, and any creature brave enough to fend the rats off was met with gleeful brutality. Tostig still remembered the humiliation of being forced out of his own lands like it was yesterday. Now he was forcing other creatures to run.

I will be earl again, Tostig swore. *Whether through love and loyalty, or by power and fear, I will retake what is mine.*

The fox did not see what became of the mole he had struck down. Instead he marched through the village with a flaming torch. He was setting fire to a thatched hut when he heard the horn.

Long, ceremonial, pretentious. It could only have been the hares.

From all sides armoured Northumbrians came trooping into the village. Four divisions of heavyweight badgers, thick-skinned otters, and archer squirrels soon surrounded Tostig at every angle.

"Wha-" said Tostig.

"They knew we were coming!" Copsi cried.

"Into lines! Into lines!" Tostig shouted at his rats, but few seemed to hear him over the horns. They were spread out throughout the village, too busy hunting for treasures. Arrows began to fly and many rats bolted. They scurried back to the ships, clutching whatever treasures they could manage close to their chests.

"Cowards!" Tostig screamed after them. "Stand and fight!"

Some did, but most didn't. The fox could not stop the stampede of fleeing rats as they rushed past him, back to their ships.

"What shall we do?" said Copsi, ducking under a whizzing arrow.

If Tostig allowed himself to panic, he knew all would be lost. He grabbed the duck.

"Get out of here! Fly!"

"Sir?" asked Copsi. "You are saving me?"

"What? Of course not! We need fire! Get a torch and burn."

"Burn what?"

"Everything. Now go!" he threw the duck into the air. Copsi flapped and wobbled in the sky. A couple of arrows missed him by inches as he went. Tostig didn't much like the idea of relying on the duck in battle but desperate times called for desperate measures.

If Copsi could create enough mayhem there might be a chance for an escape, but Tostig wasn't about to sit around and wait, not when there was a chance to kill the jumped-up rabbit who had stolen his life. The Northumbrian army converged on Tostig's position. The limping hare led them from the front.

"Morcar," snarled Tostig. He recognised some of the other creatures from his time in Northumbria. Some of them had been the ones to march against Tostig when he had been the Earl of Northumbria. The fox had fantasised about returning home and bringing them to justice, but here he was, caught off guard again.

It wasn't supposed to be this way this time.

"With me!" the fox screamed at any rat who had not yet run to safety. "If you want to be paid, you will fight!"

Tostig ran at the Northumbrians, not daring to see how many rats joined him. The two forces collided. The rats were small and quickly infiltrated the opposing army's defences. Tostig saw a dozen of them overrun a fat badger whose fur was covered in so much flab that their knives barely made a scratch. One leaped into the air and gnawed at an otter's neck whilst Tostig sliced through any creature that approached him.

All of the northern warriors knew they were here for the fox and they all wanted the glory of being the creature to bring him down.

Tostig stood out amongst the mass of rats, yet no fighter could match his speed and skill. One by one the Northumbrians fell.

The fox had his own eyes set on the hare, who was busy battling off a cluster of rats. Tostig blocked the attack of a muscular rabbit and then slit its body open with his sword, painting the white fur red. Two otters engaged Tostig but he blocked both attacks and ended their lives with a graceful spin of his weapon.

An acrid smell of burning hay and timber began to overwhelm the copper stench of blood. Copsi had set fire to the tops of multiple houses. Smoke drowned the battlefield as the wooden huts burnt and crumbled all around them.

"Morcar!" Tostig shouted when he reached the hare.

The hare looked around for the fox, struggling to see through the clouds of smoke. Tostig lunged for him, but his sword clanged off the hare's armour.

"The fox is mine!"

The battlefield ceased to be filled with the sounds of clashing steel and instead filled with coughing creatures. Tostig tried to keep track of the silhouette of the hare in the smoke. He stabbed in that direction and this time he struck fur.

"I got him! I got him!" Tostig roared madly. "I got the hare! Northumbria is saved!"

He swung his sword again but struck nothing but air.

"Let's get outta 'ere!" a nearby rat begged him.

Tostig blinked and looked around. He could only see a handful of creatures in front of him, but could hear the many screams of both sides. Whether Morcar was dead or not, the village was ablaze and the rat was right.

"To the ships!" Tostig roared.

The rat mercenaries didn't need telling twice. They ran through the mask of the smoke, each holding the tail of the one in front so they didn't lose one another. One rat leapt on Tostig's neck, sinking its claws through his flesh to cling on. The fox barged his way through the obscured battleground, his eyes stinging and his throat burning. He stabbed at any creature in his way and his enemies fell without ever seeing their attacker. The fires Copsi had started had no intention of stopping. Each house set its neighbour alight, and as the creatures hurried to put it out Tostig and his rats were free to race back to the ships.

Once out of the smoke they charged back down the hill towards the river. The fear of death made many rats shove and claw their friends and family out of the way. When Tostig reached the *Vindicta* he saw much of the fleet had already left. There couldn't have been more than half of the sixty ships still there.

"Hey!" Tostig yelled. None of the rats paid him any attention. Any survivors dove headfirst into their ships and began rowing back up the river.

Copsi's fire had all but engulfed the entire village. Rats still poured out of the smoke, black and bruised, coughing and bleeding. They took up their oars at once. The rat that had escaped on Tostig's back jumped onto the *Vindicta* and grabbed his own oar.

"Stop," Tostig told him. "Not yet."

"I'm outta 'ere," said the rat. Tostig hopped on to the ship himself. He grabbed the rat around the neck and lifted him up.

"I said wait."

"You are crazee!" shouted the rat, thrashing around in Tostig's paw. The rat next to them recoiled as an arrow struck his chest. He slumped over his oar and was still.

Tostig looked towards the village and the plumes of dark smoke which circled over it like thunderclouds preparing to strike.

"Come on," he whispered. "Come on."

As he stared into the distant smoke another arrow whistled past his head.

"What are you waiting for?" shrieked the squirming rat.

As it spoke a ball of fire soared through the smoke cloud towards them.

"Aaaaahhhhh!" it shouted before landing with a great *thud!* onto the *Vindicta* deck.

Tostig tossed the rat away and ran over to the burning creature. He patted away the flames on the poor creature's feathers.

"Thank you, sir," said Copsi.

"What are you doing, setting yourself on fire?" said Tostig.

"Sorry, sir."

Tostig ducked another arrow before turning on the rats. "What are you waiting for? Get us out of here!"

Only twenty sea-rats from the *Vindicta* survived the ambush, yet the ship sailed just as fast as Tostig had ever seen it. With the threat of being chased down the river looming behind them, the rats heaved harder than ever before.

The Humber River got wider and wider until the *Vindicta* spilled out into the North Sea. At this stage they could be safe in the knowledge that they weren't being followed. Some rats threw up from exhaustion and the fox granted them rest.

Tostig stood at the bow, where an arrow had found its mark in the fox figurehead he'd had carved in the wood. He looked out across the waters at his decimated fleet.

Only twelve of his sixty ships remained. There had been a mass desertion and Tostig had no means of stopping them. Even now he could see a handful of ships sailing south, back to Flanders where he had found them.

"Damn mercenaries," said Tostig. "No honour."

The North Sea was in a boisterous mood and it had started to rain. Copsi was moaning about seasickness again on the deck and every other creature was too focused on their own aches and pains to notice Tostig's bottom lip start to wobble.

Harold and the hares have poisoned everyone against me.

Tostig slid to the floor next to Copsi. He curled up into a ball and held his tail close to his chest with both paws, like a cub holding its favourite toy. The rain hid his tears.

"Are you ok, sir?" said the duck, rising into a precarious sitting position. He shook his glossy green head to quell his seasickness but it only made it worse.

"It's over, Copsi," Tostig whispered. "I failed."

"Well, we tried our best, that's all we can do."

"They don't want me," he mumbled.

"What's that?"

"The Northumbrians hate me."

"No, no!" said Copsi. He rested a wing on Tostig's head. "Don't say that. You said you killed Morcar? That's a start."

"I'm not sure, maybe," said Tostig, smiling weakly. "It was a strong thrust."

"Shall we return to Flanders, sir?" the duck stroked Tostig's fur. "It's nice there."

"No," muttered Tostig. "I am Earl of Northumbria. The true northern creatures raise a toast to me and wait for my return...." his voice tailed off.

"It seems we cannot do it all ourselves, sir. We need more help."

Tostig scowled and sat up. He leant against the side of the ship.

"We need to take our time, build a proper army, and get some strong allies," said Copsi. "There must be someone."

Tostig's orange ear perked up a little. He rubbed his tears away.

"There... there is one who might be able to..."

"Who, sir?"

Tostig grinned and life sparked behind his glistening blue eyes. "The most fearsome creature alive..."

"Who?"

"It would be dangerous..." Tostig seemed to be talking to himself now. He rose to his paws.

"I don't think William will reconsider joining us, if that is-"

"Pah! No, you fool," laughed Tostig, his usual zest reappearing as quickly as it had departed. "There are far more formidable creatures than the lynx out there."

"Then who?"

"Yes, yes, this could work," Tostig began pacing up and down. He drew his sword and swiped at the air as he schemed away. "I just have to convince him...that shouldn't be too hard...England is quite the prize...he can be king...I get Northumbria back...yes...yes..."

"Sir, please, where are we going?"

"Set course to Norway," Tostig said proudly.

"*Pourquoi?*" an eavesdropping rat moaned exasperatedly.

"There is one more potential ally that I have not considered. We will find King Harald Hardrada, the last true Viking. The beast will make short work of these northern traitors, and my brother too. Then everything will be put right, and I can finally go home."

SPRING

The Owl

A slender shadow was perched on the altar table, facing away from Lanfranc. Its feathers were mostly brown but beset with white streaks, like a branch that had lost strips of its bark. It was draped in a white and gold robe with a tiara nestled atop its head.

Lanfranc twisted the hazelnuts in his pockets thrice over for good luck, and cleared his throat.

"Holy Father," said the red squirrel, bending low.

The body of the tawny owl did not move. His head rotated around with the slow precision of a creature that hadn't had to rush in a long time. The pope's face was round and, other than the stooping, yellow-green worm of a beak, totally flat. It stared at Lanfranc with its dark, empty eyes. Birds were notoriously hard to read and the squirrel panicked for a moment in the face of Alexander's vacant expression; had he done something to upset him?

"Brother Lanfranc!" Pope Alexander's face didn't change, but his voice was hearty and welcoming. "How are you, dear fellow?"

"I'm very well!" Lanfranc beamed, puffing out his cheeks in relief. "It makes an old squirrel very proud to see you here!"

"I could never have achieved it without your teachings." If the pope could have fashioned his beak into a smile he would have. It was simple flattery but Lanfranc rejoiced nonetheless. Alexander had been a top student of his all those years ago, and Lanfranc had known to keep good relations with the owl.

"*Per favore,* your successes are all your own," said the squirrel with another bow.

"You're too kind. So, what can I do for you?"

"I come on behalf of Duke William."

"Ah," Alexander hopped down from the table with a single flapping of his wings to ease his landing. "What does he want this time?"

The owl's voice still sounded cheery but partnered with his emotionless face it made Lanfranc uncomfortable. He dug at a scratch on his ear with his paw.

"Your support," said the squirrel.

"In what?"

"Invading England."

The owl stood perfectly still in contemplative silence. The moment stretched into minutes. Lanfranc turned the hazelnut thrice over again.

"May I ask what you are thinking, Your Holiness?" said the squirrel when it became apparent that the owl would have no qualms not moving all night.

"What is there to say, Lanfranc?" His voice lacked its original euphoria, but hadn't slipped to hostile just yet. Lanfranc saw that as a win.

"I can think of two things: *si* or *no*?" Lanfranc smiled, but this time there was a hint of enmity in the owl's silence. "You will want to hear why William wishes to invade first, of course..."

The owl blinked and watched him.

"There are many reasons for this crusade we are proposing, Holy Father."

The owl blinked again.

"Where to start?" Lanfranc said aloud, a little flustered. "Perhaps at the beginning, hmm?" The owl didn't join in with the squirrel's nervous laughter. "The badger king, King Edward, spoke with William before he died. It was agreed that the kingdom of England would go to him if Edward never had cubs with the vixen."

Finally, the owl spoke.

"You are mistaken. The badger proposed Harold be the next king on his deathbed. Perhaps you have the wrong information there." Pope Alexander spoke with the unpleasant confidence of a creature who was accustomed to correcting others. Lanfranc relished dealing with such creatures. The more stubborn they were, the easier the squirrel found he could manoeuvre them to his will.

"Ah, but the badger had already promised the kingdom to William."

"I see."

Silence resumed.

"You could see why William would be upset then, hmm?" Lanfranc prompted.

"Certamente."

Breathing was the only sound in the grand chapel for a moment. This time Lanfranc would not speak, he could not let the pope continue to dominate the conversation. The squirrel watched and waited.

"I am sure William understands how things are done in England?" said the owl eventually.

"I'm not sure I follow, Your Holiness."

"The Witan decides who will rule. Not the previous king. The kingdom was not Edward's to give away to Harold, or indeed, to William. The lynx is Duke of Normandy because his father was the duke before him. England is quite different."

"This is true," Lanfranc knew it was better to agree than to press the matter. The pope didn't seem impressed so far.

"This is not enough to warrant my support. The English have paid 'Peter's Pence' ever since Alfred the Great. Very generous donations too; Rome cannot turn away from all that money."

"If William was king, I'm sure he would arrange to still make the payments - more even!" Lanfranc decided to run with it. "Yes, he told me he would make even larger payments, in fact!"

"Hmm," the owl was forever impossible to read, but his voice was softening.

"This new king broke a sacred oath!" squeaked Lanfranc.

"Harold? Go on..."

"The fox swore on holy relics that he would serve William loyally when the lynx became king. Then he betrayed his honour and disgraced God when he stole the crown."

"Hmm...this is not good...not good at all..."

The owl used its long legs to begin pacing up and down the atrium. Lanfranc followed him as calmly as he could manage. He scratched frantically at his ear with one paw and fiddled with his hazelnut with the other. He had the pope exactly where he wanted him.

"If you will give William your support, Holy Father, creatures will flock to our cause. Then we will be able to bring Harold to justice in the name of Pope Alexander – in the name of God!"

The owl stopped pacing. He nodded, and looked ready to agree, before he scowled and resumed his agitated wandering.

"William is a fine warrior, but so is Harold. How could the lynx possibly defeat the fox? You see my trouble, Lanfranc? If I am to pit two Christian dominions against one another, I have to be absolutely sure that the one I back will be the one that comes out on top. Otherwise the risk is too great."

"I think it best we leave the war planning to the warriors, Your Holiness. William has some sensational plans that have never been attempted before-"

Lanfranc stopped himself. He winced at his own misstep. William's vision of taking the notoriously wild horses with him across the Channel was unheard of.

"Never been attempted before? I'm not sure I like the sound of that. Is that supposed to assure me of his victory?"

"Your Holiness-"

"The English can afford to lose battle after battle, so long as they win the last," the pope spoke with a grave finality in his voice. "If William loses one, he is finished."

Lanfranc opened his mouth but nothing came out.

"I will discuss with the Council of Cardinals tomorrow. Thank you for bringing this to me, Lanfranc."

The owl gestured a wing to the exit. Lanfranc sloped away with the owl at his side. The squirrel's mind was racing; he hadn't done enough. The pope wasn't convinced, and the prize of Canterbury had never seemed further away.

They left the cathedral together. There weren't any clouds and the moon lit them well.

"Where are you staying tonight, old friend?" asked the pope.

"Alexander," said Lanfranc abruptly. "Think seriously about what I have said. The time to make change is now. You know as well as I do, popes should not be elected by kings, kings should be elected by popes."

Lanfranc left without another word. The owl stood where he was for a long time before taking a long overdue flight. His wings had become rusty from too many years of diplomacy and not enough exercise. The air was cleaner above the city, and his thoughts were sharper. He took a few laps around the sleeping Rome and when he landed, he had made his decision on this small matter of Harold, William, and the future of England.

SPRING
A Holy War

Duke William had been tossing and turning all night. He made loud tutting noises and scowls but his wildcat wife didn't stir.

"Are you awake?" he whispered to her in the dark.

"No," Matilda grumbled. "Shh."

The lynx smiled. "Then wake up, I can't sleep."

"Not my problem," she rolled around and turned her back to him.

"Oh, Mora," he said, using his affectionate name for her. "My mind is always awake, wondering about where we will live in England when it is mine. Where would you want to be, *mon amour*?"

"Wherever, dear."

"Wherever? C'mon, say something."

"I'll just stay here," she said.

"What?" William said, grabbing her shoulder. "What do you mean?"

"I mean I like it in Normandy, England is cold..."

"*Mon amour!* I am taking England for you, for us, for the kittens."

"Hm, ok."

"What? You don't believe me?"

She twisted back around and put a paw to his face. "In part it is for us, yes. But mainly..."

"What?"

"It's for you."

William didn't say anything. She didn't raise her voice or change her tone, but something about her words stung.

There was a knock at the door.

"What?" William called.

"It's Lanfranc, sir, he's returned," responded the creature from the other side of the door. "You said to bring him no matter the time or-"

"Yes, yes, let him through!" William leapt off the bed.

The door creaked open and the red squirrel stepped through. A rat servant brought in a torch and lit the bedside candles before leaving hurriedly.

"What's happening?" said Matilda, squinting at the entry of the squirrel.

"I apologise for the late hour, my Duke, my Duchess," said Lanfranc, though the energy and excitement in his voice suggested he wasn't sorry at all. William's heart was beating fast in his chest; he could see what the squirrel was holding.

"How did it go, Lanfranc?" said William, his voice shaking.

"Pope Alexander listened to my sage advice. He has bestowed upon you this," Lanfranc offered up a large, folded piece of fabric. William took it and opened it up on the bed. Sowed into the fabric was the image of an owl and besides it the Holy Cross.

"You did it..." said William, adrenaline coursing through his body. "I can't believe you did it..."

"Of course I did," Lanfranc boasted. "He also gave you this." The squirrel yanked a large box free of his pocket and gave it to the lynx. Inside was a ring with another cross. He slipped it onto his paw.

"A ring and a flag?" said Matilda. "What is all this?"

William was staring speechlessly at the ring in awe and seemed not to hear her.

"Duchess Matilda," Lanfranc beamed. "The pope has offered support to William. The invasion is now a Holy War. We have secured the support of God in our attack. The balance has now shifted in our favour."

Matilda put a paw to her open mouth. "Is this true, *mon amour*?"

William looked at her and tears fell unabashed from his eyes. "Yes. This changes everything. With Pope Alexander and God on my side, nothing will stand in my way."

PART TWO
THE LAST VIKING

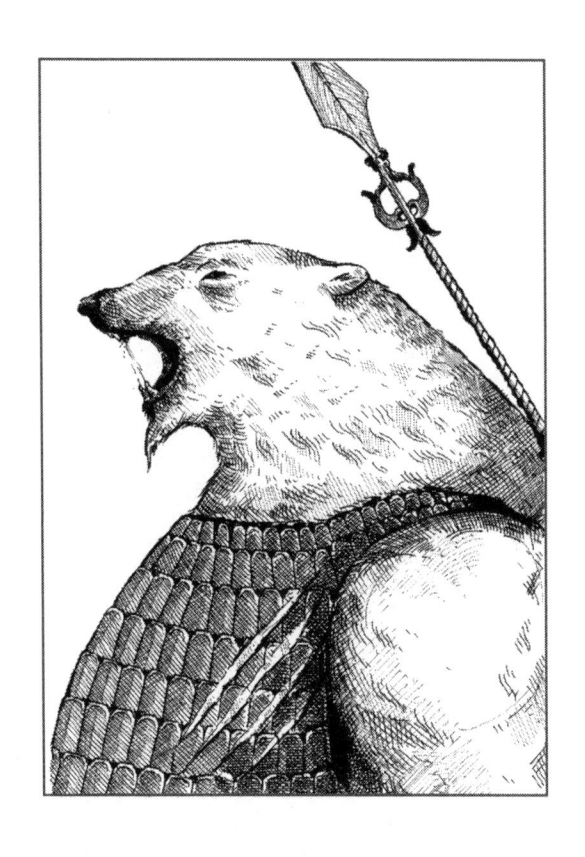

SUMMER

The Hard Ruler

The great hulking shadow of the king was growing long and thin as the sun dipped in between the crevice of two sloping mountains. The glistening, damp mud was hardening as the warmth of the day slipped away with each passing moment. The polar bear was unperturbed by the creeping frosty cold, and quite protected from it by his enormous, shaggy white coat of fur.

"Keep going, Thjoldolf," said the king, trudging determinedly forward on all four paws.

Thjoldolf had bright orange feet and a striking red and grey coloured beak. His feathers were black on the back, and pure white at his breast. He was a brittle-looking thing with morose looking eyes and a sort of stuffy, pompous complexion. He cleared his throat and spoke in a dry voice;

All creatures know Harald
fought eighteen savage battles;
wherever the warrior went
all hope of peace was broken.
The grey-

"'Shattered'," said Hardrada. "Try 'shattered'."

The puffin, shivering somewhat in the mounting cold, nodded and cleared his throat again.

Wherever the warrior went
all hope of peace was shattered.
The grey eagle's talons

You reddened with blood, great king;
On all your expeditions
the hungry wolves were feasted.

"Good," Hardrada's lips twisted upwards for a half second before sliding back down. The king believed a creature should be as comfortable wielding words as they should a sword. While his flesh would one day perish, his words would live on. It didn't hurt his relationships with both of his wives either; both creatures loved listening to him regaling his great victories in battle in lavish, grand verses.

Thjoldolf opened his beak to continue but Hardrada suddenly raised his great white paw to his mouth in a shushing gesture.

"Wait," growled Hardrada in a whisper. He stopped his pounding strides and the puffin took the time to take a much needed breather from the extreme pace they had maintained since the morning. Hardrada, meanwhile, had his eyes squinted in concentration. His ears were twitching independently from each other as they hunted down the source of a sound that Thjoldolf had not yet heard.

The king looked up and the puffin followed his gaze. A circle of pink sky was visible between the wilting branches of gently bristling, spindly trees. The hectic sounds of flapping wings approached, and a moment later flocks of geese and ducks could be seen soaring overhead. There was much squawking and laughter as both families tried to outdo the other with their arrow formations. The ducks seemed less organised and one or two resorted to flying into and knocking the geese off course. There was faux outrage from the geese as their formation broke and more laughter from the ducks.

Hardrada grinned, reaching for the two metre long spear that was strapped to his back. He shifted his paw along the shaft, feeling its weight.

"This way," he said to Thjoldolf, pointing the spear after the geese and ducks.

The king picked up the pace further still, leaving Thjoldolf to wheeze and struggle behind. His heart fluttered with the familiar ecstasy of bubbling bloodlust. He'd been hunting the families for hours. He cut through the forest shrubbery and stopped as the trees opened out to a great lake surrounded by a grey stony shore.

The two families of geese and ducks had joined hundreds, if not thousands, of others. Some swam in the dark, moody surface of the lake and others sat chatting lazily on the pebbled beach, each blissfully unaware of the predator in their midst. The surrounding mountains were mirrored in the shimmering water; Hardrada watched the sun's reflection sink behind the mountains and disappear into the lake's black depths.

The king's black snout flared and air poured into his canyon-like nostrils. He rose to stand on his hind legs and relaxed his shoulders. More deep breathing settled his heart and focused his mind. He pointed a black-tipped claw at the heart of the birds and selected an unsuspecting target.

Thjoldolf appeared at his side but the king ignored him. He took one slow step with his left paw and another with his right, holding his spear behind him. On the third step he leant back, transitioned all his weight forward, and launched the spear through the air. The steel-capped weapon whistled as it ate the distance between Hardrada and his target in less than a second. The spear never wobbled or deviated off course. The throw was true and unstoppable. When it struck it severed the head of the duck and carried on into the chest of the goose behind. Both creatures were dead before they could prepare to be scared, the ghosts of their laughter still on their faces.

Time was suspended for just a moment as the jovial atmosphere of the birds lingered. Creatures turned to face the commotion and stared blankly at the dead creatures, their minds catching up with their eyes. One scream was enough to light the fire of fear, and soon the lake was a cauldron of panic and chaos. Hundreds of birds scattered into the sky until there were only a few weeping creatures left - those who had known the victims best, Hardrada figured.

The king sloped back down to all fours and marched over to the water's surface. It had been a fine throw and he was soothed with the knowledge that he still had the strength and eye to do it, despite now being over fifty years old.

The last of the ducks and geese also took flight as the giant beast-king approached. Two geese tried to drag the body of their own into the sky, but the dead weight was too much and they dropped the body as Hardrada arrived beneath them. It landed with a dull thud on the pebbled floor.

The king absorbed the scene. Blood was still pouring from the headless duck, and the goose still had the spear embedded in its chest. He spotted the duck's green head floating in the lake some ten metres away.

"Exceptional," Thjoldolf breathed beside him, taking in the devastation. "Would you like me to compose a verse about it?"

Hardrada gave a resentful grunt. Something about the puffin's words irritated him. The king's life and career as a warrior were unparalleled with any creature Hardrada knew or had heard of. Thousands of pages could be written about his victories, but was this really how the book would end? Hunting helpless creatures was a poor substitute for war, but after the treaty with Denmark was signed two years ago, Hardrada had been without a conflict for the first time in his life.

The king sighed, the enjoyment of a clean kill vanishing. He ripped the spear from the goose's flesh and strapped the weapon onto his back. He grabbed the duck's body too and slung it over his shoulder, knowing his beloved friend Orre would like to see the perfect decapitation when he got back.

"We are going back, Your Majesty?" said Thjoldolf as the king trod back towards the treeline.

"Aye," he said. "Best not keep the fox waiting too long."

"The English are not to be trusted," Thjoldolf said haughtily. "Safest just to send him back now."

"Always the cynic, Thjoldolf," Hardrada snorted. "Let's see what the fox is sniffing around for, so far from home."

Something interesting, I hope, thought the king.

SUMMER

The Chevalier

William trampled through the untamed Forêt d'Écouves determinedly, scanning for hoof prints on the dry ground or any other sign of travelling horses.

"Sire," a voice called from the trees. "They've fallen behind again."

William looked up to see an albino polecat hanging upside down from a branch; the jongleur Taillefer.

"What?" the lynx barked. He spun around and saw that the party's third and fourth members had indeed grown small in the distance once more.

I would never have embarrassed my father so, thought William, as rage bubbled to the surface like a pot of water left over fire too long.

"How 'bout a song?" chimed the polecat from the trees, its beguiling pink eyes shining.

William grunted.

"It's not a no," Taillefer winked. He jumped from branch to branch as he sang, his eyes wild and his soft voice high.

The badger saw black and it's fur went red,
As life slipped out the hole in the back of his head!
The fox struck true and hid its sly knife,
As the vixen bawled tears - what a nice wife!
The English placed the crown on that soft ginger head,
As the helpless badger lay murdered in his bed!
Now the killer-thief Harold is king,
And all our hopes lie with Duke William,
His great steel sword and his shiny Papal ring!

William smiled reluctantly.

"It's getting better," he snorted.

"I try," the polecat landed on the ground and bowed.

Just then, the lynx turned to see a fuzzy-furred, stocky marmot rolling its way towards them. He looked like a sort of large, chunky squirrel with leaves dangling out of his round cheeks as he chewed noisily. He had multiple satchel bags strapped around his waist and was carrying a lengthy roll of parchment and quill.

"S-s-so s-s-sorry, s-s-sir," Bill the marmot babbled, leaves spewing from his mouth. "C-can't k-keep up. S-so fast you are, s-so n-noble-"

"That's enough," William silenced him.

Bill had been tasked to record all of William's actions so that future generations could one day learn of his great achievements. The marmot was certainly in awe of the lynx and his tendency for exaggeration rivalled that of a family of gossiping pigeons. William watched the creature catch his breath sourly, already regretting the decision to bring him along on this particular quest.

Moments later, the final member of their group crashed through the undergrowth towards them.

"Is it time for luncheon?" William's oldest son whined.

The fur of both the lynxes had turned a similar shade of reddish brown in the summer heat, though where William's dark spots still stood out, Robert's were nearly invisible. This was never a good sign for a lynx, and William often doubted his son's ability to represent the family after he was gone. William's third son, William Rufus, though much younger, was already showing more of the qualities he was looking for. William wished he had chosen to bring Rufus along with him for the mission, but it was Robert who was first in line to be duke, and he had to make some effort to build a relationship with the petulant teenager.

"We've barely started," said William, his patience wafer thin.

"I really don't see the point," huffed Robert.

"I will not explain myself again," William growled.

William's horse, a beast he considered a friend and ally, had fallen ill. The honest truth was that the great thing would not survive the voyage to England. Of course, he could have taken an already tamed steed, but that was not what his father had taught him. One needed to be bonded to one's horse to be sure it would not bolt at the first sign of battle.

"You should be excited to find a steed. Many fine beasts have been found in these woods."

"Right," Robert nodded dismissively.

"Just do as I say, *Curthose*," said William scathingly. Robert's mother had begged him not to use the nickname that insulted his son's thick, short legs. But she wasn't here, and the boy was irritating him.

William spun on his heel and led the party of four further into the depths of the forest. As he did so the lynx endeavoured to push thoughts of his errant son from his mind. There was something far more important at stake.

After word had spread that the pope had blessed the lynx, support for his invasion had come flooding in from all areas. Previously unsure Norman creatures were swiftly convinced. Even the craven chamois, Count Eustace, had offered up his creatures to the cause.

Many knights from across surrounding territories had come in their droves to offer their services to the "Chosen Lynx", as he was now being dubbed. Believing that the duke's attack was being overseen by God, they thought that success was already determined. Those who died in battle would be assured a pathway to heaven for their noble work, and those who survived would be honoured to defeat the corrupt English in God's name.

Construction of the duke's fleet was underway and his army was close to being fully assembled. There was just one thing he needed now: a ride worthy and willing enough to carry William forth on his journey to win back the country he was promised.

I know you're out here, William licked his nose in anticipation. *I can feel you.*

Whilst Bill and Robert were far from ideal companions, Taillefer proved himself to be an entertaining and worthwhile addition as the day wore on. The polecat improvised many flattering songs about the duke that cheered his spirits.

Oh duke what an honour,
it is to walk with you!
Oh Harold you're a goner,
the brave lynx gon' get you!

William was taken with the strange little creature and even let the polecat share some of the mead he'd brought with him. Not only highly amusing, Taillefer was sharp enough of snout to find an old and rather unpleasant pile of horse droppings (Robert point-blank refused to go near it) which set the small company off in the right direction. Other than this discovery, and a brief, uncomfortable run-in with a protective stag, the day was an uneventful one.

Night fell. William lay resting by a crudely constructed fire, staring at the pope's ring in the dim firelight. Bill lay on his front, shifting uncomfortably and trying to find a flat bit of earth to write on. Taillefer was juggling with two flaming logs, his energy unceasing, whilst Robert laid a little way away from the group, snoring lightly.

"And d-do you think that H-Ha-Har- the fox a-always wanted E-England?" The marmot was reeling off a list of seemingly never-ending questions.

"Who knows?" said William absently. He hadn't blinked or looked away from the ring for two minutes.

"Why is having h-horses s-s-so imp-p-portant?"

"Harold cannot be underestimated, he is..." William wanted to say 'brilliant' and scowled at himself for even thinking it. "We fought together in the Battle of Dinan last year. He has a keen eye for strategy...and he was a competent chess player too."

"B-b-but why-"

"I will need to be at full force if I am to defeat him," William said impatiently. "If we fight on his terms we will lose, but the fox will not expect the horses. It has not been done before," William smiled to himself. "They will talk about us for a thousand years."

Bill nodded urgently in agreement and began scribbling notes down on the page.

"They will talk about you, sweet duke," said Taillefer, still juggling. "But the rest of us I am not so sure."

"This is the way," William shrugged. "It is not impossible for a creature such as yourself to make a stamp on history."

"Oh, quite right," the polecat grinned impishly. "When the battle comes, I will find a way for the world to remember the name Taillefer, don't you worry about that."

William wrested his eyes from the ring and smiled at the polecat. "I can't wait to see it."

Bill looked up from his writings, oblivious that any conversation had continued without him.

"And w-why is it imp-p-portant for you to find y-your o-o-own horse?"

William looked over towards the back of his sleeping son. "Because of my father," he whispered.

"Go on," whispered Bill back, his quill hovering over the page.

"My father, the duke, taught me what it meant to be a Norman, a knight, a *chevalier*. He took me to tame my first horse, and we have fought together ever since. All knights must be able to ride into battle. For one to do that, the knight must be at one with the horse; they need to trust and understand each other. On the battlefield, their lives are linked, and one cannot survive without the other."

"Tell me m-more about your f-father."

"He died when I was eight, far away on a pilgrimage to Jerusalem. My father and my mother were not married. I was deemed an illegitimate kitten, and not his true heir. *William le bâtard* they called me," he laughed mirthlessly. "For ten years I had to fight for my right to be duke. I never imagined I would have to do it all over again with England." The lynx sighed and played with his ring. "I am a creature of war. I would not know what to do without one."

"Do you m-m-miss your father?"

"No," said William. "Creatures die, this is the way of the world. Though I would not wish the turmoil I endured onto my sons. They should not have to fight for the right to rule as I did."

At that moment, Robert spun around looking dazed and irritated. "Can you be quiet? Some of us are trying to sleep."

The young lynx turned back around in a sulk and silence duly fell on the camp.

They began the next day on the right paw by finding multiple sets of recent hoof tracks in the dirt. By noon they spotted a straggler, but the horse was too small for William's liking. The horse was brown with a shaggy black mane that was tangled with small twigs, thorns and leaves. It was the first time *Curthose* had seen a wild horse. The beasts of Forêt d'Écouves were nothing like the groomed, already broken creatures he had come to expect. The lynx's sharp ears perked up at the sight of it.

"Go get it, Dad," whispered Robert as they lay hidden in the bushes, watching the wild beast feed on some grass.

"A horse is not to be caught, son," said William. "It is a mutual union."

Robert nodded. He was staring at the horse with fascination.

"Good lad," said William. "Now, let's move on."

"Wait," Robert whispered. "Maybe – maybe I could have this one?"

William looked back at the beast. It seemed to have a slightly dodgy hind leg and would be more suited for a smaller creature than a lynx, but William was pleased to see Robert engaged.

"Let's see what you've got then," said William.

Robert nervously stepped out from behind the bush and approached the beast. He slowly drew his sword from its sheath and displayed it to the horse, who backed away nervously.

"I'm not here to hurt you," Robert whispered. "Look," he used his blade to cut open his own paw, just as William had shown him, and placed the sword back out of reach.

"Good...good..." muttered William, watching from out of sight.

"Beast seems jittery," whispered Taillefer nearby.

"Hmm," agreed William.

Robert approached the horse with his bleeding paw outstretched. The horse continued to back away. The young lynx, ever impatient, rushed the first touch. The horse snorted aggressively. Sensing the beast was preparing to run, Robert risked it all by trying to leap onto its back. He managed to get on and cling to the beast's neck for longer than expected, but the horse bolted away and Robert was knocked to the ground by a low-hanging branch.

William stepped out to help his son back to his paws. Once standing, Robert yelled and swore at the back of the departing horse.

"It's ok," said William. "You weren't compatible. It happens."

"Stupid creature," said Robert. Blood was trickling from his wobbling, lower lip.

"Onwards," said William, slapping his son's shoulders.

After that first meeting, it took two further days to find any other horses, enough time to seriously threaten Robert's glimpse of interest. William was relishing the time in the wild and the rekindling of his natural, predatory instincts, though it was actually the jongleur who found the horse.

"This way," Taillefer hissed, his pink nose reappearing through the shrubbery after the group had split up to follow diverging tracks. The polecat led the two lynxes and the marmot (who had written so much at this point that he had become tangled up in his own sprawling parchments) to where he had spotted the beast.

This horse was all white, and standing in a shimmering haze of gold. Sunlight fell in shafts through the crowded treetops, beautifully highlighting the horse's striking athleticism. It was the largest horse William had ever seen, with an enormous trunk of a neck and thick, muscular legs.

"It's perfect," said William, breathless with excitement.

"Can I try again, father?" said Robert eagerly.

"No," said William, not lifting his eyes from the horse. The beast was standing perfectly still, bathing quietly in golden sunlight, as if waiting for its partner.

"But-"

"This beast is meant for me. See how it waits in the sun? God is showing the way."

"But you said-"

"Quiet," said William. "We will find you another; this creature is meant for war. My war."

"It's not f-"

"Do not disturb me." William left his son and took steps out towards the horse. Bill immediately grabbed his papers and began to write, and Taillefer scrambled up a tree so as to get a better view. Robert was torn between his curiosity to see and his instincts to sulk, but eventually the former took precedence and he settled himself quietly beside a wild rose bush to watch his father tackle the beast.

William took several long, silent steps before stopping six metres from the horse. Up close, the lynx marvelled at the creature's magnificent size all the more. It turned to face William and stared him down. Where the horse that Robert had tried to mount was skittish from the off, this one was still and quite unperturbed by William's presence.

The duke maintained eye contact with the beast, as his father had taught him thirty years ago, and slowly drew his sword with a high pitched screech as the metal scythed the air. The horse snorted and flared its dark nostrils at the sight of the glinting blade. It raised its head in open defiance, as if challenging the lynx to attack. William held out his non-sword paw and ran the blade along it, creating a deep gash that dripped scarlet beads on the ground. He put the sword back away before inching ever closer to the beast.

The horse allowed him to approach, but didn't adjust its tense stance as it prepared itself to fight or flee if necessary. William felt his pulse pounding in his chest, neck and ears. He focused on keeping his trembling paw still as he reached out to touch the wild beast. The lynx was dwarfed beneath the horse but William fought off the urge to shudder in its dominant shadow. He could not show fear or weakness. The forest was deadly silent, save for the steady, rattling breaths of the great beast in front of him.

William reached up and hovered his paw over the horse's neck. Once he was sure it wasn't going to lash out at his touch, he placed his paw down. He ran his paw along it, feeling the muscles ripple beneath its skin and leaving a red stain on the white. At the same time the horse bent its great head and began sniffing William's fur. It tickled the lynx but he did not resist. The horse then licked the bleeding paw several times. William gritted his fangs against the stinging pain but again did not resist.

For some minutes, the two creatures became accustomed to one another's presence. The lynx stroked the beast's unkempt mane and plucked any stray, tangled thorns from it. He knew Robert, Bill and Taillefer watched on but he did not see them, nor did he try to look for them. He maintained eye contact with the beast when he could and gaped at the breath-taking marvel he had before him. William's heartbeat subsided as the horse warmed to his touch, but the hangover of the adrenaline and fear left the lynx hypersensitive to his surroundings. The beam of sunlight was warming the back of his fur, a slight breeze was blowing leaves over his paws like a tickling tide, and his eyes were stinging gently beneath the horse's hot breath. William knew he would remember every detail of his first encounter with this magnificent beast for as long as he lived.

An angel, he thought as the horse's white skin continued to glow in the sun. *A protector sent from God.*

One could never be totally sure that a wild beast would allow itself to be ridden, and for some creatures it took weeks or even months for the bond to be secure enough. William, however, never doubted it. Like him, the beast was clearly a creature of war, and the lynx had never been so sure of his victory as he was in its fierce presence. He took a couple of slow steps to the beast's side, and made to leap on its back.

The beast whinnied and rumbled its protests in an ancient language William knew nothing of. The pair spun as the lynx clung on to the horse's hair around its neck. William attempted to dig a claw into it but the horse's strength was too much. He crashed to the floor in a dusty heap.

William winced and got back to his paws. Out of the corner of his vision he saw yellow eyes in the shade. He cursed at his son Robert silently.

Don't move, Curthose.

The horse was restless and William knew it was a vital moment. If the beast sensed they weren't alone the whole thing could crumble.

Before Robert could ruin it all, William strode purposefully back to the horse, staring it down and hoping to assert some dominance.

The horse didn't even allow him to get by its side this time; it struck him with the side of its head and William went sprawling backwards. The lynx was winded and gasped desperately for air.

No, thought William. *Destiny will not be denied.*

He got to his paws and coughed. The pain in his side spasmed but he dismissed the thought that he may have seriously hurt himself. He took two steps towards the horse who had made itself large and looked ready to strike him again.

William took a deep breath, locking the pain far away from his mind. He closed his eyes and stepped forward. All he could see was a pinkish black behind the lids, but he could sense the erratic movement of the horse beyond it. He approached slowly, with both paws outstretched. The horse snorted warnings for the lynx to back away, but he carried on forward. He reached out and touched the horse again, and this time it grew still once more. He leapt upwards, swinging around its great neck and landing painfully on its muscly back. The horse struggled again but this time William dug his claws deep into its skin and refused to budge. The horse flailed and kicked and whinnied but the lynx could not be thrown from its back. Only after a minute had passed did it relent, and William opened his eyes.

He let out a breath of relief and smiled. Very carefully and nervously, Bill the marmot stepped out into the clearing, his mouth agape and rolls of parchment curling around his hind paws. Taillefer leapt from the treetop and landed gracefully without a sound in front of them. He grinned and bowed to William exaggeratedly. The lynx looked around for his son and was pleased to feel the horse respond to the gestures of his paws at its side.

Young Robert stepped out from behind the rose bush. He had to crane his neck to look up at his father, sitting so high above them all. For once, he was speechless.

William drew his sword once more from its sheath and raised it above his head, feeling like a giant, feeling unstoppable, feeling as if he truly was Chosen.

SUMMER

Isle of Wight

The sun was at its highest point in the sky. Alfie the hedgehog felt its piercing rays on his spikes and wondered in a distant sort of way if it was really safe for him to be out here this long. The chill of the sea breeze whipped around his body and disguised the sun's heat. Alfie stared absentmindedly around the beach at the thousands of gathered creatures. A legion of fierce-looking wolves that were sworn to protect the king jogged past in glinting suits of chainmail armour. They followed each other in perfect unison. Alfie watched each of their paws land in the sand exactly where the wolf in front had done.

Alfie knew he was on an adventure that his daughter Faye would have done anything to enjoy herself. So why did it fill him with such disappointment?

The day of the summer solstice was approaching. If Alfie had been home that would have meant another feast and plentiful celebrations. The hedgehog couldn't help but imagine his wife Eleanor stressing over the preparations for the day. His hoglets Hugo and Benedict would be making mayhem, chasing after one another and crashing into anything that could break, whilst Faye would be dragged away from her slingshot and forced to help. He imagined his clumsy daughter dropping plates and pans and the ensuing arguments. He sighed fondly and tried to push thoughts of them from his mind. It would only make it harder.

Despite only being honour-bound to serve two months with the fyrd, Alfie had already been with the army far longer. King Harold had assembled his armies into an almighty force on the Isle of Wight just off the south coast. Small numbers were left stationed at other tactical ports, but the main host formed the largest united army England had ever seen.

The core of the army was made up of the housecarls: the trained professionals who had sworn their lives to their infamous battle-axes. Harold had his own housecarls when he was Earl of Wessex, but he had also inherited the King's Wolves that had once protected King Edward. The king's fox brothers, Earl Gyrth and Earl Leofwine, had their own housecarls too. Combining these trained creatures with the common creatures of the fyrd, such as Alfie, the English army stood at something like 10,000 creatures.

Alongside the creatures ready to fight, four hundred ships were beached on the sand, waiting to be deployed if word came that the lynx had taken to the seas.

So far there hadn't even been a whisper.

The mood of the camp was divided. Some creatures were eager for the fight, for the chance to defend England and win glory. Others thought quite differently, and counted their lucky stars that no battle had been forthcoming. Some said that the king was paranoid. Some said the lynx was taunting them all and would never set sail.

On the day before the solstice, Alfie and his friend from Hooe, Tata, were at the back of two hundred assembled creatures on one of the isle's white sanded beaches. Dunstan the bear, constable of the Wessex housecarls, was leading combat drills at the front. Alfie struggled to see him over the backs of other creatures.

"Whath he thaying?" asked Tata. The fat beaver managed to balance on the tips of his paws before slumping back down again. Tata had been called up to serve the fyrd just as Alfie had been. The hedgehog thought the chubby beaver was the only creature that might be as hopeless as him if it came to a battle.

"Hedgehogs aren't soldiers!" Alfie's wife's words echoed in his mind. He grimaced fondly at the thought.

"I dunno," said Alfie, who could only see Dunstan's ears over the taller creatures who stood in front of him.

A CLASH OF CLAWS

Dunstan was clearly showing them something important but as neither Alfie nor Tata could see or hear properly they soon lost interest. Almost at the same time, the hedgehog and beaver caught sight of three foxes and a wolf appear someway down the beach.

"Lookie, ith the king." Tata pointed.

King Harold was walking with his brothers. Alfie recognised the king as the one in the middle, typically adorned in his red cloak. Alfie recognised the slightly taller fox by his side as Lord Gyrth. Gyrth had a large pole and flag that he carried over his shoulder. He stabbed the shaft into the sand and twisted it deep until it could stand by itself. Afterwards the fox stepped back and the small group watched the flag flutter violently in the breeze.

"Bit odd, innit?" frowned Tata.

"Ain't it obvious?" said Alfie. "S'all about the wind n' that."

"Huh?" said Tata, mouth open.

"You two!" a voice shouted. "Enough talking!"

Alfie looked back towards the front. All the other creatures had turned to look back at them and Dunstan's grisly face was murderous.

"Sorry, sir."

"Thorry, thir."

"Up the front," said Dunstan.

"Beg pardon?" said Alfie, his heart lurching.

"Both of you, up the front now."

Alfie and Tata looked at each other.

"I'm not asking!" shouted the bear.

The other creatures of the fyrd cheered teasingly as the hedgehog and beaver made their way meekly to the front of the group.

"It's time to put what you've learnt to the test," said Dunstan loudly.

Alfie chewed his lip.

What are we supposed to 'ave learned?

"Sometimes you may lose your weapons in battle," said Dunstan, stripping them of their weapons. The hedgehog always carried a slingshot and the beaver used a short club. The crowd jeered when the bear threw them into the sand. "Sometimes you have to fight paw to paw."

Alfie and Tata looked at each other again.

"You want uth to fight each other?" Tata's eyes were bulging.

"You *are* soldiers, aren't you?" said Dunstan. The crowd of creatures laughed and Alfie didn't even blame them for it. "Create a ring, boys!"

With much pushing and shoving the creatures quickly circled around Alfie and Tata.

"A silver on the 'hog!" a squirrel shouted.

"Are you mad?" laughed an otter.

"We're very thorry for talking, thir," pleaded Tata.

"Three rounds," Dunstan boomed, not listening to him. "A round only ends by submission...or knock out!"

The fyrd creatures cheered.

"But he'th got tho many thpiketh!" wailed Tata. "It'th not fair!"

"Find a way around it, '*tholdier*'!" laughed Dunstan.

Alfie hardly thought he had the advantage; a normal beaver might have been twenty times as heavy as him, let alone a beaver that ate as much as Tata did.

"Let's get this over with," said Alfie quietly to Tata.

"From three," said Dunstan, conducting the crowd.

"Three!" the crowd said together.

The beaver was rigid with anxiety and looked ready to cry.

"Don't worry, Tata," said Alfie.

"Two!"

"This will all be over soon!" said Alfie.

"One-"

"Aaaah!" Tata screamed. He ran at Alfie and spun on the spot, swinging his enormous flat tail at the hedgehog's face. In the split second before it struck, Alfie was reminded of the time his wife slapped him with a pan after he'd burped at the dinner table. The leathery tail collided and Alfie flew backwards through the air, his vision going black in an instant.

Alfie grumbled as his eyes fluttered back open. The warm sand was a comfortable bed and he would have been quite happy to stay there.

"You with us?" said a voice Alfie knew but couldn't place.

He squinted as his eyes adjusted to the bright light. An orange furred creature came into view.

It was the king.

"Aye, yes, sorry sir, Yer Majesty, sir," Alfie rambled, trying to sit up.

"Easy, you took quite the whack," smiled King Harold, helping the hedgehog up.

Dunstan, Tata and all the other fyrd creatures were around him.

"I'm thorry," Tata twiddled his paws together. "I don't know what came over me."

"It's fine," said Alfie, rubbing his aching snout.

"What's your name?" said the king.

"Me Ma named me Alfred, though most call me Alfie," the hedgehog mumbled to the floor. He couldn't face the embarrassment of making eye contact with the fox.

"Alfie," Harold nodded. Many of the creatures were watching him with awe. He shook paws with those he already knew and began asking the names of those he didn't.

"I know this is not easy for anyone, being away from your homes," Harold said to the group. "My brothers and I are no different; we wish this would all end. We are forever grateful for your service."

"Even Alfie?" a rabbit with a cheeky grin joked. There was nervous laughter as creatures weren't sure what sort of teasing was allowed around the king.

"Especially Alfie," smiled Harold, looking at the hedgehog. "Every creature has their worth."

"Ta', Yer Majesty."

"When will William come, thir?" asked Tata. There was a shift in atmosphere from relaxed camaraderie to edgy cynicism.

"No questions, Tata," Dunstan intervened.

"It's alright," the fox told the bear. "It's hard to say for sure, Tata. We don't know yet if he has the ships or the creatures he needs. We know it won't be today, at least."

There were grumblings as creatures tried to work out how they could possibly know that. Harold stood like an expectant teacher waiting for his students to provide an answer.

"It's 'cos o' the wind, ain't it?" Alfie blurted out quickly.

Harold looked at him with a half-smile. His eyes glinted approvingly. "Go on, Alfie."

"It's why yer watching that flag over there, ain't it?" Alfie pointed to the pole and flag Gyrth had driven into the ground earlier. Harold's two brothers and the wolf were still standing around it. "Them Normans will have many large ships, they'll be needin' the wind to come from the south, but I ain't noticed any of late. Everythin' 'as blown down from the north."

"Tho?" said Tata blankly.

"So...without the righ' winds...the lynx and the rest of 'em are out of luck, ain't they? Stuck at Normandy. Righ' shame it be for them, and righ' 'elpful for us...no?"

All the creatures looked from Alfie to Harold.

"Very good, Alfie," King Harold twizzled his smiling whiskers and stared at the hedgehog. There was an elongated silence as the fox studied him. Alfie stood a little taller under the king's gaze and returned the stare.

"Every creature has their worth," mused the fox. He turned his back on the group and started walking down the beach. "Back to it, Dunstan!"

Alfie joined the bustling creatures as Dunstan began his next combat drill.

"Not you, Alfie," Harold called back, making the hedgehog and the rest of the creatures pause. "Walk with me."

Alfie shared a look of bemusement with Tata. All of the other creatures were looking at him with a mixture of jealousy and admiration.

"You work for me now," said the king.

The hedgehog felt a fluttering excitement in his belly and followed the fox dutifully. He attempted to walk on his hind paws as he knew was considered good etiquette, but he kept stumbling forward onto all fours. The king didn't comment on it, for which Alfie was grateful.

They continued down the beach together, the fox leaving sizeably larger paw prints in the sand. Countless battalions of housecarls and the fyrd stared as they walked past. Alfie kept his head down.

"You're a clever little thing, aren't you?" said Harold.

"O', I dunno about that, sir. I'm sure me wife would tell yer different."

"Humble too."

"I ain't sure 'ow I'm able to 'elp yer, Yer Majesty," said Alfie. "Perhaps yer've made a mistake."

"I saw that beaver knock you out with a single tail slap. I don't think England will miss you on the battlefield," Harold winked.

Alfie said nothing at that. Usually he wouldn't let any creature make him feel bad about being a hedgehog, though at times he cursed nature for giving him so little.

"I like you, Alfie," said Harold, maybe noticing the despondency in the hedgehog. "I need smart, good creatures around me."

"What for, sir?"

"To make sure I stay smart and good."

"I can give it me best shot, sir," said Alfie.

"There's something else…something I have in mind…"

"Anythin' yer need, Yer Majesty," Alfie bowed his head.

The king smiled a little. "You haven't heard it yet."

Alfie pondered these cryptic words for a moment. The two creatures approached the flag that had been stabbed into the sand. Alfie recognised Lord Gyrth, tall and brooding, and Lord Leofwine, slouched and easygoing. Between the two foxes was a white-grey wolf that was taller than all of them. It only had one eye; the other was a dark gash. Alfie had heard all about Wulfric, leader of the King's Wolves.

"This is Alfie," said Harold. "I thought he'd be perfect."

The wolf and foxes looked down on him. Alfie swallowed nervously. He felt his back ache as it wanted to bend him into a protective ball. It took everything Alfie had to fight his natural instincts.

"Does he have the guts for it?" said Wulfric, giving Alfie a penetrative stare with his remaining eye.

"Yet to be determined," conceded Harold. "But he's clever, and switched-on."

"We will need a creature with a keen eye," Gyrth said, nodding.

"And he's definitely small enough," Leofwine grinned.

"I'm not sure," growled Wulfric. "I would like to question him before we send him out."

"Agreed," said the king.

Alfie didn't much like the sound of any of this, but he was amongst the most powerful creatures in the country, and he knew they could do whatever they wanted with him. He thought of going home and telling his hoglets that he spoke directly to the king and his brothers. This warm thought burned away the cold fear that was starting to grip him.

"Of course, Alfie, you would like to know what is needed of you?" King Harold kneeled down to talk to Alfie on his own level.

"That'd be most welcome, Yer Majesty."

"We need to know what William's up to," said Harold. "We need to know what's happening over there. We need to know how many ships he has, how many soldiers. We have sent many birds but the lynx has guarded the skies with his own wings. We think a creature might be able to get through on paw, if they can keep a low profile..."

Alfie nodded slowly, already understanding. "Aye, I can lend an eye their way. I'm to be a spy, yes?"

"Yes."

Alfie thought once more of his family, and how he had promised them he would be back within two months. With sudden clarity, he realised the chances of ever seeing them again had just been halved. Or worse.

Alfie took a deep breath and drew himself to stand as tall as little legs would allow.

"Whatever England needs, I'll be there."

King Harold smiled at him. He reached out a paw to pat him on the back but hesitated over the spikes. "Thank you, Alfie. You are doing a great -"

The king stopped talking, his eyes suddenly fearful. Alfie was startled at this change in demeanour. The fox wheeled around to face the sea. He drew his sword and stepped towards the water. Alfie looked around in confusion. His eyes fell on the flag, and noticed with a sickening start that it was blowing the other way. The winds had changed and were blowing from the south.

Harold was pacing up and down the beach as if expecting the lynx to arrive at any moment.

"Harold," called Gyrth. "It's ok."

Alfie looked up at the flag again. The wind had already resumed its usual blowing.

Harold continued to stare at the horizon. Gyrth went to him and at his brother's touch, the king lowered his sword.

"Sorry, I...don't know what came over me," the king mumbled. He shook his head and gave Alfie a tight-lipped smile. "We're counting on you, Alfie. Good luck."

"Come on," Wulfric barked at Alfie, gesturing for the hedgehog to follow him. "I need to know if you're up for the task."

Alfie did as he was told. He hastened to match the wolf's fast strides, but risked one last glance back at the king.

Harold still had his sword out and his brothers were surrounding him worriedly as the flag fluttered innocently on.

SUMMER

Vikings

Tostig winced, scrunched up his eyes, and rubbed his ears. The noise was unlike anything he'd experienced before, and quite unbearable. He lurched forward as a creature brushed past him none too caringly.

"Watch it," he said, opening his eyes again. His words disappeared into the bedlam of the room as the wolf that had gone by continued barging into any creature in his way without looking back.

The room was cold, exceedingly dusty, and more crammed full of creatures than any place Tostig could ever remember seeing. The fox supposed that the room was actually quite large, and merely appeared tiny because of its suffocating crowdedness. On every side Tostig was surrounded with fierce-looking creatures. Every one of them was brandishing flagons of mead a little overzealously. Tostig's black and orange fur was damp after one creature nearby repeatedly used his paws to gesture the width of the king's spear, and kept spilling his mead all over him.

"Oh, *so-ree*!" he said in a thick accent after Tostig gave him a scathing glare.

Tostig's emotions were close to boiling point but he bit his tongue; now was not the time to go picking an argument. He was in an enclosure of sharp-clawed arctic foxes, grey, tundra wolves, stoic stags and moose, a particularly vicious-looking band of wolverines, one scowling, sly lynx, and what appeared to be a very fat, immobile walrus. Every one of them seemed to have drunk more than necessary and were continuously shooting him furtive glances with narrowed, bloodshot eyes.

A CLASH OF CLAWS

After the disaster that had been Tostig's humiliating return to Northumbria, the Stray Fox sailed first to Scotland, and then made the treacherous voyage to Norway. By some miracle Tostig's pitiful twelve remaining ships had survived it. The fox had left Copsi to oversee the ships in Viken harbour. Tostig felt oddly off balance without the duck by his side. He kept forgetting Copsi wasn't with him and often caught himself muttering under his breath to the absent creature.

It had not taken long to find King Harald Hardrada's court even without the duck. Tostig had been waiting for over a week for an introduction to the Norwegian king. He had been told today would be the day but the sun had already set and he had a nagging feeling the meeting would be postponed again.

At the far end of the room was a long table with five impressive chairs. Only the seat on the furthest left was occupied. A blind moose called Stump sat whistling to himself. Tostig couldn't decide what his name referred to as he was both missing a hoof on his right hind leg and much of his left antler. Stump seemed to be well into his second century of life judging by the tired way in which he spoke, but all the boisterous creatures treated him with a reverence and respect they didn't appear to reserve for one another.

"The king was compelled to hunt; he will be with us soon," Stump had told Tostig in perfect, albeit slow, English.

Tostig had opened his mouth to say he didn't like to be kept waiting, but had resisted the temptation when he remembered how his appeal to the lynx of Normandy had gone. As bitter and reluctant as he was to accept it, Tostig had resigned himself to the fact that he could not reclaim his place in the north of England alone. Certainly not with just the ragtag bunch of rat mercenaries he'd secured in Flanders. No, he needed a top military commander, and as legend went, there weren't any more formidable than the warrior king of Norway. The creature who made Vikings shiver in their graves when he walked by.

If he could just persuade Hardrada that a Norwegian invasion was best for all parties, everything would be different. He would not be forced out of England a third time, Tostig had decided. The next time he was in Northumbria, he would be one of two things: reinstated as earl, or dead.

Beyond the table that Stump occupied alone was an open archway. Three creatures walked in one after the other, and the chaotic atmosphere subsided somewhat into a gentler, buzzing din. First came a limping wolf. It had all white fur with a single stripe of black running up from his snout and down his back to his tail. The colouring was so striking it appeared as if it was intentional war paint. Tostig had always believed that everything you needed to know about a creature came from their fur patterns. Tostig's own black and orange, for instance, was one of a kind. The fox smiled at the wolf as it sat down in the seat next to Stump. The wolf didn't smile back.

The second new entrant was a youthful, wicked-looking wolverine. England didn't have any wolverines, not even in the north where many Vikings had settled in the past. It looked like a sort of small bear, with brown fur, long, stocky arms and legs, and powerful paws. Tostig was wary of the creatures and their throat-ripping capabilities. The one that sat at the table (at the right of the centre chair) seemed to be twice the weight of Tostig himself. It seemed cheery and relaxed, and when it yawned Tostig balked at its wide, fanged jaw.

The wolverine was talking heartily to the creature that had come in behind it. This creature was even larger than the wolverine and Tostig swallowed nervously. This *was* a bear, a polar bear. All white and enormous, it trudged in on all fours.

Hardrada, Tostig thought immediately. But when the shock of seeing the king wore off, Tostig felt unnaturally calm.

Is that it?

The polar bear was large, yes, but looked clean, well groomed, and lacked the scars that marked the faces of the wolf and the wolverine. Perhaps the rumours of the warrior king were exaggerated? This one certainly didn't look like the one the rumours had told Tostig to expect. Was this really the creature who had been sentenced to death by lion attack, and had lived to tell the tale?

A CLASH OF CLAWS

The polar bear sat on the far end of the table next to the wolverine. The middle chair remained empty. As the three newcomers properly settled into their seats there was a great creaking of a floorboard, and the raucous crowd went utterly silent.

A fourth shadow was approaching through the archway. Slow echoing thuds made their way into the now quiet room. The wooden floor wailed under the weight of the oncoming creature and Tostig was sure it was about to crack.

A giant, white head emerged into the light of the room. This polar bear was nearly twice as big as the first. The fur around its mouth was frayed and unkempt, and coloured a murky brown; the remnants of blood stains that could never be washed clear.

"My God," Tostig muttered out of the corner of his mouth to where Copsi would usually stand.

Fresh from his recent hunting, Hardrada rose from four muddy paws onto two. He couldn't even extend properly before his great head brushed the ceiling. He drew an enormous, dragon tooth of a spear from his back and rested it casually on the table. He then reached for something at his shoulder Tostig had not noticed before. He threw the carcass and trophy from the hunt onto the floor in front of everyone.

"Copsi!" Tostig shouted, as the headless duck rolled towards him.

His sudden shrillness stunned those around him. Tostig started forward, barging through two arctic foxes in his way. As he got closer he noticed the dead duck's unkempt feathers. Copsi always kept himself well groomed.

Wait a minute, that's not...

Tostig looked around. Everyone was staring at him. The wolf with the dark stripe of fur examined him with something close to disgust. King Hardrada's mouth was contorting in a growl.

"*Copsi!*" Tostig cried again. "*Copsi* is an English term for 'great kill'."

Hardrada didn't take his eyes off Tostig as Stump the moose translated in his slow, quaking tone.

"Hmph," the polar bear king nodded, and then to Tostig's great relief, smiled.

"The king is impressed with your term, and thanks you for it," said Stump, turning his milky, blind eyes straight at Tostig.

"My pleasure, Your Majesty," Tostig bowed low to hide the look of relief.

The wolverine that sat next to Hardrada looked at the duck and shared a laugh with the king. The younger polar bear rolled his eyes at their excitement over the kill.

"The council has been convened to hear what you have to say, Lord Tostig," croaked Stump. "The king is very interested to learn what you have to offer."

So, it seemed, was everyone else. Evidently word had spread that an English fox of noble birth had arrived on their shores. This was not a particularly frequent occurrence. Tostig detected a sensation of excitement and fear in the room. The wolf at the table looked as if he wanted to sink his teeth into Tostig's flesh, but the wolverine and younger polar bear seemed much more open and curious.

Tostig drew himself up to full height and stared resolutely at the giant king. He knew he could not show weakness if these brutish creatures were to join him.

"Why... are you... here?" Hardrada grunted in clunky English. Tostig responded with as much assurance and confidence as he could muster in the wake of such a fearsome creature. He took pauses after every sentence to allow Stump to translate for the king when necessary.

"I come to you with an offer. My beloved England is in a desperate state. We suffer under the paws of a tyrant, my misled brother, Harold. He shares your name but none of your might. I believe that if we stood together, we could defeat him and yet salvage my home by placing a more worthy king on the throne," said Tostig grandly. The king was nodding slowly. "You," Tostig added, "If that wasn't clear."

"You wish to destroy your own brother?" the striped wolf growled.

"This is Marshal Ulf Ospaksson," said Stump, gesturing to the wolf.

"That's right, Marshal," said Tostig coolly.

Ulf spoke out of the corner of his mouth to the king, revealing a yellow fang.

"And...why...would I... help you?" rumbled the king.

"Because it is your right," said Tostig. The fox didn't consider this a lie, but understood it was very much a push. He and Copsi had worked on the best way to persuade Hardrada on the voyage to Norway, and had come up with this rather bold theory that linked back to 1042, when King Edward had been crowned.

Before the badger, England was ruled by the Viking stag, Harthacanute. After Harthacanute's abrupt death, Edward was chosen by the Witan to succeed him. The crown had been returned to the royal line of English badgers, and all was well.

When Harthacanute had been alive, however, he had named the king of Norway, Magnus the polar bear, as his heir. This was where Tostig's biggest hope to ensnare Hardrada lay.

"When I was a young fox King Magnus wrote to Edward, telling him of his intention to invade. The invasion never came."

Hardrada grunted dismissively in his own foreign tongue.

"Magnus died. What's your point?" Stump translated.

Tostig, of course, knew this already. Norway had crowned Hardrada, and the threat of invasion disappeared. Now Tostig was hoping to bring the threat back.

"It was Magnus' hope to rebuild the Scandinavian Empire of Norway, Denmark and England. I know you yourself have been warring over Denmark for many, many years."

"There's a treaty," Hardrada barked. He looked positively sick at the thought of the peace he had now arranged with Denmark. Tostig hid a smile.

"Magnus did not have the capacity or strength of will to conquer England. You, on the other paw, are the creature for the job. Word of your victories, of the blood on your blade and the piles of gold in your treasury, has reached every corner of the earth. My brother is a fearsome soldier, but he is not King Harald 'Hardrada' – the last true Viking alive. Will you join me in this expedition for glory, gold, and conquest? Do not let the last pages of your tale be dry of ink and blood. Keep on writing, Your Majesty. Fulfil your destiny!" Tostig spoke with enormous gusto and ended with a flourish, flinging his paws out by his side. The effect was dampened somewhat as Stump's croaky translation continued in his wake. Nevertheless, the king's eyes were shifting excitedly as the old moose spoke in his ear. Ulf the wolf snorted derisively but the wolverine and younger polar bear looked at each other with a knowing smile.

"You speak well, fox," said the fresh-faced polar bear on the right of the table. His voice was calm and serene. "My father always appreciates a creature with a tongue as sharp as its claws."

"Prince Olaf," Stump announced, gesturing to the bear.

"Thank you, Prince," said Tostig with a paw over his heart. There were many murmurings in the room as creatures discussed what had been said. The hubbub covered the sounds of Marshal Ulf whispering aggressively in Hardrada's ear. Tostig watched the striped wolf with growing disdain.

What's your problem, you old dog?

Ulf's body began to convulse with hoarse coughs. Hardrada placed a pacifying paw on the wolf's back before speaking. Stump duly translated.

"Yes, you speak well. Glory is a fine motivator for war, and the hunt for it often provides a worthy opportunity for death."

Tostig gulped slightly, hoping that there was a slight mix-up in the translation and that the king wasn't actively seeking the perfect moment to die.

"The patterns of your fur show that you are bred for war," Stump continued, translating the deep snarls of the king. "But Marshal Ulf believes your black and orange complexion shows treachery too."

The wolf coughed again, looking at Tostig. The fox's face contorted into an ugly shape as he fought the urge to snap back.

"This is the first issue," said Hardrada. "You English have come to fear us, but we have learned to distrust you. Secondly, it would be a most difficult journey to the island, and the English know their lands far better than us. Thirdly, there are the housecarls to contend with. Each is worth two of our fighting creatures."

Tostig watched the king closely as he listened to Stump's dry translation. Was this really what the polar bear believed? Each of these supposed "issues" seemed flimsy at best, and the warrior king had a longing in his eyes. If it was a test, Tostig was happy to play the game.

"Your distrust is expected, Your Majesty. I can only hope to prove myself worthy over time."

Ulf coughed and growled.

"On your second point," Tostig said, ignoring the sour wolf. "Do not worry – you have me. I will be at your side in every moment of the conquest, and I can assure you there aren't any who know the north better than I."

"This is where you would land?" said Prince Olaf sharply.

"It is," nodded Tostig. "Northumbria is, shall we say, not a priority for the king. The gates are open for us, Your Majesty."

There were more intrigued rumblings from around the room and Tostig's confidence continued to build.

"Which leads me to my third point. I have to laugh, Your Majesty, at your insistence that the housecarls need be feared. We would say the same about your *berserker* warriors. Yes, the King's Wolves are capable fighters, but we needn't worry about them, or even the king himself," Tostig looked around the room and paused for dramatic effect. He felt the Norwegian creatures hanging on his every word and delighted in the attention. "Harold will not be there. He is distracted by the lynx of Normandy in the south. He wastes time and resources; his army is spread thin. By the time Harold knows we are there, the north will be ours, and there is nothing he can do about it."

The clamour of the room rose again. Some were cheering and shouting and Tostig was again splashed with mead after forceful gestures of assent. The fox smiled to himself. For all he knew, William had already landed and the war was underway, or even finished for that matter. Tostig found he didn't care either way; looking around at the ferocious creatures that surrounded him, he believed they had the power to destroy William and Harold both.

"North...is...empty?" said Hardrada, returning to his basic grasp of English. The crowd went quiet to allow the king to speak.

"The hare is there," Tostig waved a dismissive paw. "I have already killed the brother, Morcar, in battle. Earl Edwin is young, not fully grown; he will be easy prey for our combined forces."

"How... you kill?" asked Hardrada with a look of grisly satisfaction.

Tostig drew his sword and plunged it into the imaginary hare in front of him. "Straight to the heart."

Hardrada gave two booming laughs and stopped abruptly. Tostig wasn't totally sure that Morcar was in the ground, but if it endeared him to the king he would be happy to exaggerate the story ten times over.

"I am loved in Northumbria, creatures will join us when we arrive. Our forces will be doubled – tripled even!" Tostig smiled but realised immediately this had been his first mistake. Hardrada suddenly looked deadly serious.

"And what is it you want?" barked Ulf the wolf.

"Me?" delayed Tostig. "Well, what is best for my people."

Ulf snorted again.

"You want be king!" Hardrada shouted. His voice reverberated around the room and Tostig felt as if he'd been hit over the head with a club. The polar bear was leaning forward off his chair and pointing at him with a colossal, meaty paw. Tostig saw what looked like chunks of flesh in his teeth and felt a shiver go down his spine. He wondered how many other helpless creatures had felt the same fear in the presence of the beast, and how many had lived beyond it.

"No, no," said Tostig earnestly. "Only Northumbria. I wish to be earl again."

The bear slumped back down in his seat, still unconvinced. The wolverine on his right and Ulf on his left leant in to whisper in either ear. If Ulf's was the voice of the devil, Tostig hoped that the wolverine was his angel.

Do I want to be king? Tostig asked himself as the council continued their hostile whispering. *King Tostig does have a certain ring to it.*

At the table, Marshal Ulf descended into another coughing fit and Tostig took the opportunity to speak.

"Your Majesty, please believe my words."

Hardrada's not the youngest; perhaps he would fall ill before long.

Tostig cast an eye over to Prince Olaf, the king's tranquil-looking son. Olaf didn't seem nearly as intimidating as the father.

I could have him, Tostig repressed a grin.

"I would only want to be your right-paw creature in the realm, but you would sit atop the throne."

Stump translated as hurriedly as he could manage. The creatures on the council fell silent and looked to the king. The whole room waited on bated breath for his response. The king looked Tostig up and down, and then nodded once.

"No!" cried Ulf as the room erupted in excitable cheers again. The wolf got up and pointed a claw at Tostig. "I do not trust it! Why is it here? We are to rely on an English creature to honour their word?" The wolf spat on the floor.

"I was banished for speaking out against my brother, I do not regret it! I did what was right, and I will continue to do so!" Tostig shouted back at the wolf.

"Lies! His heart is blacker than his fur!" the wolf got to his paws.

The noise in the room was so loud that Tostig hadn't a clue if the creatures at his back were cheering for or against him.

"You would have us never go to war again!" the wolverine on Hardrada's right stood up. It turned and raised his paws to the room. "We have spent fifteen long years fighting Denmark, only to end up with peace!" Now the wolverine spat on the floor. More cheers and flying mead came with it.

"You are too young to understand what you are talking about, Orre!" shouted the wolf back at him.

"And you are too old to seize the opportunity of the future!" Orre the wolverine shouted back.

Hardrada stood and the table in front of him crashed to the floor. Both Ulf and Orre sat down immediately on either side of him, knowing their place. The polar bear closed his eyes and began to speak. Stump translated it quietly into English for the fox, but Tostig was struck by the beauty of the king's words in his own tongue.

Now I go creeping from forest
To forest with little honour;
Who knows, my name may yet become
Renowned far and wide in the end.

Tostig didn't understand but suddenly felt he didn't need to. Stood beneath the great polar bear Tostig felt an unexpected and overwhelming deference to the king. Without thinking, he knelt before him. Hardrada was a God amongst creatures, and more worthy of fear and respect than any creature he had ever known.

The polar bear explained emphatically to the room and Stump's translation sounded like a murmur after it.

"I wrote this stanza when I was fifteen. My brother the king was dead, and I was forced to flee the battlefield like a common rodent. I knew then that I would continue to fight, and now, thirty-six years later, my name is renowned far and wide as I predicted. Our lives are not dissimilar, Lord Tostig. You too have had to flee your lands, but you are not willing to give up. Perhaps your name will one day be renowned too."

"Thank you, Your Majesty," muttered Tostig, tears forming in his eyes.

"I judge your words to be true. The entrance to England is open, and we shall go through it together. I will be king, and you will have your wish. If you can assist our conquest as you promised, you shall be hereafter known as "Duke of the English", and indeed Earl of Northumbria once more."

Tostig's jaw slid open a little. There was a period of extended silence. Had he really done it?

King Hardrada raised a clenched paw and shouted "TO WAR!"

The room exploded in noise. Suddenly Tostig wasn't kneeling or standing, but half suspended in the air as creatures grabbed him and cheered and roared. Some creature thrust a flagon of ale into his paws and he gulped it down ferociously. Shouts of "To war!" and "England is ours!" filled the room as howling creatures raised flasks or weapons into the air.

What have I done? Tostig thought briefly before another flagon was forced into his paws. He laughed and poured both drinks into his mouth at the same time, postponing any fears of the threat he was unleashing on England's shores for the moment.

SUMMER

Far From Home

A sweltering summer in Normandy was coming to an end. Autumn winds arrived crudely uninvited. The rowing boat bobbed in the oscillating waves.

"This is it," said Alfie quietly. "This be the one."

The hedgehog crawled to the edge of the rowing boat and peeked over it. The harbour in the distance was the nucleus of a rippling mass of countless dark, moving specks.

"How can you be thure?" asked Tata behind him. The heavyset beaver didn't have as keen an eye as Alfie.

"Ships, 'undreds of 'em!"

"Hundredth?"

"Maybe the king ain't so paranoid after all, eh?"

"Hmm..." Tata groaned noncommittally.

Alfie and Tata had been searching for sight of William's army for a long time. After Wulfric had brutally questioned the hedgehog, and reluctantly concluded that the tiny spiked creature did indeed have what it takes to be their chosen spy, Alfie had been sent to Normandy without any further delay. The hedgehog's size was a plus when it came to spying on the enemy, but unfortunately a minus when it came to rowing. As such, he was allowed to bring another creature with him. Although Tata had consistently proved himself to be a bit of a liability as a standing soldier, he performed his role of rower admirably. Alfie knew that the wind was blowing their small boat towards Normandy and so the odds were greatly stacked in Tata's favour, but he didn't mention it.

"Get us close, Tata," Alfie found himself whispering for some reason, despite still being a way off shore. "But not too close, mind!"

The hedgehog and beaver had spent much of the last month hunting for signs of William's invasion. Several of the ports they had come across had been eerily empty. Now Alfie understood why. It seemed every last vessel in Normandy had been gathered here. As Tata drew their little boat nearer, Alfie did his best to count the ships.

"Thereth so many!" whined Tata.

"Shut up a minute I'm tryna count!"

All the ships were so clustered together that they formed one giant, swelling form. It was impossible to get a good estimate. Hundreds of squawking birds clogged up the airways above the port, blocking any of Harold's winged spies from getting through.

"Leth get out of here, Alf," said Tata.

Tata was rowing the other way now, against the wind. With great effort he managed to keep the boat where it was, despite the waves desperate to take them forward to Normandy.

Alfie shook his head. "No."

"Huh?"

"Gemme closer."

"You what?"

Alfie turned around with a severe look on his face. "The king 'as given me a job to do, and I'm gunna do it righ'!"

"We have! We've theen the army! We can tell him he wath right!"

Alfie faced the distant harbour again. He thought of turning home, safe and sound, no risk taken. He thought of seeing his hoglets again.

What would Faye do?

"Take me to shore."

"Are you crathy?"

"C'mon," Alfie grinned. "Ain't never too old for an adventure, eh?"

As the pair of English creatures drew nearer they found they were perfectly able to blend in. More ships were entering the harbour all the time, and no one paid them any attention, taking them for a pair of merchants looking to capitalise on all the commotion. Tata beached them alongside a slightly larger boat of mice which were flogging boxes of cheese.

Alfie trembled as he placed a paw down on Norman sand. He licked his snout nervously. The rowing boat creaked beside him.

"What you doin'?" he hissed to Tata.

"I'm coming with ya!" whispered Tata, who was halfway through clambering out of the boat.

"I don't think so!" said Alfie. Tata looked offended. "This calls for a... *smaller* creature."

"Oh," Tata slunk back into the boat and it shifted in the sand. "Ok."

Alfie looked around. The mice were busy struggling to unload their cheese and didn't seem interested in them.

"Just be ready for a quick getaway, eh?" said Alfie, checking his two satchel bags for his slingshot and stones.

"Will do," said Tata. "And Alf?"

"Yeah?"

"Be careful."

"Yeah."

Alfie left Tata there, his heart hammering in his brittle chest. He tried his best to appear confident as he passed the mice. They were yapping at each other in French as one of the cheese boxes fell and split open on the beach. They quickly took to whacking each other and one of them caught Alfie's eye watching them. The mouse said something to Alfie, and Alfie, not understanding what it was saying, offered a nod and hoped it would suffice.

Alfie didn't look back as he left Tata and the mice behind. He hoped they didn't try to have a conversation with the clumsy beaver and suddenly wished he'd told Tata to wait out at sea.

Don't be thinkin' about that now, Alfie told himself. *Yer got a job to be gettin' on with.*

He continued into the depths of the harbour with renewed steeliness; sneaking further into the heart of an enemy that had King Harold so scared.

He had every right to be, Alfie soon understood. The fleet William had gathered was spectacular and seemingly never-ending. The hedgehog found that being closer to the ships didn't give him a clearer idea of how many there were, as everywhere he looked was a jumbled wall of coloured sails bobbing up against each other in the water.

Alfie kept to the shadows as much as he could and despite the odd passing glance he slipped around the camp unseen and unopposed. The Norman soldiers laughed and joked, sometimes practising their swordplay or attending to their ships. They were in their thousands, Alfie was sure of that, perhaps even breaking ten thousand. Alfie recognised certain creatures that they had in England, but also creatures that he had never seen before. There was one moody-looking creature which had the stripes of a badger but two curling horns on its head and oddly long legs. This was one of those that squinted suspiciously at Alfie when it caught him looking, but with a quick trot into the shadows Alfie had swiftly disappeared from view.

Somewhere amongst Alfie's ongoing, bubbling fear, the hedgehog revelled in seeing a plainly French creature up close. He silently pledged to describe its features in full to Faye and the twins if he ever got back to seeing them. However, the memory of the horned badger was swiftly pushed from his mind as he was suddenly forced to roll out from under an oncoming hoof.

The creature before him was so large, its legs so tall, that at first Alfie had looked directly under it, and hadn't noticed its approach. Alfie's little neck could barely crane so high up to see it. The creature had a long face and four legs of immense size and strength. It had a brown and smooth coat, with a dark swishing tail that didn't quite dangle low enough to brush Alfie's spikes.

The hedgehog had heard rumours of horses; magnificent beasts that communed in their own language and roamed free in the woodlands. He had never known they would be so beautiful.

The horse that had nearly crushed him walked by, oblivious to the spiky shape that stared from below. A second followed, and a third, and then more, one after the other. They were dressed in metal coats of armour themselves and on one, Alfie spotted a beaver riding it confidently.

Do the Normans mean to ride 'em into battle?

Alfie doubted he had ever had a more frightening thought, except perhaps when his wife had nearly passed away after the birth of the twins.

A cloud passed over the sun above and Alfie shivered. He doubted it had much to do with the cold. He continued on, hoping his theory would be proved wrong. Sadly, it was only further confirmed with many more sightings of horses and their riders. Alfie noted how some of the ships in the fleet were larger, with open centres ready to hold battalions of horses as well as ordinary creatures.

How are we gunna figh' those things?

The hedgehog had seen enough. He turned to head back to Tata, and yet again, his eyes fell on creatures he had never seen before.

Marching his way was a family of nine creatures. There were many little ones at the front, fuzzy little creatures with playful hearts. What Alfie took to be the parents followed them all. The mother was tiny, a wildcat with brown fur and smiling, green eyes. The father was the tallest of the lot, and broad. It walked with slow, important deliberation. It had a pair of sharp ears pointed with black tips. Its white goatee of fur drooped low, and it had several prominent dark spots marking its red and white fur.

Alfie didn't need to have seen a lynx before to know what it looked like. He knew it was the duke. It was William.

The hedgehog stared as the family approached. They were all speaking together in French. Every soldier nearby drew silent as they came closer. William's stoic face was unmoving and Alfie could not help but join the Normans in looking up at their duke with a sense of awe. There was a great sword swinging by his hip, and he wore a glittering ring on his right paw.

When the duke passed by him Alfie looked up, struck with an indescribable wish to be seen. He wanted to make eye contact with the fearsome lynx. He wanted his approval; he wanted to be known by such a creature.

William did not even notice the hedgehog's presence. He continued down the beach and Alfie blinked out of his stupor.

Without conscious thought, Alfie followed him. He slipped both paws into each of his satchels. He brought out a jagged stone and his slingshot.

Somewhere a far off voice in his mind told him no, but he ignored it.

He stopped walking and slipped the stone into his slingshot.

Don't do it, one voice warned him.

One good shot, and it all ends, another voice argued.

He raised his paws and aimed.

One miss, and yer life goes with it!

Think of the lives yer could save!

William was getting further away. He had still not fired.

'e's with 'is family!

What about yer family? What will this creature do to them if yer let 'im live?

William was nearly out of reach. Alfie stretched the slingshot back further.

"For Faye," he whispered. He made to release his shot-

"*Bonjour,*" said a voice by his side. His paw slipped and the pebble flew off at an angle, ricocheting harmlessly off the bow of a ship and falling in the water.

Alfie turned to see two mice, the ones who he had seen with Tata when they arrived.

"*Fromage?*" asked one of them, offering him a block of cheese.

Alfie ignored him, looking back towards William. The family of lynxes were too far away.

"Err...*non*," said Alfie in his best French accent. The mice were looking at him with confused looks. They looked up the beach, trying to see what he had been aiming at. Their voices got louder and more outraged.

Alfie started walking away but the one who had offered him cheese came around and blocked his path.

"*Qui es-tu?*" it demanded.

Alfie didn't hesitate. He lunged forward and jabbed the mouse with his spikes. It yelled out in pain and its white-brown fur was soon blotched with red. Alfie darted away, scampering along the sand as quickly as he could. Behind him he could hear the mice yelling angrily after him. He didn't turn, he didn't stop. He couldn't. He raced past scowling soldiers that were forced to dodge out of the way and zipped in between horses' legs, all the while pursued by the mice who were yelling at every warrior they passed. At one point he felt a pair of paws try to grab him but his spikes put a stop to that.

You better be ready, Tata, he thought desperately.

The horses rose on to their back hoofs and made panicked snorts as the spiky ball bolted in unpredictable zig zags beneath them. Their skittishness caused chaos as creatures had to focus on getting them back under control. The beaver-rider that Alfie had seen earlier fell from the horse's back and landed with a wheezing grunt. Pandemonium built and soon any creature in the vicinity was looking his way.

The horned badger-looking creature appeared in front of him. Alfie quickly slipped another stone into his slingshot and fired. The pebble struck right above the eye and the creature wailed out in pain. Alfie slipped under its legs and continued on. He had never run so fast.

Alfie fired three more pebbles as Norman soldiers attempted to block his path. The first two missed but the third struck true, sending an otter colliding into the others and allowing Alfie to sprint by.

Tata's rowing boat was in reach now. The sight of it doubled his spirits. He was so close. All sounds of pursuers behind him seemed to be growing quiet. He was going to make it.

When he reached the small boat he leapt into it in a feat of athleticism he never knew he had.

"Row, Tata! Row!" he yelled as he landed on his stomach painfully.

He had winded himself with his hard landing and scrunched up his eyes to the pain. He wheezed and gasped for air. As the aching faded he managed to pry one eye open.

The boat was empty. Tata was gone.

"No," Alfie groaned, sitting up. "You didn't follow me, you stupid beaver..." The waves lapped against the boat angrily. The winds that had been keeping William's fleet in the harbour whistled in his ears. There was no way he could get home without Tata.

Alfie crawled to the edge of the boat and peered back along the beach. A few dozen or so creatures were looking back at him. The horned badger was nursing a bloody head, the two cheese-selling mice were watching on excitedly, and a large feline creature that looked like it shared blood with the duke was standing in front of them all. It was smaller than William but also had a fierce constellation of spots on its fur. In one paw it held a long club, and in the other, it gripped the fur on the back of Tata's head. The beaver was kneeling in the sand, and weeping.

"Oh, Tata," Alfie sighed, as many Norman creatures converged on the boat. "You weren't ready."

SUMMER

Mora

A large, oblivious cloud wandered rudely across the sun, and the harbour went dark for a fleeting moment. William noticed his youngest kittens shiver.

"Agatha! Constance!" Duchess Matilda shouted at two very fair, very small bundles of fur. "Be still!"

All four of William and Matilda's girls were playing at their mother's paws. Their sons, Robert, Richard and William 'Rufus', stood behind their mother. Robert looked typically on edge, whilst his younger brother Rufus looked up at him, talking enthusiastically about something or other. The quiet Richard was twisting his whiskers absentmindedly. He had his head bowed and appeared to be keeping out of sight of his father.

"What is the meaning of this?" William's deep voice cut through the chatter of the kittens.

"You'll see, *mon amour*," his wildcat wife purred with a smile. "This way," she stumbled forward, impeded by two of her kittens holding on to her legs.

The family had come to see William at Dives, the port in which the lynx had decided to gather his army. The Stray Fox, Tostig, would have passed it when he had arrived to meet William several months earlier. Had Tostig seen it now, William imagined the fox would find it unrecognisable. What once had been a dwelling place with market stalls and creatures patiently fishing off the coast had now become nothing less than a war camp. Hundreds of warships were bobbing in the shallow water, waiting to be deployed, whilst thousands of soldiers prepared for the imminent invasion.

"Good day," Robert *Curthose* said repeatedly to the soldiers, lowering his voice several octaves.

Most of the kittens were scared into silence by the presence of the immense strutting horses and grisly-looking warriors that passed by. Rufus, meanwhile, was as excitable as ever. When he was not giving gasps of wonder at the largest weapons or ships he saw, he was continually bugging his older brother Robert for details about their father's taming of the wild beast in the forest. William smiled, being reminded of himself when he was Rufus' age.

"I call him Leroy," William slowed down to join the conversation. "It means '*the king*'."

"*Leroy*," Rufus repeated with glazed eyes and a look of wonder. "Is he really the biggest horse you've ever seen?"

"A king for a king," William winked.

"Come on, keep up!" called Matilda up ahead.

William sidled up to his wife, who he noticed was peeking between the sails of the assembled fleet to get a glimpse of the blue waters of the English Channel.

"What is this all about, *mon a-*"

"Shh," her green eyes had lit up suddenly. She had seen whatever it was she had hoped to. "Come on! Quickly!" Her kittens, save for Robert, hurriedly followed her.

"Why are we here?" Robert asked his father.

William bristled at his son's lazy tone. "Don't ask stupid questions, *Curthose*," he snapped back.

The two lynxes followed the others as they turned onto a slippery wooden dock that stretched deep into the water some thirty metres from the beach. William's dormant fleet surrounded them, but at the end of the dock there was a rare stretch of open water as yet unoccupied by a ship. Matilda and the kittens were already there, jumping up and down excitedly and pointing out to sea.

A ship was drawing nearer. The sails were multi-coloured with the owl, Pope Alexander, and the Holy Cross stitched into the fabric. The lynx mouthed the word that was emblazoned across the wood.

"Mora..."

"What do you think, *mon amour*?" Matilda whispered. "It's my gift to you."

William nodded tersely. It would not serve well to show his emotions with so many of his soldiers nearby.

"You've done well, Mora," he said, using his loving nickname for his wife and hoping that secretly conveyed his gratitude to her.

"Look at the front!" Rufus tugged his father's short tail.

The figurehead of the ship was spectacular in its detail and size. A young lynx had been carved into the wood. It smiled with a fiendish look of triumph and cheek, and William knew immediately who it was supposed to be.

"It's me, isn't it Dad?" said Rufus.

William ruffled his son's ears with a hesitant look towards his oldest son. Robert was frowning at the figurehead.

"It's the largest and fastest of the fleet, I've been assured," said Matilda proudly.

"Harold and England will quiver when I land on this fierce vessel, *mon amour*," William smiled. "Now," he turned to his kittens. His tone told them all to be still and listen. "As you know, I am going away for a while. Today will be the last day you see me for a long time."

There were worried groans from the littlest kittens.

Did Robert just smile?

"When we are together next, I shall be king of England," William paused there but got little reaction. Little Agatha's attention was already drawing away to the hovering water flies that danced in front of them all. "Whilst I am gone you are all to look after one another. Listen to your mother, she will be acting as duchess for all of Normandy and doesn't need you bothering her."

"What?" said Robert suddenly.

"What?" William barked back.

"I thought *I* would be left in charge."

William stared at his son. His first thought was to laugh but the faint-spotted lynx had never looked more serious.

"And why would you think that?" said William calmly.

"Because!" Robert bristled. "Because I am heir to be duke, of course. If you die out there I will be."

"I am not going to die."

"You might."

"You are not ready for the role."

"You promised."

William fell silent. The voices of the two lynxes had risen considerably and creatures on the surrounding ships struck up loud conversations to hide their eavesdropping.

"It's in writing, you've already agreed to it – I will be duke!" Robert ploughed ahead obliviously.

William raised a balled paw, preparing to strike him.

"William," said Matilda sharply.

The duke scowled and dropped his paw. It was true; William had already signed Normandy away to Robert.

I'll be damned if he has England though, William thought scathingly. He looked at his second son, Richard, and then down towards Rufus smiling up at him. He smiled at the ginger little thing, and silently promised then that when he was king of England, Rufus would be heir.

Robert followed William's gaze and turned away scowling.

"This is rubbish," said the young lynx. He began walking back down the dock.

"Come back here, *Curthose!*"

"Leave him," said Matilda as their oldest kitten ignored William's words. She turned to the rest of her kittens. "Come on, we should leave your father too."

One by one they all said goodbye to their father.

"Kill them all Papa," said Rufus, hugging William's leg. "I'll look after mother."

"Good lad," said William. "I will."

The tall lynx bent down to receive a kiss from his wildcat wife.

"When will you sail?" asked Matilda, a hint of nervousness in her voice.

"When God allows," said William. "There must be a reason we are made to wait. God is protecting and preparing us for the fight."

The fleet was ready to sail, but the winds had still not turned in his favour. He was running out of time. The Channel would soon be too dangerous to travel with autumn just around the corner. William's invasion might have to be pushed back to next year.

"I see," Mora muttered.

"It will be soon, I am sure."

It has to be.

"Good luck, *mon amour*," said Matilda. She then whispered in his ear. "When you return there may well be another kitten running around."

"You're pregnant?"

"I am," she smiled.

"Yet another. I shall be king of England when he is born."

"I know you will."

The duke and duchess embraced. When they broke apart she put a paw to his cheek and played affectionately with his drooping whiskers. Her eyes began to water.

"I-"

"William!" a distant voice cut Matilda off short. The duke and duchess turned to see the approach of William's brother, the ferocious bobcat Odo. He had his club drawn and two creatures stumbling ahead of him. The kittens began to surround their uncle.

"Get the kittens out of here," William said.

Matilda leapt into action, gathering all of her kittens and leading them down the dock and out of sight.

"What have you brought for me, brother?" said William, looking down at the trembling hedgehog and beaver. The beaver in particular looked on the brink of breakdown. Its fat gut bounced as he shivered uncontrollably. The hedgehog was breathing heavily, but had the good grace to keep his little chin up. Where the beaver had its eyes closed, the hedgehog stared at William with defiance.

"What have they done? Broken the Truce of God?"

"No," growled Odo. "They're English."

William revealed his fangs. The beaver's bottom lip wobbled so much William was sure it was about to fall off.

"This one was spying," Odo pointed his club at the hedgehog. "He shot Eustace with a stone."

"Really?" William couldn't deny he was a little pleased to hear the chamois had been hurt. "And what about the fat one?"

"Found him trying to steal some cheese."

The beaver started to wail at this point. His English protests fell on deaf ears. William felt sick to see such cowardice brought to him. At one point the beaver reached out his paws to touch William's leg in a show of total submission. The lynx dodged out of the way with growing disgust.

"How shall we do it?" asked Odo. William looked at his square-faced brother. The bishop was twisting his club eagerly in his paw. As a worshipper of God, Odo was forbidden to spill blood. The bobcat got around this particular inconvenience by using a club to shatter the bones of his enemies.

"I will do it myself," said William, drawing his sword. The beaver screamed as the blade cut the air. He scrambled across the wet deck, his paws slipping and sliding as he tried to escape. There was nowhere to go, and Odo swiftly forced him down. He rested a dominant paw on its back and pinned it to the floor.

Whilst this mad scramble was happening with the beaver, William's gaze was drawn to the hedgehog. The spiky creature now had its eyes closed, with his tiny, dark paws interlocked in prayer. He muttered his last words to God in a language William could not follow.

The lynx squatted down to examine the hedgehog. When the prayer was finished, the hog opened its eyes. Its breathing was settled and calm and he looked at William with neither defiance nor fear, but something stronger.

"This one has heart," William stood up.

Odo shrugged. "All spies are cravens."

William ignored him, considering the hedgehog. "We will not harm him."

"What?" Odo blustered in outrage. For a moment he relinquished the grip on the beaver, who duly tried to run away. Odo whacked him with the club and the beaver crashed back down.

"Perhaps an English creature will come in useful when we land on their shores, perhaps not. I would like the chance to find out."

Odo shook his head. "I don't believe it. You're going to let them get away with it."

William gave his brother a murderous look. He looked down at the crying beaver below and raised his great sword high above his head. With one enormous, pounding strike, William struck the beaver with his blade. The sword cut through the flesh with ease and got stuck in the wood of the deck. The beaver did not scream for a moment, the shock delaying the pain. William wrenched the blade free from the wood and stared down at his victim. Both of his front paws had been severed cleanly away from the body, and as the beaver recoiled in terror, the paws stayed where they were on the deck.

"Tata!" the hedgehog screamed.

William kicked the beaver and swung his sword again, taking his remaining two paws.

"No!" the hedgehog wailed.

The fat beaver writhed in pain, his watery eyes bright orbs of horror. William calmly strode over to it, placed a boot on its belly, and rolled it into the sea.

There was a splash and the screams were silenced.

"Do not test me, Odo," said William, brushing past his brother. He pointed his bloody sword at the sobbing hedgehog. "And lock that one up."

The duke turned away from the bloodshed to watch as the *Mora* ship anchored before him. Odo ushered the weeping hedgehog away and the Norman soldiers watched curiously as they went by. Rumours and gossip soon spread of the capture of two spies, and the four severed paws that William's wrath had left behind.

AUTUMN

Omens

Dark clouds were drawing near. A light drizzle began to blanket the field and hundreds of mourning creatures turned the ground to a squelching mush. Three wolves panted as they pushed spades into the soft earth. They cast wet mud over their heads but the dirt kept slipping back in the hole and they were making little progress. King Hardrada scowled and snatched one of the spades from an apologetic wolf.

"A bad omen," said Prince Olaf quietly as he watched his father hack huge chunks out of the earth with his spade.

"He was old, he'd been ill for a while," whispered Eystein Orre, the young and feisty wolverine. "Don't read too much into it."

"Ulf survived many wars, Orre. He didn't support this war, and now he's dead," said the prince, shaking his head despondently.

"A coincidence," shrugged the wolverine.

"Makes you think though," said Olaf, stealing a glance to the two creatures that stood at the edge of the gathered crowd.

Orre followed Olaf's gaze and found the English fox. Tostig had his head bowed but seemed to be whispering to the duck that followed him everywhere.

"What? You think the fox killed him?" smirked Orre.

"No, it's not that. I don't know, I just-" the prince looked disturbed but fell silent as his father clambered out of the cavernous grave he had just dug.

Four wolves walked through the crowd with the Marshal's corpse held aloft. When they reached the grave Hardrada took the body from them with ease. He lowered the dead wolf gently into the earth with a pained look.

"Marshal Ulf Ospaksson," he boomed. "There lies the most loyal and trusty liege-creature a lord ever had. Rest easy, my friend."

Tostig kept his head down throughout the funeral to hide his pleasure.

"I told you God was with us, Copsi," he muttered to his lieutenant.

"How'd you mean, sir?" Copsi whispered.

"That wolf was a problem. When I convinced Hardrada to join my cause, Ulf was the one who argued against it. He doubted my intentions, and was quickly struck down because of it."

"Quite right, sir," Copsi said tiredly.

The service didn't last long. All creatures began to disperse in a dour malaise.

"C'mon!" Tostig made a beeline towards the king with Copsi in tow.

"Your Majesty," said the fox. The polar bear stood looking over the grave as the wolves tossed mud back on Ulf's body. Soil splashed over the dead wolf's black striped face and Tostig couldn't deny he was pleased to see it. "I am sorry for your loss. I knew he was sick but I didn't know it was so serious."

Hardrada grunted and turned away. It had been many weeks since their first meeting and Tostig had barely seen the king since. He had noticed many warriors pouring in from the Norwegian countryside but had no idea how the rest of war preparations were coming along.

"I was only wondering," said Tostig, trotting into an ungainly skip as he tried to keep up with the polar bear's long strides. "When will we be ready to sail? This year, I hope?"

Hardrada stopped and looked down at the fox. He looked grave and Tostig wondered if he'd push his luck too far to discuss war on a day of mourning.

"We...have...begun," said the king.

"And the fleet – the ships – the boat things?" Tostig tried to mime rowing.

Hardrada thrust three claws in the air.

"Three...three...three hundred ships?"

The king nodded and continued walking away. Tostig shared a look with Copsi. Both had their eyes widened in surprise.

"When?" Tostig shouted after the departing bear.

"Week," boomed the king.

"How many weeks?"

"One."

"Oh, boy," puffed Copsi quietly as Hardrada disappeared from sight.

Tostig, who had been standing stunned, suddenly laughed and grabbed the duck. He swung him around in the air.

"No, stop!" squealed Copsi.

"We're going home!" Tostig cheered.

"Put me down!" Copsi yelped with an edge of impatience not often found in his voice.

Tostig dropped him instantly. "What's your problem?"

"This is hardly a time to celebrate," snapped Copsi, combing his ruffled feathers down with his beak.

"What do you mean?"

"I..." Copsi opened his beak before closing it again. He averted his eyes from Tostig and started waddling away with his head down. "Creatures are looking at us, is all."

This was true. The wolves who had buried Ulf in particular were watching the jubilant Tostig with disdain.

"Fine," Tostig called after Copsi. The duck hadn't been his usual self for a while.

Does he not want to go home? Tostig scowled. *This is the only way. Hardrada is my only way.*

Hardrada wasn't a creature to break promises lightly. The fleet set sail, just as he said it would, one week later. His call to war was answered with vigour by thousands of Norwegian creatures, and those who didn't volunteer were conscripted into the cause instead. There was some talk of rashness, of this not being a risk worth taking, but these voices fell silent under the polar bear king's withering gaze. With the greatest warrior in the world leading the charge, doubts were soon burned away. Talk of the king's destiny was rife in the camp, and creatures wanted a paw in making it a reality. Glory awaited them on the far-off foreign island of England, if they only had the gumption to seize it.

On the morning they were due to depart, Hardrada was struck with an urge to visit his brother. Tostig and some eight thousand creatures were forced to wait as the king entered the shrine.

The polar bear didn't carry a flame as he set paw into the crypt. Stump the blind moose sealed the door shut behind him. The tomb cascaded into near total darkness and the sounds of distant waves were silenced. Light from the grey sky on the outside world did its best to slip under the door, enough to outline the giant coffin at the room's centre. Hardrada could barely move in the tight space, and his fur was wet from rubbing up against the moist stone that surrounded him.

The king felt for the coffin as his eyes adjusted. He needed two paws to prise it open. Inside was his brother, who they called St Olaf, dead for thirty-five years and yet perfectly preserved. His white fur almost seemed to light the shrine.

"It's good to see you, brother," said the king, smiling wistfully at the passing of time. Had it really been thirty-five years since the Battle of Stiklestead when Hardrada had fled and Olaf had died? He had killed more creatures and won more battles than any creature since that fateful day.

"Watch over me," Hardrada whispered. The king brought a crude blade from his cloak and trimmed Olaf's ragged fur and claws. "One last time."

When he stepped out of the shrine the first of five waiting creatures to greet him was his son. The king was proud of Prince Olaf, named after his saint brother. The prince would be accompanying him to England, a gifted opportunity to prove his worth. How would he fare against the housecarls of England?

Behind Olaf was the wolverine, Eystein Orre. Hardrada loved the creature more than any other and had promised him marriage to one of his daughters. The wolverine would never let him down, he knew that.

As Stump locked the shrine door, Hardrada looked at the remaining two creatures. The black and orange fox Ulf had not trusted and his 'lieutenant' duck that seemed more like a servant. Could he rely on the English to honour their words? It seemed only time would tell.

"Good luck, Your Majesty," said Stump, offering the king the key to St Olaf's shrine. "We look forward to your return, as king of Norway and England both."

When Hardrada later stepped onto his ship he took a deep, rattling breath, enjoying the taste of sea salt in the air. He cast the key into the ocean, closing distracting thoughts from his mind and turning all focus towards England and war. He turned to Orre. They shared a savage grin, both eager for bloodshed.

"Let's begin."

A fork of lightning split the sky in two. A single, cannoning clap followed. Tostig felt twice as heavy as usual because his fur was so weighed down with rain. He shook his head back and forth, flinging water everywhere and yet achieving nothing. Hardrada's ship laughed in the face of the sea's endeavours to hurl all the creatures overboard. It charged up a wave and crashed down the other side of it. Tostig had to dig his claws into the deck to stop from being thrown from one side of the ship to the other. Nature had failed to provide Copsi with such a tool. Consequently, the duck had spent much of the voyage sliding uncontrollably across the wet deck.

Whilst Copsi was doing an excellent job of embarrassing them both, the fox understood international politics enough to know that he couldn't afford to look so weak, especially in front of Hardrada. The two English creatures were surrounded by Norse creatures that were as comfortable standing on the deck of a ship as they were on grass. Scandinavia, after all, was so mountainous that it was far easier to sail across the sea-flooded valleys than to attempt to scale the many snow-capped peaks themselves.

Tostig had no choice but to trust in the Vikings' ability at sea. To his untrained eye they were quite lost, but the other creatures on board seemed confident in where they were. With no land in sight in any direction, the Vikings were using the sun and stars to direct their way. The storm had blocked the sun from vision, but those at the front of the fleet had already broken through the reach of the dark clouds and were leading them out of danger.

Despite the frightening circumstances (every stroke of lightning made Tostig jump), many of the Vikings were taking their turn to rest. Tostig himself hadn't slept in nearly two days. He stared longingly at an arctic fox snoring blissfully away. With such drastic weather conditions there was no need to have creatures operate the oars. Instead, forceful winds had been blowing incessantly from the north, sending them racing towards England. Tostig thought dimly of the lynx at Normandy. He wondered if he had had such luck in his voyage across the Channel. Tostig pictured his three brothers and William doing battle on the southern coast. What would he and Hardrada find when they landed? A war-weary Harold? Or a triumphant William? It did not matter which was the victor; both creatures and their armies would surely be tired after a summer of war, while Hardrada's army were fresh and raring to go.

Tostig continued to mentally play out the potential different outcomes. Whenever the notion that Harold may already be dead came to mind, he swiftly dismissed it with a lurch in his stomach. The ambition to kill his brother himself and the memory of their time as cubs was an ugly concoction that made him sicker than even riding up the steepest of waves.

Whilst the common creatures dutifully operated the giant, billowing sails, the likes of Prince Olaf and Eystein Orre sat around drinking. They invited Tostig to join the conversation, impressed with the amount of mead the fox was able to drink. Tostig failed to mention that it was less for pleasure and more for necessity – the more he drank the less he felt the violent cold.

Conversation led characteristically to war. Tostig spoke of his invasion of North Wales and the subsequent beheading of the fearsome mountain goat, Gruffydd ap Llyewlyn. He left out the information that he was one half of a pincer movement, with Harold leading an army into the south of Wales at the same time. Orre in particular enjoyed the retelling with avid bloodlust. The wolverine howled in delight at all of Tostig's bloody, detailed descriptions. Even King Hardrada (who was so big he had to sit in the ship alone so as to not affect the weight too badly) seemed to be leaning forward to listen to his story.

"What have the English heard of my father? I'm always interested to know what stories have made it across the sea," Prince Olaf said thoughtfully.

"Victories," said Tostig simply.

"And gold," whimpered Copsi, sliding past them as the ship surfed up another wave.

"There must be more," said Olaf, his eyes shining. There was an innocence in the young polar bear's eye that Tostig doubted his father ever had.

"Of course there are legends too," said Tostig. "I liked the one where Hardrada and his creatures were stranded on an island without anything to drink. They say he caught a snake and put it over the fire. Then he set it loose, and the thirsty snake led them to water."

Olaf and Orre smiled knowingly.

"And another," said Tostig, getting excited. "He intercepted messenger birds and set them alight. They flew home and the village went up in flames. And another siege story, where he had creatures playing and exercising right outside the gates without any armour, teasing the enemy out to their deaths."

"The fools," Orre laughed savagely, looking up as if to watch the fond memory.

There was the creaking of wood as Hardrada stood and shuffled over. He barked a strangled jumble of words to Orre and Olaf who smiled appreciatively.

"What did he say?" said Tostig.

"His favourite siege story," said Orre, "is when he pretended to be dead. He was in the coffin, and when the enemy opened the gates to let him in – you know, for an honourable burial – we wedged the coffin in the door. The king jumped out and his army stormed through. The town burned and was his."

"Amazing," said Tostig, watching the king. The fur around his mouth, usually a faded murky brown, was darker than usual with all the rainfall. Tostig wondered how many times the white king had needed to bite into flesh to permanently stain his fur with blood. "What about the lion? You were sentenced to death by mauling, but killed it with your bare paws. They say your captors were so impressed they set you free after that."

Olaf translated for his father. Hardrada smiled and began to speak, but was cut off by a bloodcurdling scream. All creatures looked to the corner of sleeping creatures. The arctic fox was now awake, its eyes wide and fearful.

"I had a vision!" he shouted. "A dream!"

"What is it?" Olaf said quickly.

"I saw an island...wolves...and a voice... it said we are to fill the soil with our dead," the arctic fox looked on the brink of tears. All around whiskers trembled and tails flailed.

"How ridiculous," snorted Tostig. Nobody else spoke. There had been many reports of bad dreams amongst the fleet.

"Another bad-" started Prince Olaf.

"I know," snapped Orre.

They looked towards the king for direction on how to react. Hardrada was already lying down, seemingly undisturbed, trying to get some sleep of his own.

A circle of pink sky was visible between the wilting branches of gently bristling, spindly trees. Flocks of geese and ducks could be seen soaring overhead. Hardrada unhinged the spear from his back and followed the birds to a black lake. The sun set behind the mountains as he selected a victim. The white king sent the javelin soaring through the air and two birds fell down dead.

Hardrada approached the bloody scene. He stood over a decapitated duck with his paws in the shallow water.

"I've been here before," he said vaguely. "Thjoldolf?" the king turned, expecting to see his poet beside him. The puffin wasn't there. Instead, a giant polar bear was stalking across the pebbles. Its fur glowed an ethereal white, but its eyes were grey and unseeing.

"Brother," Hardrada gasped. "You're alive."

St Olaf stopped just ahead of Hardrada. His face was blank and his voice empty.

> *"The warrior King Olaf*
> *Won many famous victories;*
> *I died a creature of holiness*
> *Because I stayed in Norway.*
> *But now I fear, great Harald,*
> *That death at last awaits you,*
> *And wolves will rend your body;*
> *God is not to blame."*

Olaf was glowing brighter still, his physical body fading into light. Hardrada looked at his own paws. The chilled touch of the water was fading, a certain numbness was spreading. His own fur began to glow and become transparent.

A CLASH OF CLAWS

"No," Hardrada barked, looking back up at his brother. "Not yet."

St Olaf became a sparkling orb of light and disappeared in silence.

"I'm not ready!" Hardrada shouted, his voice echoing across the icy bowl of water. His glowing fur became so bright he had to shut his eyes to cope.

When he opened them, he was back on his ship. He sat up quickly.

"What is it father?" said Prince Olaf, his son.

The sun was rising on the horizon. The storm had long passed and many creatures were resting. The English duck was leaning against his master, Tostig, and both creatures were snoring lightly.

"Did you have a dream?" said Olaf, noticing his father's distress and duly panicking.

"It's nothing."

"There have been many bad omens. Maybe we should have stayed at home."

Hardrada lurched towards his son and gripped him around the neck, startling him.

"Omens hold no power over us," he growled. "*We* hold our future in our own paws. You remember that."

Prince Olaf smiled sheepishly. "Of course, father."

Together they watched the sun climb in silence. The orb of light in the sky was uncomfortably reminiscent of his brother's saintly visit. Hardrada struggled to bury the memory of Olaf's words: "Death at last awaits you, and wolves will rend your body."

Not yet, Hardrada vowed again.

The Norwegian fleet sailed first to the Orkney Islands, and then continued south with the Scottish coast on their right. Northumbria was soon in their sights, and so the Vikings turned to Tostig. Fresh from Hardrada's declaration that the Stray Fox would be known as the "Duke of the English" once they conquered England, Tostig spoke with confidence and authority when giving directions on the best place to land.

"We are close," Tostig told Hardrada on one misty, autumn morning.

The king spoke brusquely and Olaf translated for him.

"What would you have us do?"

"We must deal with the hares first," said Tostig at once. "They are the puppets of Harold, and the ones who turfed me out of my own home. I killed Morcar, but Edwin is still alive."

Hardrada spat a lump of saliva into the sea and Tostig took it as a show of support.

"They were always arrogant," Tostig said scathingly. "The fool will seek to meet us on open ground, which is all the better for us. York will fall. Once we have this base it will be impossible for Harold to stop us. I'd suggest making York the new capital of the country, if it pleases Your Majesty."

"Edwin is...hare?" grunted Hardrada.

"That's right, not very scary."

"Not...wolf?"

"Wolf?" said Tostig in surprise. Surely the king wasn't frightened? "The wolves are the king's housecarls, they will be south with Harold."

Hardrada nodded with a stifled look of relief. He spoke to Olaf again.

"Then lead us to this hare, my father says," said Olaf. "He's looking forward to battle."

"Aren't we all?" laughed Tostig.

The king didn't have his hunting spear with him. Instead he had a great sword that was taller than Tostig himself. He drew the blade and licked the steel with a laugh.

"What did he say that time?" said Tostig.

Olaf hesitated for a second. "He says he hasn't tasted English before."

"Ah," said Tostig. "Excellent."

As the mist cleared and the green coast of England came clearer into vision the Vikings cheered. The sails rippled as the winds continued to blow kindly. The fleet skipped across the waves at a great pace and Tostig felt suddenly breathless. It had all happened so quickly. Copsi, meanwhile, had only disappeared further and further into his quiet shell the nearer they got.

"Go on," said Tostig quietly. "Spit it out."

"What?" said Copsi.

"You're clearly upset about something."

"No, sir." Copsi's voice was unnaturally high.

"You were the one who said we needed allies," Tostig seethed out of the corner of his mouth.

"I know," said Copsi. The duck hung his head in what looked like shame. "It's just - I have always been scared when looking out to sea. What if a Viking ship appears on the horizon? I never thought that I..."

"Look-" Tostig was interrupted as all the creatures aboard started shouting and hollering gleefully. They raised their weapons above their heads, looking berserk and yelling indiscriminate insults and threats. Tostig wheeled around, hunting for what all the creatures were looking at. Peeking through the mist was a single orange flame. It was growing larger and larger every second. More fires erupted all along the coastline and screams could be heard. The first ships at the head of the fleet had already landed. The unsuspecting village went up in flames. Houses were burnt and creatures were killed. The king shouted "TO WAR!" and his Vikings bellowed their approval. Copsi sighed a little and Tostig blinked.

"It's ok, we're ok..." mumbled Tostig. Nobody heard the fox's words over the mad hollers of the Vikings on the ships and the pleading cries from the English villagers at shore. Tostig smiled a little hollowly when his paws touched English soil once more.

"Home," he said simply, looking blankly as chaos reigned around him. He watched as Hardrada charged into the smoke, his great sword aloft. The polar bear roared in delight when he struck down his first creature, an unaware mole that had emerged from beneath the earth.

"Well done," the polar bear told Tostig later, when the village was naught but ashes. The north of England, it seemed, was just as open and undefended as the fox had promised it would be.

AUTUMN

The Wrong Coast

It was a moonless night at the Isle of Wight. The only light that filled the deep black came from a stout wooden cabin that perched just off the ledge of a white cliff. Inside, three of the four candles that adorned a long table were no more than mounds of stiff wax, with the last sagging and flickering, about to go out.

Three foxes were sitting around them. King Harold was at the table's head, slumped in his chair and rubbing his eyes. His red cloak was creased and dangling off one shoulder. The second fox brother, Lord Gyrth, sat at the other end, his posture vigilantly straight, his whiskers trimmed neatly. The third brother, Lord Leofwine, was using a knife to dig chunks of wood from the table as he watched his older brothers argue. The one-eyed warrior of the King's Wolves, Wulfric, observed them all in silence. He stood masked in shadow behind Harold, steadfastly refusing the honour of a seat.

"This cannot continue," Gyrth repeated stiffly.

Harold's tail twitched involuntarily.

"You think I don't know that? What would you-"

The fox was interrupted by a wispy snore. Curled up in front of him on the table was Mabel. The mousemaid had fallen asleep on a pile of parchments and letters. Harold watched her miniature frame rise and fall as she took miniscule sips of breath. Her face looked at peace and Harold decided to let her sleep. He turned back to Gyrth.

"What would you have me do?" he hissed. Harold noticed the note of desperation in his own voice. His first year as king hadn't been the one of lavish living he had imagined when he was a cub. He had received William's letter promising to seize the throne way back in the depths of winter, and now September had already begun. He had gathered the largest army England had ever seen to protect it from the lynx, yet for what? William had not come, and it seemed more and more likely that he never would.

Northern winds had blown for an unnaturally long time. Tempting as it was to consider this as God intervening on his behalf, it was starting to make Harold feel uneasy. After all, the wind could only delay a battle, not prevent it. The fyrd were exhausted from months of waiting. No enemy had even been glimpsed and Harold could feel their belief in him slipping through his claws. Worst of all, they were growing hungry. The food reserves were all but empty.

It had no longer become a question of *if* they should sail home, but *when*?

"It is time for decisive action," said Gyrth.

"That's helpful," Harold snorted derisively. Leofwine leaned back on his chair, yawning.

"As far as I see it, we have few options remaining to us," Gyrth ploughed on. "The first is obvious. We go home. The equinox is in one week. If the lynx has not arrived by then, he never will."

Everybody knew summer was the season of war. The September equinox, when day and night are the same length, was nature's announcement that winter was coming. The otters had assured Harold that William wouldn't dare to test the dangers of the sea beyond this date. The conditions were too unpredictable. Already the autumn waves were starting to rise, becoming more and more intimidating with every day.

"I don't like it. You do not know William like I do. He would sail on Christmas Day if the winds were with him."

"Then he is a fool."

"Ha!" Harold laughed without humour. "William is many things; a fool is not one of them."

"Fine," snapped Gyrth with uncharacteristic irritation. "Then there is only one option."

"Which is?"

"We take the fight to them," said Gyrth.

The repetitive sounds of knife on wood stopped as Leofwine stared. Harold said nothing, but twisted his smiling whiskers thoughtfully.

"We have our ships and we have the wind. Let us sail to Normandy and attack. They will not be expecting this."

For a moment life seemed to surge back into the king's eyes, but perhaps it was merely the reflection of a bright flare from the flailing candle as a look of hopelessness reappeared on his face.

"No," said Harold, staring at the candle. "No, it is too risky."

Gyrth's paw clenched in anger. "At least consider it."

"Not until Alfie returns," whispered Harold as Mabel stirred. "We don't know what we'd be getting into."

"Brother," Gyrth started, his voice struggling to stay even. "I think we all know the hedgehog will not be returning."

Harold's tail wrapped itself around his leg. He did not want to think about this.

"It was always an outside shot," said Gyrth. "I'm sure he and the beaver did the best they could. But we don't want their deaths to-"

"Don't say that," Harold scowled. The tail was starting to make his leg go numb.

"You can't save everyone, Harold."

Harold didn't say anything. He stared at the candle until it burned a white spot on his vision.

"It's late. Let's do this tomorrow. I'm sure William will still be there in the morning," Leofwine said lightly. His brothers ignored him.

"If you will not even entertain attacking Normandy," said Gyrth loudly. "Then we must leave. It is time."

"And leave England unprotected?" Harold sneered.

"You must decide," said Gyrth, nearly shouting now. One of Mabel's eyes flickered open. "One way or another."

"I will not charge into an enemy I still do not fully understand, and no, I shall not abandon England's defences either!"

A paw struck the table from Gyrth's dark corner. His chair fell to the floor with a thud as the fox got to his paws. Harold looked up in shock.

"You would rather stay here whilst our creatures starve," Gyrth said scathingly.

"Watch your tone," said Harold warningly, also standing. Gyrth was not a creature to show emotion lightly. It made Harold very wary when he did.

"I didn't take you for a coward, Harold," said Gyrth.

Harold couldn't see his brother's face clearly in the dark, but saw the outline of his body breathing heavily.

"Calm down."

Gyrth stepped towards Harold, pointing with a well sharpened claw.

"You are-"

Whatever Gyrth hoped to say Harold never knew. As soon as he made a movement towards the king Wulfric leaped into action. All three of the foxes had forgotten he was there, standing sentinel in the shadows. He seized Gyrth and pinned him against the wall.

"Hey!" cried Leofwine. "Get off him!"

"Wulfric!" yelled Harold.

"Apologise to the king," growled Wulfric.

"Stand down," Harold demanded. Wulfric relinquished his control of Gyrth and stepped back, standing in between the two brothers.

There were a few moments of elongated silence.

"I'm sorry," said Gyrth quietly. A door opened and closed in the dark.

"He didn't mean anything by it, Harold, honest!" whined Leofwine.

Harold was panting hard himself, his heart drum-rolling. For a moment he considered what punishments he could muster for Gyrth and delighted in their multitude.

No, that's not the king I want to be.

"Leave me," he said shortly. "Both of you."

Wulfric strode towards the door immediately. He waited in its frame as Leofwine lingered. With a wary glance at the wolf staring him down, Leofwine stepped outside. Wulfric closed the door behind them both.

Harold slumped back into his chair. He leaned down and wrenched the tail free from its grip of his leg.

"Darn thing," he muttered.

"Sorry, sir, I think I fell asleep, sir! I will punish myself, if it pleases you, Your Majesty!" Mabel rolled onto her paws tiredly.

Harold leaned on the table, putting his face close to hers.

"Not necessary, my dear," his smile was more of a wince.

"I've crumpled your letters too!" she said, standing off the parchment she'd been resting on. Harold picked it up and began ironing out the creases. The dim candlelight strived to illuminate it and he re-read the letter that had arrived some months earlier.

King Harold,

After my decisive victory, I have scoured the seas for any sight of the Stray Fox, but none of my creatures have seen a whisker of him. With any luck, Tostig is dead by now. If not, and if he should return, do not fear that I will put him in the ground myself. I rather think my speedy return to health shows my resolve against the fox. I shall never surrender to his tyranny.

Lord Morcar, Earl of Northumbria.

Harold leant forward and burnt the letter on the candle. It flared up brilliantly and lit the room brighter than it had been for hours. He saw Mabel was watching him closely.

"So much to worry about, so few solutions," puffed Harold.

"W-where is Tostig now, sir?"

"Your guess is as good as mine."

"I'm sure everything will be made right soon, sir."

"And how can you be sure?"

"Because you are a great king, and you will find a way."

"I'm not sure, Mabel, I haven't done much great of late."

"You're a protector, as all kings should be. I-I'm not sure that..." her voice wavered. She looked nervous.

"Go on."

"I'm not sure Edward was much of a good king, is all..."

Harold cocked his head. "No?"

"If he told you *and* William you could be king, then really, this is all his fault."

Harold smiled. The mouse had a point. "Come on." He let Mabel run up his arm and nestle in the fur underneath his crown.

The King left his cabin and strode along the ridge of the cliff. The grass and bed of lavenders swayed in the breeze. Harold walked for hours, and the memory of battling the blizzard on the night Edward had died came to him. He wondered what might have happened had he not returned when he did. What if Mabel had not found him, and Edward had died without him there? Who would be king then?

Every quarter mile he saw creatures of the fyrd at their stations, watching the black, empty horizon for William. He saw a shivering rabbit standing beside a common pale-furred fox. They pointed their weapons at him as his tall frame materialised out of the dark. Both of their faces looked to be in a panic, and they rushed over to him once they realised who it was.

"Your Majesty-"

"Please help us-"

"We don't know what to do-"

"He won't wake-"

"Settle down," he said sternly. "Show me."

The rabbit and fox turned and ran over to a small bundle on the floor Harold had not previously noticed. A very frail, not fully grown badger was lying there. Harold blinked, thinking of the badger-king, weak and frail, tangled in his bedsheets in Westminster.

"What's wrong with him?" demanded Harold.

"We dunno! Is he dead?" the common fox said nervously.

Mabel hopped down from Harold's head and felt for the badger's pulse. "He's alive."

"He ain't ate for three days, Your Majesty, sir," said the rabbit.

"Three days..." Harold repeated, his face burning with shame. His tail threatened to strangle his leg again.

"Will he be ok?" asked the rabbit.

"I'll make sure of it," said Harold. He leant forward and scooped up the light badger into his arms.

Decisive action.

Harold pondered these words. He cast a glance at the wall of black sky. Somewhere in its depths the lynx was lurking. A gust of wind blew at the fox's back, resolutely, defiantly keeping the duke trapped in Normandy.

The wind will have to protect us, he thought with sudden clarity. *Gyrth was right; it is time we all went home.*

The following morning, the fyrd disbanded. The southern creatures boarded the ships that had been idle for so long, and sailed back to the English mainland. As if to prove Gyrth's point about the equinox and dangers of sailing so late in the year, many of Harold's forces got caught in a storm and several vessels suffered nasty shipwrecks. When the king returned to London, he was still awaiting confirmation on how many creatures they had lost.

Harold travelled up the Thames with his brothers and wolves, the guilt playing heavily on his mind. He thought of Alfie and the beaver, and how he had likely sent them to their deaths for what felt like nothing. As Gyrth and Leofwine took their housecarls to their respective homes, Harold travelled back to Westminster.

Harold went to Edward's Westminster Abbey to pray. He almost ran into Stigand, the Archbishop of Canterbury, who was also visiting.

"Who's there?" asked the nearly blind mole, his voice echoing loudly around the chamber.

Harold backed slowly out of the abbey and hurried across the courtyard. His mood could not face the test of dealing with the mole.

Instead he ended up in the King's Dormitory, which he supposed was now his. The room looked much the same as the night in which King Edward had died. Harold wanted nothing more than to rest but it felt wrong to sleep where the badger had spent his final moments. He collapsed onto a hard chair that faced it. His head lolled against his chest and he drifted off within moments.

When he awoke he felt heavy. The room was dark; it was clearly the middle of the night. He tried to rise but there was a sharp pain in his leg. He could not stand. He looked around, trying to shake the sense of impending doom.

The sound of pawsteps approached. He searched the darkness for the door. It swung open. A vixen holding a candle under her chin raced towards him.

"There you are!" she cried.

"Edith?"

"You need to come with me right now!" she said, grasping his paw with her own.

"What is it?" he demanded as she hauled him up.

"Invasion," she trembled. Her whiskers were vibrating, her whole body was shaking.

"No," he whispered. His legs folded in on themselves and he sank to the floor, feeling empty and yet heavier than the sea. "I should never have left."

His sister slumped next to him.

"It is not what you think."

A CLASH OF CLAWS

"I have failed."

"Harold," she gripped his ear and twisted it painfully. He looked up at her, shocked and affronted. "You have been guarding the wrong coast. Word has come from the north. Scarborough burns. It's Hardrada."

Harold's mouth slid open. He had nothing left. His tail did not even have the energy to constrict around his leg.

"I-"

"Tostig is said to be with him. I'm sorry. I was wrong about him," the vixen looked on the point of tears.

Her look of fear was enough to stir Harold's strength. He clambered on to his paws and found he could stand. The pain in his leg was gone.

"I will do what I must," he helped her up as well. "I will ride north tonight."

"It's impossible. The polar bear is too strong."

"No," said Harold, and he was pleased to hear the firmness in his voice had returned. Anger flared in the empty space inside him. "I am king, and I will protect England to the last."

He left the King's Dormitory and ran down the stairs. Morcar had stopped Tostig retaking Northumbria once. But the king of Norway was another beast entirely.

This was something he would have to do himself.

AUTUMN

The Hares

Lord Edwin was hopping too fast. He bounded into a pair of rat servants and they both yelped as he stood on their exposed tails.

"Oi!" one of them shouted.

"Shh!" said the other to his friend. "It's the Earl of Mercia!"

Edwin paid neither rat any attention. He continued to race down the corridor towards the door at the far end. A rabble of mousemaids stood in his way. They all screamed at the oncoming hare.

"Watch out!" Edwin cried. The mice ducked and scattered as he propelled over them with a high jump and flip. Under normal circumstances he would have paused to wink at the mousemaids, or perhaps run a casual paw through his floppy ears upon landing. Unusually, the hare found he didn't have the time to pose. There was something far more pressing at stake.

"Vikings!" Edwin shouted as he thrust open the doors and entered his brother's office. "Vikings at Scarborough!"

The room was clean, wide, and mostly empty. When Morcar had been made Earl of Northumbria he had thrown out all of Tostig's possessions and burnt them in the street. Even now, almost a year since Tostig had been forced to flee the city of York, Morcar had failed to fill the office with many possessions of his own. As it was, there was only a small wooden table positioned under the light of one small window. Sitting at it was Lord Morcar, his already crumpled face arranged in absolute misery. Standing opposite him was a beaver in fine white robes, the Archbishop of York.

"Yeth," Ealdred the beaver scowled at Edwin's dramatic appearance. "We are aware of thith."

"What are you doing here?" asked Edwin haughtily, catching his breath. He knew the beaver was a friend to the foxes of the south and didn't trust him for it.

"I am here to atthith in any way I can."

"What? What's 'atthith'? You mean 'assist'?" Edwin said coldly.

Ealdred opened his mouth in outrage but Morcar grunted "enough" and the beaver was silent.

"You have already heard then?" said Edwin, looking at his brother.

"Pigeon came this morning," said Morcar.

"He wanted plenty of gold for hith troubleth," sniffed Ealdred. "Vermin with wingth, I alwayth thay."

"You have heard...I mean to say... you know who it is we're dealing with?" Edwin said tentatively, trying to catch his brother's solemn eye. The ugly hare was staring off into nothing and hadn't blinked for a long time. His eyes were watering and he looked slightly possessed.

"The Stray Fox is back," said Morcar.

"Tostig is the least of our problems," said Edwin a little meekly. "Two polar bears were seen with the fleet..."

Morcar continued to stare blankly into the corner of the room.

"You know what this means?" Edwin urged. "It's Hardrad-"

"I know," Morcar snapped, blinking out of his stupor. The crouched-over hare got to his paws and winced a little, feeling his side. It still ached from where Tostig had stabbed him earlier that year.

"I theem to recall, Lord Edwin," pronounced Ealdred, as Morcar began to pace ungraciously around the room, "when the Witan wath gathered in January, *you* thaid to uth all that you would never thubmit to a foreign ruler. Thurely you are not thcared, Mathter hare?"

Ealdred bared his great orange teeth to Edwin in open dislike. Edwin thought about punching him.

"Of course I'm not *thcared*," he said bitterly. "I am merely not fool enough to underestimate what we have ahead of us."

"Thuch bravery," the beaver said sarcastically.

Edwin turned away from the archbishop and went to stand by his younger brother, who stood looking out of the small window. He slung a paw around Morcar's neck.

"Once more we must take to the battlefield, little brother. Summon your creatures. This is our final test. Together, Mercia and Northumbria can defeat the white beast and the Stray Fox. And then, finally, we will be able to claim the north entirely for ourselves. A new nation, united under the hare flag."

"I thay!" cried Ealdred from behind them. "Thith ith propethterouth!"

"Be quiet," hissed Edwin.

"Hardrada cannot be conquered on the battlefield!" Ealdred shouted. "We muth lock the gateth of York and let winter defeat them!"

Edwin laughed harshly. "If the rumours about the polar bear are true, we would do well to avoid a siege. No, we must leave York and head out to meet him!"

"No, no," the beaver was shaking his head. His heavy tail slapped against the floor in subconscious aggravation. "We muth wait for King Harold."

Edwin spat on the floor.

"I thay!" Ealdred cried again. "That ith treathon!"

Edwin ignored him. "C'mon brother. Fight with me."

"We muth thiege the city!" Ealdred pleaded.

Morcar's crumpled face was unmoving. There was an extended silence but for the irregular slapping of Ealdred's tail. Morcar turned from the window. He grabbed Edwin's paw.

"Together?"

"Together," Edwin smiled.

They hugged bracingly, and somewhere unseen behind them, the beaver sank to the floor.

"We're doomed."

AUTUMN

The Burning North

Tostig, Hardrada and the rest of the Viking fleet left the town of Scarborough with coats of ash on their furs. The polar bear king was entirely cloaked in grey except for his wet, red muzzle which was drenched in the blood of his enemies. The polar bear's foes had started their day quite unaware that they would be adversaries to anyone. The peasant creatures that had busied themselves with thoughts of the oncoming winter and potential hibernation in the morning were subject to a cruel and swift end in the afternoon. The Vikings had set balls of wood alight and sent them rolling down the surrounding hills and into the town. When creatures spilled out of their burning houses onto the street, the polar bear led the vicious killing himself.

Tostig could not help but admire Hadrada's gift for ingenious violence and cruelty, and delighted in the ease in which their war campaign had begun. When the Stray Fox had been Earl of Northumbria, Scarborough would have been his to protect. Tostig was still unsure whether Morcar had survived his sword in the spring, but whoever was earl now had so far failed to muster a single creature to resist them. This both pleased the fox, and unsettled him. He had underestimated the hares before, with disastrous consequences.

After the burning, the fleet sailed up the Humber River as Tostig had done with his sixty pirate ships in May. The river had many fingers, each spiralling deep into the heart of Northumbria. Even those that narrowed into nothing more than trickling streams were of potential use to Hardrada. If the boats could not cross then the Vikings were more than happy to get out and merely move the ships across the land until the water widened once more. This was a rather exhausting experience for Tostig, and he used his new position as "Duke of the English"' to dissuade Hardrada from attempting to sail into York itself. Instead they banked at Riccall, nine miles outside of the city.

"My son," Hardrada gestured to Prince Olaf to draw near as thousands of Norwegian creatures poured off the boats and onto the soggy grass.

"Yes, father?" said Olaf.

"You are to stay here and mind the ships," Hardrada ordered. This demotion wasn't entirely an insult to the young prince as the protection of their fleet was still of utmost importance to the king. Olaf had seemed to waver when killing the innocent villagers at Scarborough, and Hardrada was keen to keep him away from the battlefield for now. War was no time for hesitation.

"Of course, father," said Olaf, looking a little relieved. "What will you do?"

"Orre and Tostig will come with me at daybreak. We are to march on York."

Olaf nodded, looking a little shaken.

"Do not fear," Hardrada growled. "I will destroy every English creature that stands in my path."

The Viking army marched next morning, before the sun had fully given outlines to the shapeless shadows. They ate up the miles of open fields between their camp and the city of York swiftly; the paws at the front crushed mud and grass into a hard-packed floor for those at the back. The king brought with him six thousand creatures, a little over half of the total warriors that had voyaged from Norway. Despite the youth of the day there was no trace of tiredness in the ranks. The excitement for war was a palpable, electric companion in the dark.

Tostig was joined by what remained of his mercenaries. The two hundred rats followed him closely in a crudely formed line. Their whispers to one another blurred into a single, hissing mass that made Tostig turn up his snout in disgust. Many of Hardrada's creatures were looking at the stinking, sweaty rats with revulsion and the fox wished he hadn't brought them along.

Tostig hurried away from the rats and caught up with Copsi, who had been waddling alone. The duck's battle helmet wobbled with every step and nearly fell off.

"You ready for this?" asked Tostig, pushing the helmet down into position.

"I guess so," said Copsi. The duck had been subdued for weeks. It was starting to get on Tostig's nerves.

"What's with the raven?" asked the fox, pointing ahead.

Hardrada was leading the march on all fours. His huge coat of armoured steel glistened as the sun breached the top of the hills. A mammoth-sized sword that Tostig doubted he would be able to lift an inch off the ground was strapped to his back. Poised on the fat blade was a raven with two black, dead-looking eyes.

"They call it the *Landøyðan*," said Copsi.

"What's a Landohyawn?"

"It means *Landwaster*. Supposedly it blesses victory on whoever it battles with."

"Works for me," Tostig shrugged. The raven twisted his neck and looked back at the fox, as if it knew he had been talking about it. Tostig could not seem to hold the raven's blank and yet piercing gaze for long. He averted his eyes, and when he looked up again, the raven was arching its neck to the sky. The polar bear king had stopped and was also looking up.

A flock of grey specks were coming over the horizon. They flew circles around the army, just out of arrow fire.

"Edwin's birds?" said Copsi.

"Got to be."

"What's it mean?"

"Looks like the hare isn't hiding behind his high walls."

"You think-"

"Yes," Tostig grimaced. "Battle. Today."

Hardrada obviously thought the same thing. The polar bear didn't seem fazed that any element of surprise was lost. He ordered the army to pick up their pace with cub-like excitement in his voice.

It was not long before they found the English. The Vikings were climbing a steep hill, and Tostig had his head down against a nasty wind when he heard a sort of whooping cheer. Hardrada had already made it to the top and seemed to be unable to hide his delight. The polar bear reached for his sword and swung it hungrily. The raven stayed close, hovering just above him.

"Finally," the king grinned.

When Tostig had made it to the top of the hill he saw what had excited Hardrada so, though he didn't feel the urge to cheer about it.

Less than quarter of a mile away, and gathered on the top of the opposing hill, a vast English army stood lying in wait. The morning sun struggled to illuminate the full scope of their forces, many thousands at least.

"This is it," said Tostig to no one in particular. He felt the moment needed recognition of some kind.

Whilst hard to see clearly, it seemed the English were already organised into the traditional shield wall combat position. The Vikings seemed unperturbed. The common soldiers shouted abuse to the distant English, and Hardrada looked ready to charge headfirst down the hill at a moment's notice.

Tostig didn't know whether to be emboldened by their bravery, or concerned by their enthusiasm tantamount to overconfidence. It seemed Copsi was surer of his own feelings than the fox. Hurried breathing echoed in the duck's oversized helmet.

"Oh no, oh no, oh no..."

"Shut it," snapped Tostig. The fox knew war, and knew fear was a good shortcut to death, or sometimes even worse: surrender. He focused on keeping his own mind clear, and began to take in his environment properly.

The two armies were facing each other atop two opposing hill banks. Over to the far right, the fields of tall, tangled grass transformed into a deep marshland. Over to the left there was a large gushing river bending in and out of sight. A small strip of water had split away from the river's main body and snaked between the two hills that the English and Vikings stood upon, separating the two armies.

"Where to cross..." Tostig muttered.

"There?" Copsi pointed a wing to a muddy spot in between the hills where the ground had drunk all the water.

With every passing minute more of Hardrada's creatures were reaching the top of their hill. The king's generals were already ordering them into position. Tostig ran to the polar bear's side with Copsi jangling in his armour behind him.

"Your Majesty," Tostig bowed. "What is our plan of action?"

The king wasn't listening to him. Instead he was conferring with the *Landøyðan* raven in the bird's own mangled squawk. Eystein Orre appeared next to the black fox and white bear.

"Tostig," the wolverine wheezed slightly after climbing the steep hill. He revealed two yellow fangs like a pair of jagged stalactites hanging from the roof of a dark cave. "Friends of yours?" he nodded to the English army.

Tostig gave him a cold look. "Not exactly."

"Didn't you say the creatures of Northumbria would come to join you? Join us?"

"Edwin and Morcar have poisoned their minds against me."

"The hares? Aren't you supposed to have killed one?"

"I – well, yes."

"You said you struck your blade through its chest."

"Yes."

"Then who-"

"Quiet," Hardrada interrupted. Orre fell silent. "It... no...matter."

Tostig felt an odd prickling sensation on the back of his neck and looked up. The black raven was easily suspending itself in the air, and watching Tostig with its dead eyes.

The polar bear king placed a paw on Tostig's back and pulled him closer. Hardrada's black claws dug into his fur and the fox wasn't sure if this was intentional or not.

The bear barked an order.

"The king says you are to lead the charge," translated Orre.

"Me?" Tostig baulked. He felt the polar bear's great strength and knew that he could be snapped in two if the king so wished.

"You are to meet the English head on. We will take our best forces and sneak around the left, along the river bank."

"I see."

So I am to be the bait, Tostig thought. *Wonderful.*

"I would be honoured, though my rats and I will not be enough."

The king whistled to one of his generals, a lean wolverine called Kit.

"Together," Hardrada growled.

Kit looked eager enough, but young and lacking in battle scars.

"As you say, Your Majesty," said Tostig ruefully. He, Copsi and Kit left the king, Orre and the *Landøyðan* raven. Kit dashed away to gather his troops and Tostig looked around for his rats.

"We are going in. Get ready."

"I'm not ready for this," Copsi whimpered, breathing heavily. Tostig grabbed the duck's helmet with both paws.

"Stop whining," he shook the helmet.

"I don't think I can help much, sir."

"Just stay close to me."

"Can't I just-"

"Don't embarrass me, Copsi."

"Yes, sir."

"Now come on, we're fighting for England here."

"Are we?" Copsi looked over at the opposing army. "What if we're on the wrong hill?"

Tostig knelt down beside the duck. "Those hares over there, Copsi, those hares killed our friends. Destroyed our lives. Enough of this noble nonsense. We deserve what is ours. We are here to put things right. Are you with me?"

Copsi's eyes shimmered in the slits of his helmet.

"I am."

Tostig smiled. "Then let's do this."

Tostig marched down the hill with Copsi and his rats behind him. On his right was Kit the wolverine with a thousand or so of Hardrada's least experienced warriors. As they strode down the hill bank Tostig glanced behind. From this angle there was no way of seeing Hardrada and the rest of his creatures. God only knew if they were still there, had headed towards the river bank, or turned and left them completely.

He's sending me to my death. He wants me out of the picture.

Tostig shook his head and scowled. Fear was a sly beast. He had no choice but to trust in Hardrada's honour.

Tonight we shall dine together in the halls of York.

The water that had gathered in the crevice of the two hills drained away as the morning wore on, turning it into a muddy trench. The English had made their way down their hill as well and were waiting on the other side of it. The armies were close enough to hear each other's taunts now. Tostig could see the stitching on the red banners that were held by the English; it depicted a stout and muscly hare with poised ears, unlike their real-life counterparts.

"Morcar," Tostig spat. "He survived."

It was impossible to see the Earl of Northumbria amongst the seemingly endless shield wall. The English stood next to one another in tight formation, holding their shields up so that they protected themselves and those next to them. Tostig had fought with many of these creatures before in Wales, and knew how difficult the shield wall was to defeat. The Vikings watched the silent, impenetrable wall with bloodthirsty eyes. They jumped up and down and swung their weapons, eager to charge.

Tostig drew his sword and took a single, calming breath. The sun twinkled above him; it was just before midday.

A Viking wolf dug his heels in the ground, waiting to pounce.

An English beaver dropped his shield enough to sneak a peek at the Viking army. His giant gnashers chattered as he ducked behind the shield again.

Kit watched Tostig and nodded.

"FORWARD!" the fox cried.

AUTUMN

Battle of Fulford

He had barely finished the word when the Vikings ran. They sprinted over the trench at full pace. Tostig was soon outstripped by wolves and wolverines who charged at the English with reckless abandon.

Paws slipped and slid on the mud and slowed down the Vikings' progress. Morcar's Northumbrian army did not move – they did not have to. They held their position and waited as the Vikings stumbled towards them. The Vikings barrelled into the shield wall and the English forced them back. A crack would open in the wall for only a second as a soldier aimed an axe at an oncoming Norwegian. Once the steel had buried itself in the enemy's fur, the axe was retracted and the shield wall slid shut again.

"You!" Tostig called to one of his rat captains as he slipped to one knee on the wet mud. "Get under them!"

The pirate grinned at him. "With me!" he called to his brothers.

The English shield wall was made up of the toughest creatures: beavers, otters, badgers and foxes. For the wall to succeed, the creatures had to have the size and strength to protect those around them. This left a small window under the shields that the rats could exploit. All two hundred of the little rodents converged down the middle of the Northumbrian line. They slipped under the protection of the shields with their knives, stabbing and gnawing at the ankles of the English. Tostig saw a badger on the frontline collapse under the weight of twenty rats. Tostig charged at the chink of armour in the otherwise impenetrable shield wall with his sword aloft.

"Kit! Follow!" he called. He slipped again on the muddy ground. He clambered up, his snout dripping in mud. "Quickly!"

Tostig could not afford to allow the shield wall to seal itself. He stumbled and leaped at the break the rats had caused. The badger was struggling to get up as the rats jabbed at him. Tostig buried his sword in the badger's chest. Blood gurgled in its mouth and when the fox wrenched the blade free, its eyes emptied of life.

A second badger who had been next to the first made a cry of anguish. It appeared from behind his shield and swung its axe at Tostig. Before the curved steel could free the fox's head from his neck Kit leaped at the badger. He sunk his fangs into his arm and the badger crumpled. At the same time a bloated grey rat climbed up an otter and brought it down to the ground with a well-aimed knife to the eye. The hole in the shield wall was widening and there was chaos in the English ranks.

Tostig got to his paws. He slashed at the shield to his left and beat the creature behind it to the ground. The shield slipped briefly, revealing the face of a terrified beaver. Tostig thrust his sword downwards into its exposed neck.

The fox ploughed on. Kit was wrestling with the second badger, his large fangs now buried in the Northumbrian creature's neck. After much struggling, and a snapping sound that carried over the clanging steel and many screams of pain, the badger's head lolled blankly to one side. Tostig offered a paw to help the wolverine up. Kit didn't thank him but merely launched himself onto another shield.

The battle waged on and Tostig counted his kills up to twenty before he lost track. It was impossible to tell how long they had been fighting. Creatures were everywhere. Enemies and allies surrounded him. Copsi was nowhere to be seen. Tostig kept close to the ferocious Kit and continued driving inwards. The rats had caused the shield wall to collapse in on itself down the centre and the Vikings had forced their way through. Despite this success, the rest of the shield wall had been kept intact. Most of the Vikings had been battered away and were being held in the mud. Tostig and Kit, along with the most reckless of

Vikings, were cut away from most of their forces. They had come too far. The English began to circle those who had broken into their ranks.

"Fox!" a voice cried.

Tostig pulled his sword from the stomach of an otter barely out of adolescence and turned. A crouched hare with a crumpled face was emerging from the depths of the English forces. It hopped clumsily over the bed of dead creatures that littered the ground, its gnarled leg quivering.

"Morcar," Tostig said.

An arctic fox leaped out of nowhere. Tostig watched it in confusion, only realising at the last second it was fighting for the Northumbrians. Many Vikings had settled in the north of England hundreds of years ago, making the battle extremely confusing at times. Tostig dodged his head backwards to avoid the blade. The arctic fox had overextended himself. Tostig grabbed its neck and poked it full of holes with his sword. It wailed and crumpled.

"Nobody touch him!" Morcar growled. "The fox is mine."

Tostig threw the arctic fox aside and stepped towards the ugly hare.

"I've been looking forward to this."

The fox and hare charged at each other and their swords sang. Immediately Tostig was on the offensive. He used his height advantage to strike down on the hare, who had to use both paws on his sword to parry the fox's powerful strikes. The hare slipped in the mud and the sword dropped from his paw. The fox dimly remembered battling the lynx in the streets of Normandy.

Tostig raised his sword. The hare was crouched down and looking up at him, his face contorted with hate.

"Any last words?"

The hare sank even lower into the mud and, as Tostig made to bring his sword down, he sprang up. The fox missed his attack as the hare leaped over him. Morcar pirouetted in mid-air and landed behind him. Tostig turned and Morcar jumped again, this time with his bottom paws aimed at the fox's chest. The hare kicked Tostig with the might of a bear's punch. The Stray Fox flew backwards and tripped over a dead beaver's tail.

Morcar appeared above him, his sword back in his paw. Tostig struggled to get up off the ground but Morcar stood on his chest. None of his rats were anywhere to be seen and Kit was engaged in a duel with a crazed badger.

"Copsi! Help me!"

Nobody answered the fox's calls.

"You are alone," the hare's crumpled face spread into a smile, and for the first time, Morcar looked as handsome as his brother. "Any last words?"

Tostig struggled against Morcar's paws until a sound stopped him in his tracks. A long, dreadful screech that tore through the battlefield. All the creatures, Northumbrian and Viking alike, stopped what they were doing and hunted for the source. Tostig saw it first, behind Morcar's drooping ear.

A black raven was circling.

Only when the sounds of steel on steel began did Hardrada make his move. His forces hugged the river bank to the West, keeping out of sight.

The terrain was a squelching bog and slowed their progress. Hardrada waded through first, his heavy legs sinking deep into the mud. Far to the east the sounds of Tostig's raging battle could be heard. The Vikings crossed the bank as fast as they could, eager to be in the thick of the action.

Their plan was simple. The shield wall was indeed an effective mode of defence, but if they could open up another front of attack then it would crumble. Hardrada hoped to pincer Morcar's forces with an attack on the side. Before they could arrive, however, they were met with a small, inconvenient obstacle.

Another legion of the English was waiting in their thousands. A tall-eared hare winked at them from the fabric of a swaying blue flag.

"Edwin?" Eystein Orre asked the king. They had heard enough about the handsome hare from the fox. "The brother from Mercia?"

"I do not care," said Hardrada. He beckoned the raven down to his side and squawked. "*Kill.*"

The *Landøyðan* screeched and soared and Hardrada ran. Orre and his band of wolverines maintained the king's pace at his side, six on his left and six on his right. The raven flew above them, its earsplitting shriek making Edwin's Mercian soldiers scream and hold their paws over their ears. The screech mingled with the war cries of the Viking soldiers as they crashed into the English.

Hardrada hit the shield wall first. He ran on all fours and set his head down into a ramming position. The frontline of Edwin's shield wall quivered and backed away but those behind would not let them retreat. The polar bear collided headfirst with two otters. Their shields shattered instantly and they were sent flying backwards into the throng of English soldiers behind.

As Orre and his wolverines flew into their own attacks, the king of Norway stood. On his hind legs, he was taller than any creature there had ever been. There seemed to be a momentary pause in the fighting as the Mercians looked up at Hardrada and all his magnificence. They gaped in silence, wordless and powerless before this God amongst creatures. The king drew his sword and swung it. His first kill never even moved. The beaver merely watched as the blade came down, sliced through his shield like butter, and buried itself into his head.

After the initial shock, terror soon cut through the ranks. Hardrada swung his sword in great sweeping motions, killing all that stood before him. The bravest rushed forward, their battleaxes aloft. One badger managed to make it close enough to attack without being cut down. It could only reach his belly and the steel clanged harmlessly off his full body armour. Hardrada swiped at it as if it were a pestering bee. His claw ripped the badger's fur open and it was dead before it hit the floor.

It did not take long for Edwin's creatures to completely collapse. Nothing could be done to impede the giant bear trampling through them, and those distracted by the king were stabbed in the back by Orre and his wolverines.

The *Landøyðan*, meanwhile, was flying rings around the battlefield, its shriek terrorising the Mercians and empowering the Vikings. It stole the eyes of many creatures with its sharp beak as it carried out the mission Hardrada had given it. It did not take the raven long to find the creature he was looking for. Within ten minutes of the battle beginning it had returned to the king with the information.

Hardrada grinned when the *Landøyðan* told him. He followed the raven through the battlefield, easily chopping down any creature that dared stand against him.

The English hare wore light armour with no helmet, almost as if he wanted to be seen on the battlefield. He was useful with a blade, Hardrada was happy to concede. Edwin had just survived a nasty tussle with a wolf when the king found him.

"Back into lines!" Edwin was shouting to his creatures. His charming eyes shone behind a face covered in blood. "Regroup! Regroup! Re-"

The hare had seen Hardrada. His ears drooped and he shuffled backwards.

"Regroup..." he whispered.

Hardrada moved towards him and the hare scrambled back even further.

"Attack! Attack!" Edwin pointed at the polar bear. Two of Edwin's creatures charged at Hardrada. He beheaded them both with a single strike.

"Attack!" the hare cried again. Nobody paid him any attention this time. The English were too busy trying to get out of the polar bear's way.

Hardrada advanced and the hare fell backwards. The polar bear's shadow drowned the hare as he stood over him. The king put his sword on the hare's neck.

"No!" Edwin was crying. "Please!"

A CLASH OF CLAWS

Hardrada raised his sword. The *Landøyðan*'s screech shook the ground.

The polar bear swung and Edwin rolled out of the way. The sword hit the ground and got wedged in the mud. By the time Hardrada had pulled it free the hare was already far away, hopping away from the battle.

"Run! Run!" the hare yelled. "Retreat! Retreat! To Morcar!"

"Cowards," Hardrada sneered as the English sprinted in all directions. Hardrada pointed after Edwin and those who had followed him. "After them!"

The slowest were killed outright, and those who tripped in their haste were trampled. Edwin's hops became a blur of fur in the distance as his fleeing creatures were hunted down behind him.

The *Landøyðan*'s shriek made Morcar turn and his hold on Tostig loosen. The fox kicked Morcar away and got to his own paws. Before either hare or fox could attack the other, they turned again at another new sound.

"Run! Everybody run!" a hare was bolting towards them.

"Edwin?" said Morcar. "What is it?"

"RUN!" Edwin never stopped hopping. He bounced between Morcar and Tostig and fled east, towards the marshland that lay beyond.

"Brother!" Morcar cried. "Come back!"

"You might want to join him," Tostig grinned. The fox nodded to the direction Edwin had appeared from. The rest of Edwin's Mercian army were running towards them, with Hardrada's best warriors right on their heels. Leading the charge was Hardrada himself; enormous, majestic, unstoppable.

Morcar quivered. He swallowed and raised his sword higher.

"With me!" he yelled. The hare stepped towards the onrushing Hardrada but none of his creatures came with him. Instead they looked to the older hare and his distant hops.

"It is over!"

"Let's get out of here!"

The English resolve had crumbled. They turned and ran.

"Get back here!" Morcar roared after them. Two badgers started to drag him away. "Geroff me!"

"It's over, sir!" one badger shouted. The hare kicked and screamed as they pulled him away from the battle.

Tostig tried to follow but found his legs were tired and weak. He glanced down and noticed the patch of orange fur at his hip was red with blood. He didn't remember receiving the wound.

"Interesting," he said, suddenly feeling dizzy.

Hardrada's forces now joined with Tostig's. The surviving creatures of Northumbria and Mercia fled together. Those who valued their lives ran towards the marshland, after Edwin and the badgers who continued to drag the thrashing Morcar to safety. The polar bear led the killing of any who were foolish enough to stay.

"Are you ok, sir?" said a small voice.

Tostig turned. "Copsi! You're alive!"

"I think so," said Copsi. His helmet shone with blood but seemed undamaged.

"Well done," Tostig smiled, rubbing the blood away. He swayed a little but didn't fall.

"I don't want to do this again, sir."

Tostig looked around. Hardrada was biting into the neck of a white rabbit. Orre and Kit combined to kill an English fox. "I think...I think we won Copsi."

"I think you might be right."

Tostig put a paw on the duck's head and leaned against it. The battle was over within an hour. A thousand of the English were dead, and the rest were running and scattered. The Vikings followed the hares across the marshland and continued to kill. Creatures drowned as they tried to flee. Their bodies filled the water and acted as a footpath as the Vikings left the place known as Fulford, and continued to march on the city of York.

AUTUMN

A Causeway of Corpses

The gates of York were open when they arrived. The army drew to a halt and the polar bear king spoke for the first time since the battle.

The hares' warriors
All lay fallen
In the swampy water,
Gashed by weapons;
And the hardy
Creatures of Norway
Could cross the marsh on a causeway of corpses.

There was a smattering of applause but if Hardrada heard it he didn't show it. Instead he stared at the open gates, pondering what was waiting for him inside. After a few moments he called for Tostig and Copsi, Orre, Kit and some of his other strongest soldiers to gather. The *Landøyðan* was still at the battlefield, feasting on the flesh of the dead. The king and his guard entered the city with their weapons raised.

The band of creatures walked through the deserted streets with unwarranted wariness. They needn't have worried; it was a ghost town.

Once or twice they saw families scrambling out of their houses, or sparkling sets of cub eyes peering at them from behind hay bales. Countless fathers were dead, injured or had fled with the hares. The mothers, cubs and kittens had to make their own way. It seemed the majority had chosen to flee. Tostig could understand the impulse, but they did not need to be fearful; Hardrada wanted York as a capital, not a cemetery.

"They are all scared for the moment," said Tostig. "The creatures of the north have Viking heritage, they will be ready to accept Viking rule over a southern king from Wessex. Just wait."

"Aren't you from the south?" asked Orre with a hint of a sneer. "Why did they trust you?"

"That's different," Tostig sniffed. The fox slowed his walking to wait for Copsi to catch up with him. "That wolverine is starting to annoy me."

"Huh?" said Copsi, who had been looking around with a pensive expression. "Oh, yes, sir. Annoying."

"You good?"

"Yes, yes, it's just...strange to be back."

Tostig looked around. A deserted York was quite a different spectacle to the usual hustle and bustle. "I guess."

"I'm not sure I thought I'd ever see home again."

Tostig stopped and frowned to himself. *Home.* That was an interesting word. It had been a year since he was banished from the North, a year since the rioters had killed his soldiers and sent him running with his tail between his legs. He had spent every waking second since then working out a way to get back. He had travelled the world to ensure he did. He should be happy; he had got what he wanted.

The fox looked down at his own paws. The fur had matted with blood.

"I told you we'd do it."

"Well done, sir," the duck said quietly. Tostig's snout twitched.

Up ahead, there was clamour amongst the king's guard. The creatures were drawing their weapons. Tostig galloped on all fours to catch up with them.

"We thurrender!" a voice was shouting. "We thurrender!"

An old beaver in bright white robes was shuffling towards them holding a large white flag. The guard swiftly surrounded him with malevolent grins and glinting steel.

"It's Ealdred," Tostig told the Vikings. "Archbishop of York. There will be no need to harm him."

The beaver's eye met the fox's. Tostig looked away first.

Hardrada was swinging his sword with slow deliberation. Even standing beside him Tostig felt the heat of the polar bear's simmering power. Ealdred looked as if he was burning alive in its wake.

"We th-th-thurrender," stammered the beaver again, his voice brittle.

"Where are the hares?" said Tostig. He stared just above the archbishop, unable to face the beaver he had once known so well. "Did they return here? Are you harbouring them?"

"I told them before, I thaid we muth not fight, we muth let the H-H-Hard... let you through."

"That's not what was asked," snarled Orre. He flipped his sword in his paw and caught it on the jagged blade side. He strode over and struck the beaver in the face with the sword hilt.

Tostig looked at the ground as Ealdred wailed.

"They are...not here! I don't know...where... they are!" the beaver spoke in between sobs.

"I don't trust him," said Orre.

"He's not lying," said Copsi. The Vikings all looked at the duck.

"Who asked you?" sneered the wolverine.

"Hey," snapped Tostig. "This is our country. If we say the beaver's telling the truth, you listen."

"Ith true...we thubmit...completely... to your king..." said Ealdred, blood dribbling from his mouth.

"*Your* king?" growled Orre, raising his sword threateningly.

"M-m-m-my king..." said Ealdred, looking thoroughly ashamed of himself.

Hardrada knelt before the beaver. He traced a black claw down the side of his face. A chunk of residue flesh left under the claw stuck to the beaver's fur.

"I am...your king?" said Hardrada.

"Yeth... Your Majethty," the beaver kissed the floor at the polar bear's paws.

"What about...the *other king*?"

"How do we know you will stay loyal?" barked Orre.

"I-I-" stammered Ealdred, looking back and forth between the two frightening creatures.

"Hostages," intervened Tostig. "Give us hostages, and Harold wouldn't dare attack us."

Hardrada nodded slowly. "Five hundred," he growled at the beaver.

"Goodneth, thath a lot."

Blood dripped off the polar bear's chin as he waited.

"I- yeth – of courth. It will take time, though!"

"Harold is focused on William in the south," Tostig reminded Hardrada. "We have the time."

"You've got three days," Orre pronounced. "Gather the cubs and kittens. If you fail to do so, or we get word that you are preparing a counterattack – all of the north shall burn."

Hardrada stroked the beaver's head like a father soothes his cub. The archbishop shivered and curled into a ball, his tail frantically slapping the ground.

"Where is good?" said Hardrada to Tostig.

"We could meet at Stamford Bridge. It's not far from here. Large, open place. Hard to get ambushed there."

"You hear that?" spat Orre. He gave the beaver a kick.

"Yeth."

"Three days. Five hundred hostages. At Stamford Bridge. Noon."

The polar bear king turned away from the hapless beaver. They would return to their ships at Ricall and wait for the hostages to be gathered.

Tostig lingered as the Vikings headed back to the gates. He offered a paw to Ealdred who was weeping on the floor. When the beaver didn't take the fox's offering, Tostig grabbed him around the middle and yanked him to his paws. The beaver pushed him away.

"Geroff me, traitor!"

The beaver ran away leaving Tostig alone. The fox looked around again.

"Home sweet home," he muttered as he caught up with the departing Vikings.

AUTUMN

The Long March

The king of England was on the move. After hearing of the Viking attacks from Edith, Harold had not wasted a single moment before reaching out to his brothers.

"William?" Gyrth had said with wide eyes when Harold turned up breathless at his door. Strangely, it was Leofwine who better understood the fear in Harold's eye when the king had arrived to see him.

"It's Tostig, isn't it?" the youngest fox had said.

The fox brothers marched north that night. Edith wanted to come herself but Harold made her stay. He left Mabel to care for her; Edith had been the one closest to Tostig and the vixen was left devastated.

There was no time to reassemble the southern creatures who had served the fyrd at the Isle of Wight over the summer. Besides, it would have been a cruel stroke to recall these creatures the moment they returned to their families. Instead, Harold, Gyrth and Leofwine departed London only accompanied by their professional housecarls.

Harold had total trust in these axe-swinging soldiers, but their combined numbers reached little over two and a half thousand. The king knew it would not be enough. Luckily, the creatures of England responded.

As Harold's army marched day and night up the Roman roads that led through Mercia and into Northumbria, many creatures flocked to see the soldiers pass. Ensnared by the opportunity for adventure, lots of creatures gathered their weapons and joined the army after hearing what was at stake. On a couple of occasions, Harold stopped to give impassioned speeches about England, glory, and honour. Every village or town brought new creatures, bolstering the army into numbers Harold knew not.

After two days and nights of marching, Harold had managed a little under one hundred miles. It was unclear whether legs or minds were more tired after the exertion of such a breath-taking pace. Despite the exhaustion, there was a sense of determination around the group that persisted. Harold himself felt alert and resolute. Finally, he had a purpose; a clear plan of action. He had spent so much time as king doubting himself. Doubting his decisions as he waited for the lynx to attack. Now he was sure he was doing the right thing. He was the king of England, and now was the moment to prove it. He felt almost as if he had been an imposter king up until this point, but if he could defend his country from Viking invasion, nobody could doubt his worthiness, not even himself. He would be a true king of England, like the badger Alfred the Great all those years ago.

"What are you smiling about?" said Leofwine when Harold was pondering this thought. It was a cloudless night, and God had blessed them with a bright moon to light their way north. The two foxes were leading the way, with Gyrth, Dunstan and Wulfric shepherding the army at distant intervals.

"Nothing," said Harold a little guiltily.

"Aren't you worried?" asked Leofwine, not for the first time. "They say he's the biggest creature in the world."

Harold did not need to ask who Leofwine was talking about.

"How are we going to kill him, Harold?"

How indeed?

The steady beat of Gyrth's regimented steps approached.

"What is it?" Harold turned.

"All the creatures are tired, oughtn't we stop?" said Gyrth.

Harold was so used to long walks that he often forgot what a challenge it could be for the others, weighed down with armour and weapons.

"One hour, then we must continue."

Gyrth looked like he wanted to object but he resisted the temptation. They had been extra polite to one another after their argument at the Isle of Wight.

"I need you to bring me Dunstan," Harold told him. He turned to Leofwine. "Get me Wulfric too."

His brothers reappeared with the bear and one-eyed wolf shortly after.

"Thank you," said Harold in a voice that told Gyrth and Leofwine they were dismissed. "Walk with me," the fox said to his two generals, leading them away from prying ears.

Dunstan shook his aching paws loose. It must have been hard for the bear to march with all that weight.

"Tired yet?" said Harold.

"Please, barely getting started."

Harold smiled. "You remember Wales?"

"I remember half of it, the other is a bit fuzzy," Wulfric growled. The wolf had lost his eye in the mountains.

"You remember Gruffyd ap Llewlyn, I'm sure?" said Harold.

"Aye, I do," Wulfric nodded. The wolf had been the one to behead the Welsh goat-king.

"We were fighting alongside Tostig then, seems strange to think of it..."

There was a slightly awkward moment. All the creatures knew not to mention the Stray Fox in front of the king, but what if the king brought it up himself?

Dunstan chewed his lip.

"Speak your mind freely, Dunstan."

"Forgive me Your Majesty, only I...I never trusted the fox. Rumours of his harsh rule in Northumbria reached my ears even then."

"Yes," said Harold sadly. "Yes, me too."

There was another uncomfortable silence.

"It is unfortunate that brother must take against brother. This pain is for myself, Gyrth and Leofwine to bear, not yours. I'm afraid I am going to burden you with something else."

Wulfric and Dunstan stood a little taller, alert.

"I have a mission for you. Either, or both."

"Anything," said Dunstan.

"All reports say polar bears have been spotted. It can only mean one thing," Harold paused and twisted his whiskers. "King Harald Hardrada is from Norway. He is extremely large, extremely strong, and with much experience. He has fought many battles, has fought with the Varangian guard in the Byzantine empire, waged war on Denmark for fifteen years, and now has turned his eye upon us. If we are to succeed in-"

"You want us to kill it?" said Wulfric.

Harold thought it interesting that the wolf said 'it' as opposed to 'him'. He supposed it was easier to kill an 'it'.

"I do."

Dunstan shivered and Harold pretended not to see it. Wulfric merely nodded.

"Then it will be done," said the wolf.

"I understand what I am asking of you. Dunstan, you are the only creature close to Hardrada's size," said Harold. "And Wulfric, well," he thought of Gruffyd ap Lleywen's head. "You have killed a king before, why not again?"

A night and a day later, King Harold and his ever expanding army found the desolate battleground at Fulford. The tall grass was matted with dead creatures and scattered weapons. They scoured the land fruitlessly for survivors. Bodies bobbed for miles in the surrounding marsh. The king took off his crown and led a moment of silence for the lives lost.

"The hares decided to fight then," Leofwine said after the silence was over.

"Yes," said Harold. The fox turned to the wolf beside him. "Wulfric, see if Edwin and Morcar's bodies can be found."

The one-eyed wolf nodded with a grimace. He turned away and could be heard gathering unfortunate creatures for the ugly task of searching the faces of the many dead.

"Your Majesty," Gyrth ran over to them. "We have something."

Harold and Leofwine followed their brother to the edge of the expansive marsh. Reeds poked their way through the murky water, and lily pads and corpses floated on the surface. On the earthy mound leading into the water, a jumble of sticks and twigs had been haphazardly gathered over a cavernous hole that led under the ground. It was poorly made, but Harold recognised an otter's den when he saw one. There were remnants of bloody paw prints leading inside.

"Is anybody home?" Harold called. There was silence.

"Ceej said he saw something slither in," said Gyrth.

"I'm going in," said Harold.

"No, Harold, let me-"

The king didn't listen. He unclipped his red cloak and handed it to Leofwine before crawling in the sludge like mud. He squeezed into the dark den, momentarily feeling claustrophobic in the tight tunnel before breaking through and taking deep breaths inside a large space. Little light made it through from the outside. By the time his eyes had adjusted, there was a blade around his neck.

"Don' yer move now!" a hot breath scalded his ear.

"Easy," said Harold calmly. "You don't want to do this."

"Yer English?" the breath whispered.

"Very much so."

"Whass tha' mean?"

"I'm the king."

"Wha?"

"Please lower your blade."

Slowly but surely the knife lowered. Harold was sure not to make any sudden movements.

"Thank you."

"I'm sorry, Lor' Edward ser, Yer Majestine, ser," the creature babbled. He stepped away from the fox and Harold could see he was indeed an otter. The stranger was thin and malnourished, and seemed to have a small limp.

"That's alright, though I am not Edward."

"Oh."

"Edward died in January, I – oh, never mind – I need to ask you some questions."

The otter slumped down on the ground with a wince.

"Fire away, ser."

"What happened here? Did you fight with Edwin and Morcar?"

"Who?"

Harold bit back an impatient retort. Many simple creatures did not bother with the politics of the nobles of the country; it was not his fault.

"The hares?" Harold prompted.

"Oh, righ', yeh, we was both with the ugly one."

"*We?*"

"Yeh, please help him ser!"

For a moment Harold was truly baffled. There was a small groan and the fox spun around, his eyes falling on a limp body in the corner of the den.

"My God!" he cried.

The otter there was thin, even thinner than the first. He was sprawled lifelessly across the floor, with a great slash across his belly. His insides had spooled around his paws. His eyes were sunken, his breathing was shallow. Had Harold not heard the groan he would have assumed the poor creature long dead.

"He got hurt in the figh'! I been trying to nurse him, ser, but I don' know much about no healin'," the first otter sighed.

"Tell me what happened."

"They came. So many of 'em! We was fighting a load, led by a fox they were. Not like yer, mind, this was one was more black than orange!

We was doing alrigh' too, before the polar bear came," the otter shivered and Harold could not help but do the same.

"Then what?"

"Everyone panicked, can't much blame 'em! That bear...that's just not righ'...how could anything be that big? That powerful...that evil..." the otter shook his head. "I ran too, I grabbed me friend 'ere and brought him down into this den. T'was my father's. I was cert they was going to catch us, but no one came. I 'eard 'em passing over. Sounds like they was going to York."

"Then the city will be theirs by now," Harold licked a paw and twisted his drooping whiskers.

"It is," the dying otter wheezed. Harold turned to face him. "We heard them pass over us."

"Oh, tha's righ'!" said the first otter. "The Vikings came back that nigh'. They was talking loud and all confident like, laughin' and jokin' they were."

Harold's jaw stiffened. "Size and strength often brings about arrogance. All the better when they fall."

"I s'pose – hey, where yer going?"

"To cut down a giant."

"Yer mad!" the otter cried. "They'll do the same to yer!" he pointed at his friend.

"I'll send a nurse for him," said Harold, already scrambling out of the den. "Though there is little to be done. His life cannot be saved, but justice can still be served."

The king waited for cover of nightfall before entering York. It had taken just four days to cross the length of England. Even the fox's experienced legs were waning after something like two hundred miles of marching. Whilst most of his army were resting before a battle they knew was coming, Harold did not stop, he did not even sit. If he relented now tiredness would overcome him. He had to keep going.

"Let me go instead," said Gyrth as Leofwine fastened a dirty, black cloak around Harold's neck.

"A little tighter," Harold told Leofwine.

"You don't have to do everything yourself. This is too risky!" Gyrth pleaded.

"That's better," Harold stepped away. He handed his crown to Leofwine and pulled the hood of his cloak over his head. It was impossible to tell this was the king of England in the dark.

"Harold," Gyrth said with tired severity. "Please."

"There could be Vikings inside," Leofwine agreed.

"Relax, brothers. I'll be careful."

Harold entered York alone many hours after sunset. The streets were empty and painted a bleak picture of what had happened here. Dropped possessions littered the floor; evidence of fleeing families abandoning their homes. Harold kept his head down, and those creatures he did see paid him no attention. Distant wails and drunken arguments could be heard coming from several houses.

It did not take long to find the church. He remembered it from when he had visited Tostig a few years previously.

Simpler times, Harold sighed.

"Who goeth there?" a voice called when the church doors opened.

"Ealdred?" Harold whispered. "Is that you?"

"Reveal yourthelf!" the beaver cried.

"Shh," Harold put his arms up to show his non-threatening intentions. Ealdred rose from the floor where he had been praying and drew a small knife.

"Thtay back!"

"Ealdred-"

"I mean it!"

"Are you alone?" the fox continued to speak in hushed tones. He drew within paw reach of the beaver.

"I have a knife!"

"You are not about to spill blood in God's prese-"

Ealdred lunged and Harold only dodged the knife just in time. The blade severed a single whisker clean off. As it meandered to the ground Harold slipped behind the beaver and grabbed his neck.

"No! Help! He-"

Harold covered the beaver's mouth and whispered. "It's me. It's the king."

Ealdred stopped struggling. "Harold?"

"I'm going to let you go now," Harold gently released the beaver. He hovered around him, waiting to see if the archbishop panicked again.

"Oh, Harold!" the beaver collapsed onto the fox. He began to weep into his chest. "My king!"

Harold winced as his cloak became sodden in tears. He gently pushed the beaver away.

"I'm here, Ealdred."

"You are our thaviour!"

"Not yet. I need to know everything."

"Edwin and Morcar, they've gone! Or dead, I don't know. Tothtig and Hardrada, they're at Riccall. They demanded five hundred hothtageth."

Harold was reminded of the time Leofwine had dumped a bucket of icy water over his head when they were cubs.

I'm too late.

If Hardrada had his paws on five hundred hostages, Harold could never attack without risking their lives.

"We meet at Thamford Bridge tomorrow," the beaver began to weep again. "I'm thorry!"

Harold's ears perked up.

"Tomorrow? You mean you haven't handed over the hostages yet?"

"Yeth, thir," Ealdred nodded.

"Then there's still hope!" Harold cheered.

"There ith?"

"Oh, yes, we *will* be meeting them at Stamford Bridge tomorrow alright."

"We will?" Ealdred sniffed.

"But they won't be getting any hostages from us. Only what they deserve; only death."

AUTUMN

Home Slayer

A moose with two black eyes leant back on his chair, guffawing loudly and spilling mead on the black and orange fox that sat beside him.

"Do you mind?" Tostig snapped.

The moose grinned dopily back at him, baring several gaps in his yellow teeth. He had lost them during the battle with the English a few days earlier.

"Disgusting," Tostig showed the moose his back and looked up the table.

The Viking army was feasting under the stars, not far from where their three hundred ships were banked at Riccall. All the provisions had been plundered from nearby villages with little to no resistance. Other than those unfortunate enough to be on guard duty, the whole of the Viking army was celebrating their recent victory in style. Adjacent tables competed to drink the most and laugh the loudest. The dwindling survivors of Tostig's mercenary rats sat far away from the rest. Nobody much liked them and stayed well clear. Tostig and Copsi dined at the most prominent table, half a dozen creatures away from King Hardrada, Prince Olaf and Eystein Orre. The wolverine was standing and leading the festivities.

"To Kit!" Orre raised his flagon. "A fine performance! A fine bite that snapped the necks of many English! He shall be hereby known as Kit Iron Jaw!"

Kit, the lean wolverine who had fought closely with Tostig at Fulford, got to his paws with an assured air.

"Iron Jaw!" everyone shouted back.

Kit nodded his thanks, doing well to hide the fierce pride that came with such a name.

"Their bones snapped easily," said Iron Jaw. "The rumours of the English strength seem to have been exaggerated."

The Vikings cheered their agreement as Copsi translated. Tostig found this statement oddly irritating and was half in the mind to contradict him.

"We were all surprised with how pathetic the English resistance was!" Orre shouted over the tumult of the table. "But then many have crumbled under the shadow of King Hardrada and the black wings of the *Landøyðan*."

There was no denying this was true. The screech of the black raven was not something Tostig would be able to forget lightly. Thankfully the *Landøyðan* wasn't at the feast, though the fox didn't stop checking over his shoulder for the winged omen. Since the battle, Tostig was often struck with a swooping sensation in the pit of his stomach as if he had just fallen from a great height. After each of these moments he had turned to see the raven watching him, and had long decided there was something magical and sinister about the creature.

"The hares of England shamed their country with their hops to safety!" Orre continued. "I think any creature who could swing a sword could defeat them." His eyes glanced over Tostig tauntingly.

"What you looking at?" Tostig glared. "You got a problem?" The fox had had several meads and his voice carried doubly far with extra, unabashed venom.

"Not at all," smiled the wolverine. There was muted laughter from the Vikings.

King Hardrada spoke quietly to Prince Olaf and the younger polar bear rose to his paws with a genial expression on his face.

"My father wants to thank you, Lord Tostig," said the prince whose English was excellent. "You knew your brother would be far away in the south. Once we have our hostages, Harold won't dare challenge us. Tomorrow we will begin our plan for his demise, and your revenge will be complete."

The Vikings once again cheered their support, but the fox spoke over them.

"Revenge has nothing to do with it," Tostig scowled, half aware of how petty he sounded. "I only wanted justice."

"My mistake – justice it is," Olaf smiled at him. Tostig could tell the polar bear either didn't believe him, or didn't appreciate the difference between the two. The fox downed his drink and clicked for a rat servant to bring him another.

"Yes, we are all grateful for our English friends," said Orre. "Copsi – I hear you were a menace on the battlefield."

The duck was mid sip and coughed up mead all over his feathered breast. "Me?"

"You shall be known as...Steel Wing!"

"Steel Wing!" the Vikings roared.

"And of course, Tostig," Orre grinned impishly. It seemed only Tostig caught the sarcasm. "What can we say of your valour?"

The Vikings shouted their suggestions.

"Flaming Fox!"

"The King's Justice!"

"Brother's Demon!"

"Home...Slayer," Hardrada pronounced.

Tostig felt a lump gather in his throat. "That's...I don't know what to..."

"Thank you, Your Majesty," Copsi spoke for him.

"To Tostig Home Slayer and Copsi Steel Wing!" Olaf cried and the Vikings drank. Nobody noticed that the two English creatures didn't drink in time with this toast, and instead looked at each other with mingled expressions of pride and guilt.

Celebrations continued for hours as the autumn sky went from blue to red to black. Tostig worked his way through mead after mead, putting even the toothless moose next to him to shame. Copsi also had an uncharacteristic second flagon. Due to his size and inexperience he was soon quite as drunk as the fox. Other than those that were slumped and snoring, the two English creatures stayed on their table longer than any of the Vikings did.

"What are you thinking about, sir?" asked Copsi tentatively. Tostig had been watching the moon in silence for a few minutes. A little bit of drool had started seeping from the corner of his mouth.

"Too many things," sighed Tostig, wiping his whiskers clean. "Once we have these hostages we'll be back on the march. Time to visit my brother."

"Unless William has... you know..."

"I don't think so," said Tostig. "Harold's alive. I can feel it."

The fox didn't know where this came from, though believed more than anything that his words were the truth. There was still one more chapter in this story; a conclusion with Harold would have to be written sooner rather than later.

"Is honour a myth?" blurted Tostig suddenly.

"How do you mean, sir?"

"Edwin and Morcar didn't have it," said the fox. "Running off like they did. Harold didn't, or he wouldn't have turned on me. William claims a country he has not stepped paw in for years. Perhaps we all just do what is best for ourselves in the end. I know I do..."

"You are honourable, sir," Copsi said quietly.

"No..." the fox's eyes burned wet. "It was all true, you know?"

"What was?"

"What the Northumbrians say about me. I was harsh on them. I had my rivals assassinated when I thought I was losing control."

"I know, sir," said the duck in an even smaller voice.

"I have rarely spared a thought for what you want, Copsi."

"I want what you want."

"Pah!" Tostig laughed and wiped his tears away. "You are a liar or a fool...or perhaps the most honourable of us all."

"Yes, the honourable Steel Wing they call me," Copsi said severely. Then he laughed. It was an odd sound, a sort of strangled squeal that got lost a couple of times in his throat on its way out.

"That's funny," said Tostig. He frowned, trying to remember if he had ever heard the duck laugh before.

Copsi couldn't seem to stop giggling. Tostig dragged the duck's flagon away from him. "I think that's enough."

Over the next minute Copsi eventually hiccupped himself into silence. "I don't know what came over me," he shook his head and nearly fell off his chair from the ensuing dizziness.

"I was a bad ruler of Northumbria the first time, Copsi," said Tostig standing up. "I will be better this time. Maybe I'll listen to Steel Wing more, too."

"Steel Wing," Copsi repeated with a chuckle that was sore on his throat.

"Good night," said the fox. He didn't get much sleep that night as thoughts of honour, Harold, and his new name 'Home Slayer' fought over each other to be the centre of his troubled dreams.

The air was thick and muggy the next morning. By the time Tostig groggily awoke, the sun was beating down on the Viking encampment.

"Get up," said Tostig, rubbing his eyes.

"Nooo," Copsi groaned. "My head hurts."

The fox made to kick the duck in the side, but the memory of his promise the night before stopped him.

"Pah! You only had two flagons!" Tostig left the duck to roll and whine. His own head was a little fuzzy, but he felt a certain lightness in his step that he hadn't felt in a long time. Unlike many of his grand ideas he had once conjured under the influence of mead, his proclamation that he would endeavour to be a better Earl of Northumbria stuck with him in the morning.

The fox strolled around the Viking ships, greeting those creatures still waking up. Esytein Orre was found in a deep slumber on the deck of his ship, but the two polar bears were already cajoling creatures to prepare for the day ahead.

"Good morning, Your Majesty," Tostig bowed. "My Prince."

"Ah, Tostig, you're awake," Olaf greeted him. "You will be able to lead our forces to Stamford Bridge?"

"Of course," beamed Tostig. "We best be leaving shortly if we are to make it by noon."

After the fox had joined the white bears for breakfast, horns were blown and the army was divided. Two thirds of the forces were to go and collect the hostages. The remaining third, which included Orre, Olaf and Tostig's rats, were to remain by the ships.

Stamford Bridge was seven miles east of York. The Vikings marched under the golden rays of the sun in good spirits. Hardrada was so hot with all his fur that he had left his chainmail armour behind. The Vikings had followed their king's lead. The creatures travelled light; all chainmail was left on the ships, they carried helmets under their arms and brought with them only a sword or an axe. There were a few archers with the company, but they were also reluctant to bring anything too heavy so only came with a handful of arrows.

Tostig and Copsi were two of the first to cross the wooden bridge for which the stretch of land was named. The bridge was low over the River Derwent that ran beneath it. It was long but narrow, and the Vikings had to funnel into three or four across to get over it. Many of the Vikings were still waiting to cross an hour after Tostig had done. The bridge led onto an expansive lush meadow. The Vikings spread out far and wide waiting for their companions to join them. They rested in the sun, the merry atmosphere growing all the time.

"It's past noon," said Tostig, peering at the sun between his paws. "They're late."

"Oh, yeah?" said Copsi lazily. His eyes were drooping and Tostig knew if the duck was left unattended he would surely nod off right there.

Tostig looked around at the lounging Vikings. A sense of unease was beginning to dawn upon him. "Hmm, I don't like it."

Copsi perked up a bit. "You don't think they're planning anything silly, do you?"

"Ealdred? No way. But where are Edwin and Morcar? They were stupid enough to meet us in battle once."

Copsi shrugged and his eyes began to slouch shut again. Clearly the threat of the hares wasn't sufficiently stimulating. "Don't worry, sir. We have Hardrada."

It was at precisely this moment, as Copsi sank onto his webbed feet and sighed comfortably in the grass, that Tostig heard it. A deep, distant rumble.

The fox turned back towards the bridge. The last of the Vikings were still making their way across. All of those on this side of the river had stopped walking and turned around. They too heard the rumble. Appearing on the horizon behind them was a wall of dust.

"What is this?" Hardrada demanded. Tostig hadn't heard him approach over the sounds of the rumblings.

"I-I don't know," wheezed Tostig.

"Not...hostages," growled Hardrada.

"No...no, I don't think so..."

The dust cloud was getting bigger, getting closer. The relaxing Vikings were scrambling to their paws, craning to get a better look. The creatures at the bridge were panicking. Some stood their ground whilst others barged over each other to make it to the other side.

"Hares?" said Hardrada.

"Maybe," said Tostig.

"Not...wolves?" the polar bear's voice was soft and high. Tostig looked at him, suddenly feeling more fear than he had since the Northumbrian mob had forced him out the year before.

Wolves. Cold dread defeated the heat of the sun. *The King's Wolves?*

Tostig took a few steps towards the mounting dust. A shimmering sheet of ice glittered beneath it – the unmistakable sparkle of armour and steel.

"Impossible," Tostig gasped.

"What is it, sir?" Copsi didn't look tired now.

"I think – I think it's..."

"Speak, fox!" Hardrada grabbed Tostig off the floor and lifted him up to his eyeline.

"I think it's-" the name didn't want to come out of the fox's mouth. "H-Harold."

"He's...in...the south..." the polar bear king looked furious. "You said..."

Tostig could barely breathe in the polar bear's strangling grasp. He managed a single squeak and a shake of the head.

There was a moment when Hardrada didn't move. His face hardened as the drumming of approaching paws grew ever louder. He cast the fox aside with ease and Tostig yelped as he hit the ground. Hardrada stepped over him and drew his dragon tooth of a spear from his back.

"CREATURES OF NORWAY!" he roared. "PREPARE FOR BATTLE!"

AUTUMN

A Southerly Breeze

In the last week of September the fox and the bear, two proclaimed rulers of the kingdom, clashed in the unlikely autumn sun. At the same time, the third claimant of the English crown was made to wait.

The lynx sat rigidly in his stirrups, riding his great horse through his army. The great beast cast no shadow as the sky was blotted with black clouds. The duke received no looks of admiration as he had in the summer, only winces and resentment. The wind whipped up the lynx's cloak behind him in almost taunting fashion. The tempest-like weather that had plagued Normandy for weeks had not passed. The ships could not be launched, and no matter how many creatures the lynx had assembled, they were useless if they could not get their ships out of the Dives port.

William rode Leroy to the spot where his wife had brought him to see his ship, the *Mora*, enter the harbour months earlier. All around him ships rocked in the shallow water, restless and shackled by the weather that refused to abate.

Leroy snorted loudly. The sound reflected William's own impatience.

"Easy, boy," William stroked his steed's neck. The one thing the stormy weather had given the lynx, though unwanted, was time. William had used it to bond further with the horse he had won in the forest. Now, he and Leroy were bound together as one. The horse knew William's every thought, every emotion. The lynx merely had to lean in the slightest fashion for Leroy to respond. They were united in shared ambition to conquer. Together they watched the rough waves of the Channel torment them.

"Glory awaits us, my friend," William whispered as he stared out to sea. He had said these words so many times, had believed it so much to be true, yet now could feel his resolve starting to weaken. If he had the divine right to rule England, why was God refusing him passage to his kingdom? Why wouldn't the storm pass? After all this time, was William mistaken? Was he not meant to be king?

The sounds of hooves approached. William did not turn away from the sea as they drew nearer.

"The spy still won't talk," said Odo. The bobcat was riding a brown stallion that was dwarfed by the giant Leroy. "Eustace is with him now. I thought it time to get...*adventurous*...with our questioning."

"Typical English," scowled William. "Stubborn, obstinate, unwavering..."

"He's just a hedgehog," said Odo, sounding concerned at William's defeated tone. "We'll get him to speak."

"I don't know," said William. "Maybe he is...maybe they are..."

"Maybe they are what?"

William turned to face his half-brother. The words rose and burned his throat like vomit. "*Unconquerable!*"

Odo's face stiffened. "Do not do this now."

"Do what?"

"Doubt yourself."

It started to rain. Within seconds William's goatee of fur was drenched and drooping halfway down his body. He played with the ring the pope had given him.

"God has turned His back on me."

"Never," snarled Odo. "You are the rightful ruler of England. If God has not permitted you to set sail just yet, I am sure it is for a good reason."

"What reason?" William's voice was weak. He searched Odo's scarred face for an answer.

"It is not yet clear," said Odo, and William's shoulders sagged. "It is not our place to know. It is our place to *believe*. God is telling us we are not meant to be in England yet. He is holding us back until the right moment, until everything is in our favour."

"I want to believe you..."

"You are not listening," Odo scowled. "It is nothing to do with me. Put your faith in the Lord, and everything will be right. Let us be quiet for a moment and pray."

William didn't resist. He closed his eyes and focused first on his breathing as harsh winds fought to throw him off his horse. He had asked God many times to change the winds and allow his fleet to sail, but this time he did not. He thought about what Odo had said, and instead asked for the courage to trust. He asked that he might have the strength to follow the shrouded path that God had laid out for him.

Once he was finished, he opened his eyes and a steely calm had returned to him.

"You say the hedgehog is resisting?" the lynx growled. In his anger he did not notice the change in the breeze or the redirected flow of his cloak.

"That's right," said Odo, appreciative of William's renewed severity.

"Then take me to him," William drew his sword and Leroy snorted his approval. The horse turned in step with the lynx's thoughts.

"Of course," said Odo.

The horses had only taken a couple of steps each when they heard it.

"...brrrrrrrrrrrr"

The sound was quiet and far away. The lynx and bobcat looked at each other.

"...brrrrrrrrrrr"

This sound was closer and from a different source. It combined with the first sound.

"...brrrrrrrrrrr"

"...brrrrrrrrrrr"

"...brrrrrrrrrrr"

All across the bay horns were blown in unison until their call was heard in every corner. William and Odo looked around in momentary disbelief. Soldiers who had once been solemnly tending to their duties sprang into action. Sailors screamed at their workers to get into position. Hundreds of horses struggled to get free of their owners as they were forced onto their ships.

William's head was buzzing and not only with the sound of Norman war horns. His thoughts were slow and foggy, unable to keep up with what his eyes were telling him.

"William," Odo's voice sounded far away. "Come on."

William blinked. "To the hedgehog?"

Odo gave a rare laugh. "To hell with that spiked nuisance! The horns have been blown."

Count Eustace, the chamois, was riding up to join them on his own horse. The *jongleur* Taillefer had climbed to the top of his ship's mast and was howling like a wolf to the sky. William watched the albino polecat and saw the sky open up behind him. Caught in a forceful wind, the clouds were clearing over the port. The horns had not been blown to cheer a calming of the storm, quite the opposite; the storm was just as vitriolic as it had been a moment earlier, only this time it was blowing northwards across the Channel.

"What are your instructions?" cried Eustace when he reached the two brothers.

"Awooooooooo!" howled Taillefer.

William turned away from all of them. He looked back across the waves. The sea looked as tempestuous and treacherous as ever, but instead of seeming oppressive and impossible, it now looked tantalising. The winds that had prevented the Norman fleet from mobilising had finally changed – but for how long? A week? A day? An hour?

The lynx of Normandy was not about to wait to find out. If he was to seize England this year, now was the only time. The most ambitious invasion of any Norman army was about to begin.

He crossed his paw over his chest and swore one last prayer to his conqueror ancestor Rollo, one to his father who had died too young, and one thankful last to God.

"Board your ships. It is time."

AUTUMN

The Offer

The English army advanced. The Vikings were spread thin over opposing sides of the bridge. Tostig and Hardrada were on the east bank and, for now, safe from Harold's lethal charge. The Norwegians that had not yet crossed the bridge when the English snuck up behind them were forced to fight a helpless battle on the west bank, cut off from their friends.

The royal foxes sliced through their stranded foes. It did not take long before the Norwegians were forced back. Close-up claustrophobic fighting ensued on the bridge.

"Iron Jaw!" Hardrada called. "We need more time."

The bear-like wolverine snapped to attention. "What are your orders, Your Majesty?"

"Hold the bridge," said Hardrada grimly. The two creatures' eyes met with grave understanding. The defence of the bridge could not last indefinitely.

"It will be done," nodded Kit Iron Jaw. He gathered another thirty creatures and raced to bolster those Vikings that were being forced further and further back along the bridge.

Tostig and Copsi stood together in the middle of the field as Hardrada ordered his once lounging soldiers into position. They watched as Kit Iron Jaw and his creatures crashed into the English on the bridge. The duck was shaking his head and panicking, but the Stray Fox's heart was steady and his mind clear.

"Can you see Harold?"

"No," Copsi sniffed. "God, I should never have had that second flagon last night."

"What about Gyrth? Or Leofwine? I should quite like to see them again."

"You would?"

Tostig smiled at him and rested a paw on his head. "It seems the last chapter is here at last. It will be decided today. Which of the foxes does history have its eyes on?"

The fox drew his sword. *Let it be me.*

Like the vast majority of the Vikings, Tostig was underdressed for war. Following the lead of their king, few had bothered to bring heavy and hot armour for the supposed simple collection of hostages from the beaten York. Some of Hardrada's best forces were not even there, notably the polar bear's trusted Eystein Orre. The one thing that gave Tostig and the Vikings strength was the presence of the *Landøyðan* raven. The black bird had taken to the skies and was fortifying the soldiers with a chorus of its most horrific shrieks. Tostig had never been so grateful for its presence.

"Your Majesty," Tostig piped up nervously as the polar bear was overseeing the majority of his forces on the east bank form into their fighting divisions. Those who had brought shields were brought to the front to construct a shield wall. "What can I do?"

"Stay out ... of my way..." The king would not look at him.

"I had no idea Harold could get here so fast-"

"Clearly," Hardrada grabbed a moose who was running in the opposite direction by the antler. "Send a puffin. We need Orre...we need armour..."

The moose nodded and ran away to find a suitable messenger.

"Will there be enough time for Orre to get here?" Tostig doubted.

The polar bear king glared at Tostig. Power and fury radiated from him with such force that the fox actually took a few steps back.

"We will make time."

Harold raked his sword across the exposed chest of an arctic fox. Without armour, the blade sliced his opponent down with ease. Blood sprayed from its flapping wound. The Viking fell and Harold stepped over him.

The king cut down two more creatures and surveyed the action. So far everything was going to plan. It was evident the Vikings had no idea their approach was even a possibility, let alone an imminent threat. Their enemy was ill-equipped, stunned, and had already suffered heavy losses on the west side of the bridge. Harold stopped to catch his breath and allowed Dunstan and Wulfric to lead the charge across the wooden bridge. There were maybe forty or so creatures left alive there, although he could see Hardrada's main force gathering beyond it.

"Harold!" Leofwine had to hop over the bodies of dead Vikings to reach his brother. He looked clean and fresh-faced as ever, though his sword dripped a trail of scarlet ink behind him. "It's been a while since I've seen you swing a sword! Not bad!"

"It's been an auspicious start," replied Harold, twisting his frayed whiskers back under control. The sun was at its highest point in the sky and he had just led his army on the fastest crosscountry march he had ever heard of. He knew he needed to win victory in this battle early or his creatures would soon begin to tire. Adrenaline would only get them so far. One fatigued swing was enough to get you killed.

The two brothers watched as the Vikings on the bridge were cut down to single figures. Leofwine joked with surrounding creatures, all of whom were eager to clear the last stubborn few and take on the famous Hardrada himself. Harold stayed professional and quiet as Gyrth appeared on his other side.

"Did you see him?" asked Gyrth. Harold knew he was talking about the one brother on the wrong side of the river.

"No," said Harold. "He may not be here."

"Something tells me he is."

Harold didn't say anything. He agreed, unfortunately. The fox king had had a great deal of time to think on Tostig during the four-day march. After speaking to Ealdred at York, it seemed impossible that

Harold could trust the north to Edwin and Morcar ever again. He had a plan to make things right, but was it already too late?

There was a shriek from a Viking wolf and the last of their defenders on the bridge dropped to one. A bear-sized wolverine now stood alone. Kit Iron Jaw bared his teeth as two badgers converged on his position. They lunged at him together. The wolverine buried his battle axe into the first badger's skull, killing him instantly. The second badger mistimed his thrust and only grazed Kit's side. With his axe embedded in the first creature's corpse, Iron Jaw attacked the second with his claws. He tore open its throat and showered in its warm blood.

With the bridge being so narrow it was impossible for the English to use their advantage and surround the wolverine. Creatures attacked in twos and threes and every group fell victim to the berserker warrior. The Vikings watching on from the east bank cheered as Kit single-pawedly held up the English charge.

"IRON JAW! IRON JAW! IRON JAW!"

Ten creatures suffered either by axe, claw or fang. Then another ten, and another. At first the wolverine rolled the bodies into the River Derwent but soon the pile of carcasses was too large to clear. Foxes, badgers, beavers, otters and wolves all clambered over their fallen brothers to attack. Kit resisted them all and the mountain of dead grew taller.

"Wulfric!" Harold called for his most trusted warrior. "We have ourselves a hero. Every second he delays us gives them longer for reinforcements to arrive. I need that creature killed."

The king and his lieutenants were far from the wolverine in question. The thousands of English were useless if they could not funnel across the bridge.

"It will not be long, Your Majesty." Wulfric stared at the wolverine in the distance. His one eye shimmered with hate and admiration. "I have sent Ceej. He's my top wolf."

"He will have to be good." Harold winced as he saw a beaver struck down by Kit's axe.

Wulfric pointed a hooked claw down the River Derwent at a small makeshift raft floating towards the bridge. An excitable wolf with long, athletic limbs was paddling along with the current.

"Ceej," Wulfric grinned.

The raft drifted underneath the bridge just as Kit tossed the slain beaver into the water with a splash. The wolverine never noticed the wolf floating beneath him. Ceej unsheathed a tall spear and shoved it upwards with all his might. It pierced the wooden floor of the bridge and continued up, straight through Iron Jaw's planted paw. The wolverine shrieked in pain and shock.

Ceej was soon swept away by the current, but the spear remained lodged through the wood of the bridge and the wolverine's flesh. Kit was pinned and any attempt he made to extract himself brought with it searing pain. The English creatures seized Kit's moment of weakness and a trio of otters soon overwhelmed him.

The wolverine was down, but he had bought the Vikings time. Only after English creatures had cleared the dead off the bridge could they cross. Harold's housecarls, led by the king, Wulfric and Dunstan, went first. Then came Gyrth and his creatures, Leofwine with his, then the stragglers they had gathered over the long march.

Hardrada's creatures were waiting for them on the east bank, gathered in a tight horseshoe-shaped shield wall. Far into the sky a black raven circled them, its screech terrible and incessant. The English assembled opposite them and the two armies sized each other up. Harold had the advantage when it came to numbers, and the Vikings lacked armour and enough shields to make their defence effective. Even despite these strong odds the fox was wary. The sun continued to beat down mercilessly upon them and the English were already exhausted. The fox's mouth was dry and sore and his legs ached. He did not let his discomfort show, as was his duty.

I am the king, Harold assured himself. There was a hulking figure in the opposing army that gave cause to doubt it.

"Wulfric, Dunstan," Harold strode to his generals. "You can see him?"

"Aye," Wulfric growled and Dunstan nodded. It was impossible to miss the Norwegian king at the dead centre of the Viking army, his white fur glowing in the sunshine.

"You remember our deal?"

"We will see it dead, Your Majesty," Wulfric said.

"He is big," Dunstan puffed. The brown bear had seldom seen a creature bigger than him. "Shall we begin the advance?"

Harold hesitated, looking across at the intruders in his land, at the mad creatures from a far away land. The Vikings could not be hated for their invasion; it was in their nature to steal, plunder, seize and kill. It was to be expected. But the creature that led them here could be despised. The black and orange fox standing next to the polar bear invader had betrayed them all.

Or did I betray him? Is this God's punishment for turning on a brother?

"Fetch me a helmet," Harold said suddenly.

One of Wulfric's wolves hurriedly handed over his own.

"Creatures of Wessex!" Dunstan called to his creatures. "Prepare for battle!"

"Not yet," said Harold. He shoved the slightly oversized helmet over his pointed ears.

"Your Majesty?"

Harold did not answer. Instead he walked away from all of them, directly towards the jeering army of Vikings on the other side of the field.

A single soldier was approaching their shield wall. A heavy helmet hid the creature's identity, but Tostig recognised the red cloak that flowed behind it with a start.

"My lord," whispered Copsi. "Isn't that-"

"Shh," Tostig snapped.

Harold stopped ten feet from the Vikings' frontline. He stood opposite Hardrada but Tostig had the distinct impression that Harold's eyes were watching him from behind the slits in his helmet.

"I bring word from Harold, King of England," said the fox. Tostig recognised the voice as unmistakably his brother's. It was a bold and risky move to come so close to the Viking army. Tostig would never have expected it of his brother; he had always believed Harold to have more of Gyrth's caution than Leofwine's audaciousness.

"Speak..." Hardrada ordered, completely unaware he was talking to King Harold himself.

"Is Earl Tostig with you?" said Harold.

Earl? Does he meant to insult me?

"I am here...*messenger*," Tostig said the last word with a hint of sarcasm. He strode out from the shield wall, ignoring Copsi's desperate pleas. Harold did not move as Tostig stood before him. The two brothers stood looking at each other for a moment. A year had made the subtlest changes to the foxes. The tall Tostig was thinner, his tail more ragged and bushy. Harold's shoulders were more sloped, as if weighed down by the responsibility of playing father to a nation. His enormous, smiling whiskers peeked out from his helmet and Tostig saw that they were starting to go grey.

"Your brother sends you greetings," said Harold. "He offers you peace and all of Northumbria."

Tostig stammered, caught off guard. He turned and shared a look of disbelief with Copsi, and saw that Hardrada's face was hard and focused as he tried to understand the English.

"He does not wish to see you refuse and insist on battle. He would give you a third of his kingdom to prevent further bloodshed."

"That is different from the shame of last winter. If I had this offer then, many a creature who is dead would be alive..." Tostig closed his eyes and again was shocked by his own emotions. He did not rejoice in his brother's change of heart; he only felt pain, tiredness and remorse. "And England would be a better place."

Edwin and Morcar, it seemed, had disgraced themselves beyond reconciliation with their battle at Fulford. The hares had been exposed, uprooted, and now Tostig had the offer he had always wanted.

"If I accept," said Tostig. "What will my brother offer King Harald Hardrada for his work?"

"He said something about that too," said Harold. "Something about six feet of English earth...or perhaps ten as he is taller than most creatures."

Tostig nodded; he had thought this would be the case. He turned once more and faced the Viking army that he had bewitched with his words into invading England with him. He saw Hardrada, immense and furious as ever. Tostig did not feel much allegiance to the king of Norway, and expected the polar bear to feel little in return to him. They had used each other since the beginning: Hardrada seeking glory, Tostig "justice". The world would not miss the polar bear should he die at that very moment. He was a cruel thing, using his power to dominate others. If Tostig turned his back on Hardrada now, would all be truly forgiven? Could the fox step paw from Stamford Bridge and re-join his brother's society?

Tostig's eyes shifted down from the polar bear until he found the miniscule duck standing timidly amidst so many violent creatures. Copsi was watching him back with a half-smile that Tostig couldn't quite decipher. He thought it meant "I'm with you, whatever you decide" and so smiled back. He remembered their conversation about honour the previous night.

"Perhaps we all just do what is best for ourselves in the end."

Tostig turned back to face his brother, his mind decided.

"Then go and tell King Harold to be ready for battle," he declared. "I can never have it said among the Norse that Tostig deserted their king in the face of a fight. We shall stick together: die with honour, or win England by victory."

The Vikings roared behind him. Hurled stones bounced off Harold's helmet with a clang.

"So be it," Harold whispered, turning away.

"One last thing," Tostig called to him and Harold paused. "Copsi, come here."

The duck waddled nervously out in front of the shield wall to stand next to his master.

"You've been a good and faithful lieutenant, Copsi."

"My lord?"

Tostig picked him up around the middle and Copsi squirmed. "Be good, my friend."

The fox flung the duck at Harold. He landed with a whimper at the king's side.

"This battle is no place for a duck. Take him to safety, would you?" said Tostig. "Please?"

"I will," Harold nodded graciously.

"What? NO!" Copsi screamed, scrambling onto his webbed feet. Harold swept him up under one paw before he could fly back. The duck was helpless against the fox's grasp. He headbutted every bit of Harold he could reach, desperate to return to Tostig.

"Stop! STOP!"

"Goodbye," Tostig whispered. He did not know if he was speaking to Harold or Copsi or both. He slipped back into the shield wall and many of the Vikings clapped him on the back enthusiastically. He took his place beside the polar bear king and watched as Harold walked away with Copsi under his arm, getting smaller and smaller until he disappeared into the ranks of the English army.

The polar bear spoke over his Vikings in his own tongue.

"Forth we go in our lines
Without armour, against the blue blades.
The helmets glitter: I have no armour.
Our shrouds are down in those ships."

Hardada scowled as soon as he was finished.

"A poor verse. I shall compose another."

"We never kneel in battle

Before the storm of weapons
And crouch behind our shields;
So the noble bear told me.
She told me once to carry
My head always high in battle
Where swords seek to shatter
The skulls of doomed warriors."

AUTUMN

Battle of Stamford Bridge

Prince Olaf leaned against an old oak tree, cowering in its shade. Nobody had told him how hot England could be. He missed the lakes and fjords of Norway, the mountains and the snow. He missed his brother and sisters. He stared at the spot where his father and the Stray Fox had left a couple of hours earlier, willing them to come back quickly. If York delivered enough hostages they would have Harold the fox king in chains. He hoped a settlement could be drawn up speedily. No more creatures would have to die, and he could begin to broach the idea of returning home to his father.

"You alright there?" Eystein Orre broke away from a pack of drinking wolves and moose and approached. The wolverine was to marry Olaf's sister and their relationship had already become that of brothers.

"Fine," Olaf lied, taking the flagon that Orre offered him.

Orre laughed brutishly. He lay down on his back by Olaf's paws.

"What?" Olaf bristled.

"All this talk of names last night...Steel Wing...Home Slayer..."

"Yeah?"

"The creatures have one for you too."

Olaf frowned. "Is it bad?"

"You tell me," Orre grinned. "Olaf the Quiet."

The prince thought about this for a while, then smiled. "I don't mind it. It suggests contemplation, intelligence, control."

"Aye, it does," the wolverine laughed. It was during this laughter that a bright orange-beaked puffin landed before them.

"My God!" Orre shouted, startled, holding a paw to his heart. Olaf didn't react, already taking to his new nickname.

"English!" the puffin shouted. "Thousands!"

Orre seized the little bird and squeezed it so tight Olaf thought it might pop.

"Tell me," he growled.

"The king appeared out of nowhere...at Stamford Bridge...thousands of soldiers..."

"There is only one king." Orre tossed the puffin aside.

"They have no armour," the prince said. "What are we going to do?"

"I'm going," Orre said. "I'll take the armour, and more weapons."

"There's no time!" Olaf cried.

Orre ignored him. He ran back to the creatures he had been drinking with a moment earlier and started knocking the drinks out of their paws. Chaos ensued as the word got around that the king was in trouble. Within minutes a thousand warriors were ready to move, laden down with extra weapons and sheets of armour.

"Hey!" Orre called over to the captains of Tostig's rats. The legion of stinking creatures had not stirred from their drinking spot.

"Yes?" a rat sneered drunkenly.

"Are you ready to fight?"

"I am ready..." said the rat. "To stay and defend the ships."

Orre sneered. "Vermin."

The rat bared his black teeth. "Quite right."

Orre shook his head and turned away from the lounging rats.

"Forget them," said Prince Olaf, who had approached swinging a spear tentatively. "I'm ready."

"You stay here," Orre said, ripping the spear from the prince's paws.

"What?" Olaf balked at the suggestion. "My father is out -"

"If he's dead," hissed Orre, "then you're to be king."

"I-"

"Stay alive, Olaf the Quiet." The wolverine turned and joined the frenzied line of sprinting Vikings racing to save their king.

Harold raised his sword to block. The two blades connected and the sound disappeared in the deep vacuum of roaring armies. Harold's sword twisted loose on impact and nearly fell from his tired paw. The Viking had a second to capitalise and missed his chance. Ceej the wolf was fighting alongside the king and struck the enemy, another wolf, with his axe. As the Norwegian creature crumpled, Harold backed away from the action to catch his breath.

The battle had been raging for hours. The Vikings were outnumbered but fought together as one body, batting away the virus that was the English. Whilst the Vikings' berserkers attacked with the reckless freedom of the underdog, the English struggled to make their numbers count. They battered the Norwegian shield wall but Hardrada's creatures held firm and the losses were equal on both sides.

Harold walked across his forces, behind those who were engaged in brutal close-up combat. He didn't stop to help even those who were about to be overwhelmed. There were two creatures he needed to find more than any other. He saw Gyrth and Leofwine valiantly leading their own housecarls but strode past them too. It was the bear and wolf he needed to turn the tide of this battle.

He found Dunstan first. The bear had made the most progress in breaking through the Viking shield wall. He swung a great sword with two paws in large raking motions and any enemy creature in the vicinity was beheaded. Spears were thrown from the depths of the Viking army but they skidded off his chainmail armour.

"Dunstan!" Harold called. The bear reluctantly backed away from the front lines and this gave time for the shield wall to reassemble.

"Your Majesty? I was making good headway."

"You only have one purpose here, Dunstan," Harold shouted over the war cries of the living and the wails of the dying.

It did not take long to find Hardrada fighting at the shield wall's centre. Hundreds of English creatures were dead and piled up in front of him. Harold's forces cheered as Dunstan approached. The bear was their champion, their only hope.

"Good luck," Harold told him. Dunstan didn't make any sign he had heard the king. He opened his mouth wide enough to swallow Harold's head whole and roared. The polar bear king heard the sound and did the same. English and Vikings alike dashed out of the way of the two bears as they charged.

Dunstan still clasped his great sword in two paws as he ran on his hind legs. When Hardrada did the same he was at least a foot larger than Dunstan. The polar bear launched his spear as he ran but Dunstan brought his sword down and blocked it. The spear spun off and impaled an English beaver into the ground. Hardrada ducked down onto four paws and was suddenly a white blur. Dunstan lunged with his sword, but Hardrada slipped around it, moving faster than Harold could have imagined possible. The polar bear struck Dunstan on his black snout and sent him to the floor. He leaped atop the English bear and bit his arm with enough force to snap bone. Dunstan screamed in pain as the teeth crunched through his chainmail armour. The great sword that he was holding loosened from his paw and Hardrada made to grab it. Dunstan roared in defiance and kicked out. The two bears, one white, the other shining in silver, rolled over each other, flattening the corpses that littered the ground.

"Harold!" a voice called. The fox turned to see the one-eyed Wulfric running towards him. He had six of his best wolves with him.

"Hurry!" Harold shouted. The wolves barrelled through their own creatures as they raced to help the bear. They were only moments away when Harold heard the scream. He turned back towards the bears. Hardrada was seated atop Dunstan, his meaty paws pinning his opponent to the ground. Hardrada had his teeth in Dunstan's neck. The English bear howled in pain but then blood erupted out of his mouth like a hot mountain geyser and the screaming stopped.

King Harald Hardrada chewed at the English creature's neck. He could feel the heart pumping blood meaninglessly, not giving up despite the gaping hole in the bear's throat. Eventually the pumping slowed and the bear stopped struggling. Hardrada swallowed the excess flesh caught in his teeth and pulled away from the dead creature. He beat his chest and heard his Vikings roar behind him. He stood up, drenched in red with his paw on the still chest of his enemy, feeling invincible.

The lines of English soldiers backed away and Hardrada thought for a moment they were going to retreat entirely. It did not matter. Fight now, tomorrow, or in a year, the result would be the same. He was inescapable.

"Is there no one else?" he laughed.

An English wolf stepped forward, one-eyed and an expression devoid of fear.

Hardrada had already tossed his spear but still had a heavy blade strapped to his side. He pulled it loose and pointed it at the wolf.

"Ready?" he grinned.

Six more wolves stepped forward. They created a semi-circle around the Viking king with the one-eyed one at the centre.

Hardrada blinked. He remembered when his brother had visited his dreams.

That death at last awaits you,
And wolves will rend your body.

"No," Hardrada said. "NEVER!"

The polar bear lunged towards the wolves to his right. His blade slashed through the air but one wolf ducked and pounced. Hardada's balled paw met the wolf mid-flight and its ribs were shattered. The other six wolves flooded forward together. Hardrada slashed through the air again, cutting two. The remaining four sank their teeth just above each of his paws. Hardrada grunted and his legs flailed in an effort to throw them off. Three soon lost their grip but the last managed to cling on. Hardrada stabbed it so hard the blade came out the other end of his chest. He threw the dead wolf back into the onlooking English.

The wolves regrouped and came at him again, this time with their battle axes raised. Hardrada blocked three but two met their mark, one hitting the back of his calf, the other grazing his side. The polar bear banished the pain from his mind and moved forward. The one with the broken ribs stumbled to his paws and was swiftly cut down. He swung at the others but they did not try to fight back. They danced out of the way of his sword and reformed behind him.

There were five left, and two had nasty injuries. It was these two that came at him first. They lunged forward in open sacrifice and in the time it took for Hardrada to kill them, the other three were upon him. Two snapped at his wounded paws and the third came straight at him with his axe. The one-eyed creature hopped left and right too quickly for Hardrada to trace, then swung his axe upwards. The polar bear leant back just in time to save his head. The axe sliced Hardrada down the middle and the king roared in agony. The one-eyed wolf slid beneath the bear's legs to safety. The other two weren't so lucky. He grabbed both around the neck and pulled them away, their teeth digging craters in his fur. He crushed both their windpipes and dropped them to the floor.

"Finish him!" King Harold shouted somewhere from the battlefield.

Hardrada felt the wound on his chest. Blood was pouring but it wasn't too deep. He turned to face the one-eyed wolf. The creature was breathing heavily and also seemed to have a cut on his side. They stared each other down and as one ran towards each other. Hardrada swung the sword and Wulfric the axe. Both blades hit their mark. The polar bear's blade pierced his enemy's stomach, and the wolf struck the king directly in the neck.

Neither creature called out in pain. They only looked at each other, both knowing what had happened.

For a moment there was silence in both armies as they gawked at the two creatures locked together. There was a shriek from above as the

Landøyðan raven soared towards them. It landed on Wulfric's head and plucked his one remaining eye from its socket. This time the wolf did scream, but it was already too late. He stumbled away from Hardrada, the raven still clinging on to him. The wolf brought his axe with him as he fell to the ground. The wound in Hardrada's neck opened up and blood poured. The polar bear did not react at first and the English creatures stared in disbelief. He raised his bloody sword, mumbled a poem in Norwegian, and fell forward onto his front, quite dead.

Tostig watched as the polar bear fell. King Harald Hardrada, last of the great warrior kings that roamed the Earth, a creature that had fought more battles than some creatures have drawn breath, was defeated. There was chaos in the aftermath of his death. Some of the Vikings lunged forward, eager to avenge their fallen hero. Those who so foolishly broke ranks were swiped down by the emboldened English. Others panicked at seeing a creature they considered a God collapse; if a beast so formidable as Hardrada could suffer such an ordinary thing as death, then what hope did the rest of them have?

The Stray Fox did not flare up with sudden bloodlust as his chosen king fell. He only felt cold, and for a moment he merely watched as the battle continued around him. He was some twenty metres away from where Hardrada had died and struggled to get a clear view of the scene. Wulfric, who Tostig had once fought alongside, was also dead. The *Landøyðan* sat atop of him and was shrieking louder than ever. Tostig watched as a fox in a red cloak approached and ran its sword through the raven's chest. The *Landøyðan*'s awful cry was finally silenced.

Harold.

The glint of glory sparkled. Tostig stumbled through the battlefield like a creature dying of thirst, ensnared by a mirage of water. If he could cut his brother down the battle might yet be salvaged.

Tostig lunged forward but an English badger came out of nowhere and tackled him to the floor. Tostig skewered him with his sword and it went limp. The fox pushed upwards but his arms were weak. Eventually he slipped from underneath the heavy corpse and got to his paws. As soon as he stood he discovered why he was overcome with sudden lethargy.

A chunk of orange and black fur was missing from just above his hip. The badger had stabbed him and he was bleeding profusely.

"Oh," said the fox. He fell on one knee. "Pah! Just a scratch."

An English rabbit lunged at him and he stabbed it mid-air. The rabbit was impaled on the blade and Tostig was forced to drop the sword as an otter ran at him. He scrambled backwards as the otter beat the ground where the fox had just been with his club. Tostig searched the trampled grass for another weapon as the otter hunted him down. His paws scrambled over a Viking's fallen shield. He brought it up to cover his head just in time to block the otter's club. The shield split in two upon impact. The otter reared for a third attack and the fox leapt upwards. He struck the otter with the broken shield. The jagged wood tore open its tough skin.

Tostig did not wait to see if the otter would live. He ran backwards to the protection of the struggling Viking shield wall. Before Hardrada's death their line had been resisting the English advance but since then ill-discipline and fear had poisoned their resolve. The English were beginning to surround them. The Viking bodies were piling up and Harold's forces, smelling victory, attacked with renewed energy and belief.

The glory of striking Harold down was gone from Tostig's mind. Survival was all that mattered. Without Hardrada the Vikings were leaderless and broken. They needed a leader.

"Stick together!" Tostig shouted. "SHIELD WALL!"

If the Vikings could hear him they made no effort to listen.

"Hold them! Hold them!" the fox continued. "Orre is coming! Orre is coming! Just a little longer!"

Thousands were already dead but the battle would not finish. The Viking shield wall had become a circle. The English pressed forward on all sides. Tostig stood in the centre with panting and bloodstained creatures, watching as the front lines fought and fell. They hadn't brought enough shields for an effective defence. Creatures tried to collect the shields of fallen warriors but the English didn't give them a second. Some Vikings in the centre charged valiantly, screaming for death and glory and only receiving the first.

The fighting had been going on for hours. The Vikings were down to their last couple of hundred. A Norwegian wolf in front of Tostig fell under three stinging stabs. The Stray Fox managed to grab the wolf's fallen shield and sword and stepped into the front line of the defences.

"Hold them!" he yelled to the two creatures beside him. Their tired limbs held the shield across one another. Tostig's eyes met with the moose on his right.

"We'll get through this," Tostig snarled.

The moose nodded then screamed. An English blade had come over the shield and pierced his shoulder. Tostig lifted his shield and delivered a spray of quick jabs himself, giving just enough time for the moose's place in the shield wall to be replaced by a roaring wolverine.

"Look!"

"Over there!"

"IT'S ORRE!"

The Vikings were cheering and pointing to the wooden bridge they had crossed that morning. Many of the English heard their shouts and also looked that way. Tostig peered above his shield and squinted into the distance. Hundreds of Vikings were on the east bank and racing across the bridge to help. The wolverine Eystein Orre led them, fully gilded in armour and roaring. The reinforcements had brought with them more weapons and more armour for all of them. They had been weighed down and arrived too late to help Hardrada but Tostig hardly cared - he was saved!

"Orre!" Tostig shouted alongside his Viking brethren. It did not matter that he disliked the wolverine. The creature was a fighter almost to match Hardrada himself. "Orre!"

The English forces that had been surrounding the Viking army were turning to face the reinforcements. Tostig let his shield slip, the glimmer of hope betraying him. There were creatures everywhere, so many that it was becoming hard to know who fought for whom. Somewhere in the mass of bodies there was a flash of a red cloak and Tostig took a tired step forward.

"Harold?" he whispered, his eyes tracking the flowing red fabric. The cloak disappeared into the chaos of creatures, and Tostig's distracted eyes missed the blade that was coming towards him.

The fox felt a cold chill in his chest. He blinked and coughed. Blood dribbled from his mouth.

Tostig looked down. He watched as the thin sword was drawn out of his flesh. He did not see who had struck him. Everything went limp and he swayed forwards. He tried to steady himself and instead went the other way. He fell backwards, landing with a thump on the grass.

His fall made his head sore and his vision shimmer. His concussion masked the pain as life poured from the hole in his chest. He stared up at the blue sky. Hundreds of birds circled the battlefield, taking in information so they could sell their story to the highest bidder. Their flapping wings reminded him of Copsi and he giggled.

"Steel Wing..."

Tostig coughed again and more blood spurted. He started choking and his paws reached out for someone to help him. No creature did. Vikings fell to the ground all around him and the English continued to press in.

It was impossible to say how long he was lying there. Maybe hours, maybe minutes, maybe only seconds. Three shadows appeared above him. They were dark and shapeless before the bright sun behind them.

"Brothers?" Tostig gargled. "Harold...Gyrth...Leo..."

The three English creatures looked down at him. One was a wolf, two were badgers.

"Put him out of his misery," the wolf said.

One of the badgers nodded and brought his axe down onto Tostig's chest.

The Stray Fox felt no pain. His head rolled to one side and rested on the wet, blood-drenched Northumbrian earth.

AUTUMN

Harold Victorious

When the pigeons left the battlefield to tell their story, they spoke first of King Harald Hardrada's glorious death. Then came that of the Stray Fox, Tostig Godwinson. Thirdly they spoke of "Orre's Storm", when the Vikings rallied behind the glittering wolverine in the face of total annihilation.

Orre's reinforcements arrived too late to save the army that had fought for so long. After the Viking shield wall completely collapsed, Harold and his brothers turned to face the "Storm". Orre's creatures brawled valiantly and extended the battle into dusk. Whilst the English had suffered many casualties of their own, they had come too far and lost too much to surrender to Orre. The fighting was bloodiest at the end, and it was the English who came out victorious.

The cross-country hurried and laden march by Orre and his creatures had stolen their strength and, after seeing the desolation on the battlefield, with the loss of their king and their army, they were first to wilt. After Eystein Orre was slaughtered, the Vikings ran. The royal foxes chased the survivors back towards their ships at Riccall.

The sun set as Prince Olaf, Hardrada's meek-looking son, met Harold with his paws opened up in surrender.

"Those of you alive may keep your lives," King Harold told him. "If you promise to leave this country and never return."

Olaf the Quiet accepted these terms. The army Hardrada had assembled had been destroyed. The Norwegians rowed home, only filling twenty-four of the three hundred ships they had arrived with two weeks earlier. For the next hundred years creatures would avoid the place they called Stamford Bridge for fear of stirring the ghosts of the Viking dead.

PART THREE
CONQUEST

AUTUMN

Unwelcome Wings

Harold held a candle to light his way as he strode down a dark corridor. Waiting in the shadows were two wolves standing guard over a wooden door. The fox nodded to them and they let him through.

The room was small and mostly empty. When Tostig had been Earl of Northumbria his office in York was so clustered with trophies and expensive ornaments that it was hard to move around. Morcar had obviously thrown them all away. All that was left of the hare's time as earl was a small desk. Ink and parchments were left there in disarray as if Morcar had left in a hurry.

Harold scanned the floor with his candlelight, eventually falling on the minute body tied to a leg of the desk in rope.

"Have you calmed down?" the fox knelt down.

The duck would not look at him.

"You want me to take those off, Copsi?" Harold pointed to the ropes.

Copsi looked away, his eyes watering. Eventually he gave a guilty nod and hung his head. Harold used a claw to saw the duck loose. The ropes fell like a tired snake around Copsi's webbed feet.

"I hope they weren't too rough with you," said Harold, noticing Copsi's ruffled feathers. "I told them not to be rough with you."

The duck would still not look at him. After Tostig had asked that Harold take Copsi to safety, the king had ordered a wolf to escort the duck to York. Copsi had tried to escape three times.

"As I'm sure you're aware, the Viking army has been destroyed. The Norwegians have gone home. Those still alive, anyway..."

Copsi's eyes closed tighter.

"You brought them to our shores," Harold sighed. "What am I going to do with you, Copsi?"

"Just kill me."

Harold backed away and twisted his whiskers. The duck began to whimper softly.

"I don't want to do that," Harold said softly.

"Finish the job," Copsi croaked.

"Any time I saw my brother over the last ten years, you were with him, Copsi," said Harold. "I know he didn't always treat you nicely, but-"

"Tostig is a great friend," the duck's yellow bill began to quiver. "*Was*," he corrected himself.

Harold didn't know what to say. The two creatures sat in silence for a while as the king pondered his next steps.

"When Tostig was exiled..." Harold frowned. "When *I*...sent him away...I left him with nothing and no one. *You* stayed. For that I have to thank you, Copsi."

The duck looked up suspiciously as if waiting for a trick.

"Did he talk about me?" asked Harold.

"Sometimes."

"He wanted to kill me, didn't he?"

"Yes," said Copsi, then smiled as if laughing at some private joke. "And no."

Harold smiled too. "He was always difficult. A bit of orange, a bit of black. Who can say if anyone ever knew his true colours?"

The duck sat up. He had stopped crying.

"Some will say you are a traitor," he said. "But these people are not king. You can remain in York, Copsi, though I will have to ask you not to leave. Not until I'm sure I can trust you again."

"I-"

"Unless exile is more appealing?"

"No."

"Then you will stay?"

The duck nodded slowly.

"Excellent," Harold headed for the door. "We are feasting. You are welcome to join us-"

"I would like to see him first, Your Majesty," the duck stood up for the first time in days and nearly toppled.

"We have already sent creatures to collect the English who fell," Harold grimaced.

"Tostig was English."

"I know, that's why I asked for his body to be found too."

"And?"

"He wasn't," Harold said quietly. "There are many bodies that are now... unrecognisable."

Copsi took a deep breath, steeling himself for something unpleasant.

"With your permission," said the duck. "I will look through the bodies. I will find him. He deserves a proper burial."

Harold nodded. "You can try but-"

"Thank you," Copsi waddled past the fox and out of the door.

"Stay with him," Harold said to the two wolves who had been standing guard outside. The king smiled sadly as the loyal duck disappeared down the dark corridor. "Good luck," he whispered.

The city of York was in an exultant mood. Only one week earlier had the hare lords hopped out to tackle the threat of the polar bear invader. The Norwegian annihilation of the Northumbrian and Mercian armies at Fulford had stolen the fathers of many families and looked set to place all creatures of the north under the iron paw of Viking rule. No sooner had creatures begun to process this fact when King Harold, the fox of Wessex, came to their aid. Not even those with a longstanding distrust of southern creatures could help being grateful for their king's immediate and all powerful justice. The celebrations of the victorious English hadn't stopped for days as soldiers and civilians alike came together in the streets of York.

After Harold had spoken to Copsi he joined his brothers having luncheon in the very same hall Tostig and Morcar would have feasted in countless times. The beaver, Archbishop Ealdred, was also with them, chewing noisily with his shovel-like teeth. Even days after the battle Harold remained cautious. He stationed many armed wolves around the hall. Ceej, the new leader of the king's housecarls after Wulfric's death, stood behind Harold as he ate.

"How was the duck?" Gyrth asked. "Topsi?"

"Copsi," Harold corrected him, taking his seat. The foxes had to speak loudly to be heard over the festivities happening on the other side of the castle's wooden walls. "I don't think we need to worry about him. He's gone to the battlefield."

"Why?" Leofwine asked, then looked sour as he realised. He reached for his empty flask and drained the last dregs of ale. The young fox hadn't stopped drinking since the battle.

"I wouldn't trutht him if I were you," said the beaver.

"Why do you say that, Ealdred?" asked Harold.

"Forgive me, Your Majethty, but...any friend of Tothtig ith no friend to me."

There was silence at the table. Leofwine was staring at the beaver and digging his claws into his chair. The ongoing celebrations outside were deafening.

"We should write to Edith," said Harold. "She got on well with Tostig."

"I already have," nodded Gyrth. His slanted eyes looked even more downtrodden than usual.

"Thank you," said Harold. The question of how he felt about Tostig's death was too entangled in thorns to answer. One day he would have to pull at those vines and suffer each and every cut.

A CLASH OF CLAWS

Perhaps when winter comes, mused Harold. *I'll think of you then, my brother, when I know England will be safe.*

"Did you see him on the battlefield?" Leofwine asked softly.

"No," said Gyrth.

"Only at the beginning," said Harold.

"I saw him once," said Leofwine. "He fought well, as he always did; he was always too quick for me…"

As Leofwine spoke Harold became distracted. There was a disturbance in the cheering creatures outside. He could no longer hear drums and songs. Laughter and applause had stopped. Harold stood up.

"What ith it?" asked Ealdred worriedly.

"Brother?" Gyrth stood up too. Harold had drawn his sword.

"Something is happening out there," said the fox king.

The grumbling of the unseen crowd was getting louder and more harried.

Tostig? Harold's stomach fluttered.

The noise from outside the walls reached a crescendo. Pawsteps approached. All three foxes had their swords out when the doors to the hall opened.

"You!" Harold snarled.

There must have been a dozen or so creatures coming into the hall. All were muddy, dishevelled and showed general signs of living rough. There were a pawful of rabbits, a trio of badgers, one otter and two regal hares standing at their centre.

"Your Majesty," said Lord Edwin in his high voice. The hare's ears were tall and tense. His chest was puffed up with typical pompous energy. Lord Morcar, always the uglier of the two, at least had the good grace to look ashamed. The second hare's crumpled face was staring determinedly at the ground.

"You are alive then?" Harold's voice boomed. He strode away from his plate towards the newcomers. His chair fell and the sound of it crashing to the floor made the hares flinch.

"Through much grit and skill, yes, we have survived," said Edwin.

Harold's laughter was a crude bark. He came to stand in front of Edwin, close enough to smell the filth that encrusted the hare's fur.

"I can't wait to hear the tale," said Harold.

"We met Hardrada in battle. We held him for many hours-"

"Lies," Harold spat. "You were destroyed."

"Your M-" Edwin was cut short as Harold brushed past him.

"Quiet," snapped the king. He looked at Morcar. "What happened?"

"They were too strong," said Morcar, raising his ugly head to meet Harold's gaze.

"We ran."

"You ran?"

"I did not want to..." his ears drooped down either cheek. "But yes, we ran."

"Where?"

"North."

"How many of you survived?"

"Very few," Morcar winced.

"Why do you return to York now?"

"Your Majesty?"

"Why *now*? Because you heard that Hardrada had been defeated? Because you knew it was safe?"

"This is preposterous, Your Majesty," Edwin's high, slimy voice dripped with indignation. "York is my brother's home-"

"Not anymore."

Edwin opened his mouth up and down like a fish dying of thirst. Morcar was still.

"You wanted to be Earl of Northumbria," Harold spat at Morcar. "You made me exile my own brother. When the time came to defend it, you failed. You ran away from all those creatures you swore to protect. You could have at least had the decency to die on the battlefield."

Harold's rage was unexpected and unrelenting. All the creatures in the room looked at him with fear, and the fox was reminded with sudden savage delight that he was king. He could do just about anything he wanted.

Hang them, he thought. *Hang them both.*

Just once he could use his power for something other than good. Would God really treat him so harshly for it?

But that would not change the past, he thought just as suddenly. He immediately resented this more honourable voice.

I'd be happier if I was a fool, he concluded.

"You are no longer my Earl of Northumbria," Harold declared. He turned to Edwin. "And you are no longer-"

The fox didn't finish his sentence. For the second time in minutes he was distracted by noises from outside. A rumbling, flapping sound was building.

Harold was first out to the street, followed by his brothers and the hares. All the creatures partying on the street were looking up at the black wall that was blocking out the sun.

Hundreds, nay thousands, of birds were flying towards them. The sound of their wings and squawks crashed over them like a tidal wave.

A blackbird landed in front of Harold. It passed out on collision.

A crow landed and skidded past.

A pigeon landed next. He was panting but managed to stand and face Harold.

"The lynx of Normandy!"

Harold closed his eyes as a chill ran down the length of his spine. The thousands of winged creatures all landed before him, exhausted and terrified, each bringing the same news: William had done it – he had crossed the Channel.

AUTUMN

The Landing of the Lynx

The lynx hopped off his ship and landed on the wet sand. He leant forward and dug out a sloppy lump. It broke down into a thousand granules and fell through the cracks in his paws. He smiled and licked a claw clean. Sea salt had never tasted so sweet.

William turned to face his ship, the *Mora*. All the creatures aboard were staring at him.

"FOR NORMANDY!" the lynx cried, raising his sword into the air. His followers roared and landed on the sand beside him. It took four creatures to help Leroy, William's grand horse, off the deck and onto the Pevensey beach.

"You did well," William stroked Leroy's neck. The horse whinnied in a way the lynx took to mean *"don't make me do that again"*.

The voyage across the English Channel had gone better than William could have hoped. The lynx brought with him seven thousand creatures and a further two thousand horses. Only two ships failed to successfully cross over from Normandy. One blew off towards the port of Sandwich (its crew were killed by unwelcoming villagers), and a second was shipwrecked. This vessel had held a mystic squirrel that had claimed, "England would be taken without a battle".

"Not much of a soothsayer," William proclaimed when he heard of its fate, "if he could not foretell his own death."

During the voyage the *Mora* had been so fast that it had left all other ships behind. Where many of the other ships had been weighed down by heavy horses, William's smaller ship only took Leroy and his closest advisors.

"We are lost!" Eustace the chamois had cried when the sun rose on the second day and nothing could be seen but water and sky. William had ignored the panic and ordered a large breakfast be brought to him. He sat down to a platter of fruits and spiced wine in good spirits. When he was finished he asked Taillefer to look again for his missing fleet. The albino polecat climbed the sails for a better view and told him that four ships were appearing on the horizon. Within minutes, the sea resembled a dense forest whose trees bore sails.

It was still a couple of hours before noon when Taillefer had spotted England. It was a clear morning and the gigantic white cliff that locals called "Beachy Head" beckoned them closer. By some miracle, the stormy weather that had pinned William's fleet in Normandy did not bother them once they were on the water. The duke had never been surer of divine intervention. He kissed the ring that the owl pope had bestowed upon him. The ring had gained him his army, and now God was giving them safe passage.

I am God's chosen one, William nodded to himself. *I am the storm.*

When the lynx landed, the English creatures who lived in Pevensey did not attempt to repel him. William did not see any faces that day, only fleeing tails and wings. The lynx had been warned of what the English called the fyrd; the common army of creatures that would have been expected to defend the country's shores. William had also been told that at so late in the year, the fyrd might be preparing for winter and not thinking of war. As William oversaw his grand army promptly occupying Pevensey he knew this must be the case. Once again, he thanked God for keeping his forces in Normandy until the opportune moment.

Unfortunately, William knew the rest of England could not be so easy.

Where are you, Harold? William brooded as he strode across Pevensey beach. *Did you really believe, like everyone else, that it was impossible to cross the Channel after the equinox? Did you doubt a Norman fleet could sail like a Viking legion? Did you really doubt me? Surely you remember that my word is as strong as my iron sword?*

"What are your orders?" asked Odo, who had been following him.

Or perhaps I am underestimating you, William continued his musings. *Are you waiting around the corner, ready to pounce when I put my guard down?*

"Brother?" Odo asked forcefully.

William blinked and came back to his senses. The first thing to do for any invading army was surely to find food. The lynx set his creatures to plunder all of Pevensey and they feasted well that night. Eustace knew the land best, having visited King Edward's court years earlier, and suggested they head east to Hastings. Reluctant as he was to rely on the chamois, William agreed.

The lynx divided his forces. A portion of his ships were sent east, each laden down with equipment, weapons, and food. His infantry soldiers were sent on paw to cross the miles of surrounding marsh and his mounted cavalry were ordered to ride to Hastings by the longer route on road. William took any opportunity to spend time bonding with Leroy and so would join the knights.

"Everything we see must burn," William declared to his generals that morning. "We must draw Harold out into battle. He always wants to play the hero; he will rush to save all these poor helpless creatures. I do not fancy enduring winter here as barbarians. I want to be on my throne sipping wine well before that."

His generals all agreed wholeheartedly. As they sprang into action William's brother approached.

"What about this one?" Odo asked. The bobcat was riding his horse and was dragging a creature along the floor with a length of rope. It was the English spy they had captured in Normandy.

"Bring him with us," William ordered.

"Why?" Odo said bitterly.

"Because I said so," William snapped. He didn't know why he had brought the hedgehog back to England. The spy had a bleeding lip and many missing spikes. He had resisted answering their questions at every turn, no matter how hard they tortured him. William respected that.

He knew he would have to kill the hedgehog eventually but there was always a chance he might come in use before then.

Odo kicked his horse and joined his brother in leading the two thousand mounted creatures. Alfie the hedgehog, who had been forced into a sack, was dragged along behind them. He fell in and out of consciousness for days, only able to watch in rare fits of clarity as the Normans burned and plundered villages on their way to Hastings.

After days of such a gruelling torment Alfie was ready to give up and die. Tiredness, pain and hunger kept him in a delirium he could not escape. He begged for Odo to stop and kill him but the bobcat could not hear over the symphony of marching hooves.

"Please," Alfie yelped as the horses came to a halt. The ground was soft from morning dew. "Please…"

The hedgehog tailed off. He was lying upside down and so struggled to make out the sign that was looming over him. Something about it was familiar. With great effort the hedgehog rolled over. Like the majority of creatures, Alfie could not read or write. He crawled closer to the wooden sign and read the single word etched into it, the only word he had ever seen, the only word he knew.

It said "Hooe." Alfie stared in disbelief. He was home.

He didn't have the energy to cry. The horses continued to march into the village and Alfie was dragged along back to his hometown as screams and smoke rose in the air.

AUTUMN

Homecoming

Faye's breath made tiny little clouds appear in the air. She shivered in the cold and her spikes bristled.

"Winter is on its way," the young hedgehog told the chocolate-coloured pine marten that walked beside her.

"Hadn't noticed," lied Drefan, whose slender frame had been quivering for the last hour.

The two young creatures were returning home after another successful session of target practice in the gilded wood that ran to the north of Hooe village. They moved quickly down a path littered with yellow and golden leaves. They had to get back soon, or creatures would start to wonder where they'd gone.

"I almost had you this time!" Drefan exclaimed as they discussed their morning's work.

"Well, you only lost by thirty points, so that's definitely an improvement..."

"Hey, that last one was a bullseye!"

"If you say so..."

The two creatures had enlisted the help of the simple but friendly beaver that lived in the village earlier that year. The beaver had tied a rope to a low-hanging tree branch for them. This was much better practice as the log could be swung to represent a moving target. A "budding young archer" would be a generous description of Drefan. At this point, Faye considered herself to be a "master sling-shotter".

"I am getting better though, right?" asked Drefan seriously, who had his small bow and set of arrows strapped around his willowy back.

A CLASH OF CLAWS

"Sure you are," said Faye.

Just very slowly.

"I'm going to be a soldier, you'll see," beamed the pine marten. His fuzzy tail swung enthusiastically behind him as he picked up a stray twig and used it as a sword. "I'm going to fight with the fyrd when I'm old enough!"

Faye was lagging behind as she was weighed down with a pouch of her favourite stones. She paused at Drefan's words, her pointed snout twitching.

"Oh, I'm sorry," said the pine marten, noticing her sadness. "I shouldn't have said-"

"It's fine," Faye sniffed.

"Your Pa's going to come back, Faye, I can feel it."

"Two months. He was only supposed to be gone for two months."

Drefan winced. Nobody knew why Alfie hadn't returned. The village was distraught, but it was hardest on Faye and the rest of her family.

"There must be some explanation," Drefan said bravely.

"Yeah, he's dead," Faye brushed past the pine marten, now leading the pair to the end of the path.

"Don't say that!"

"Why not? It's the truth."

"Maybe, but maybe not. Gotta stay positive, I say!"

Faye smiled despite herself. "Yeah?"

"Yeah, you never know when it might be your time to go, so just try to be happy..." Drefan's voice tailed off. His friend Alwin had died of sickness in the summer. The two creatures walked in silence with their heads bowed as the path led out to a series of rolling hills. A large plume of smoke rose above Hooe in the distance.

They must be having a bonfire, thought Faye.

"So you're going to be a soldier, huh?" the hedgehog sighed good-naturedly.

"That's right!" said Drefan. "I'm gunna fight with the fyrd, then after that I'll fight by the king's side. I'll lead the King's Wolves into battle!"

"Except you're not a wolf."

"Details, details."

Faye laughed, something she hadn't done much since her father left all those months ago. "You're an idiot, Dre."

Faye began to take the steep decline down a dew-sodden hill towards their village. A village Faye had never left, and never would.

"You coming?" said the hedgehog. She looked back up at the pine marten who had not followed her. "Dre?"

Drefan was staring, not at Faye, but beyond. Faye followed his panic-stricken gaze to Hooe. The smoke she had seen earlier was ever growing, and three more fires had started across the village's thatched roofs. Silence fell between the two creatures. The empty space was filled with the sound of distant screams.

"Oh my God," said Faye. Her cold paw tightened around her slingshot. She began to run.

"Hey! Hey!" Drefan called after. "What are you doing?"

"We have to help!"

"But- but-" The darting pine marten easily caught up. He slid on the grass and came out in front of her.

"The twins are down there! My Ma is down there!" Faye turned left and right but Drefan blocked her way.

"We don't know what's going on, we should-"

"Dre! We're being attacked! That's what's going on!"

"You think?" the pine marten's golden eyes blinked nervously at her.

"Yes! Now out of my way before I strike you." She foraged into her ammunition pouch for a stone.

"What if it's the Vikings?" said Drefan with a voice laden with dread.

Faye frowned for a moment. She remembered what her father had told her the night before he left.

"It ain't the Vikings 'arold's worried about, so I'm told. It's Normandy."

"I think it's the Normans."

"Who?" said Drefan.

"Time to find out," she placed the stone in her slingshot in preparation but Drefan stepped to one side. He stared at the ground, chest panting and eyes shifting furiously. Faye streaked past him and a few seconds later she heard the pine marten follow her. She gripped her slingshot ever tighter and ran faster than any hedgehog dared.

Eventually the hill flattened out onto a muddy clearing. Faye and Drefan reached the edge of the village together. They could hear the sounds of swords and screams but the air was thick with black smoke and made it hard to see. Two squirrels appeared out of nowhere and collided with Drefan as they tried to escape. All three creatures yelped and landed on the ground.

"Ow!" Drefan whined.

"What's happening?" Faye asked the squirrels urgently.

"We're under attack!" one of the squirrels shouted at her. He staggered upwards and carried on running away.

"By who? How many are there?" Faye asked the second squirrel. Its black eyes spared Faye a fearful look before it ran after its fleeing friend.

"Faye," Drefan said from the floor. "I'm scared."

The hedgehog looked down at him. She could feel her heart knocking against her small chest as if it was fighting to be heard over the cries of the village.

"C'mon, soldier," she said. "We have to be brave. I'm going to find my family. Where will your sisters be?"

Drefan got back to his paws. His lower lip was wobbling but he steadied himself enough to say, "By the pond, maybe."

"Find them. Meet back here in ten minutes."

"I can barely see anything," Drefan winced. The smoke was burning their eyes.

"We know this village better than anyone, especially whoever's attacking us. Stay low and out of trouble."

Drefan gave a desperate, sarcastic laugh.

"Ten minutes, ok?" said Faye. Her house and the pond Drefan referred to were on opposite ends of Hooe. She started heading into the depths of the smoke but remembered one more thing her father had said, and turned back to Dre.

"You remember Old Monty? He had a hidey hole out by Stony Creek, covered by mud and stones. I've been keeping it stocked with supplies. It'll be safe there. If I'm not back in ten minutes I'll meet you there. Don't tell anyone else, there's only room for a few of us."

Drefan's eyes widened as he listened. He nodded enthusiastically when she was finished.

"Ok, see you — what's that?" Drefan was cut off by the sound of impending doom. Hooves pounded the earth amidst the smoke and a creature squealed in high-pitched, cruel delight. The hedgehog and pine marten stared around blankly for the source of it. Only when an autumn breeze came to their aid by blowing a swell of smoke clear did they see what was coming towards them.

A huge four-legged beast was rampaging down the road. It snorted and roared with a mouth of frothing foam. Sitting atop it was a creature dressed in a coat of steel. The gleaming soldier kicked the sides of the beast which galloped ever faster towards them.

Faye acted on instinct. She reached into her pebble pouch, keeping one eye on the charging enemy. She loaded her slingshot at speed and unloosed a stone. It clanged off the shoulder of the armoured warrior who recoiled on the impact. Faye winced as the soldier retained his seat on the beast's back. She loaded another jagged stone and thought of the swinging log they'd set up as target practice in the wood. Her tiny paws trembled as she aimed. The beast and soldier were getting closer, close enough to see a furry face behind the steel helmet of the rider. Faye fired at that exact spot. The pebble soared through the air and struck the soldier's face. Blood spattered the steel as he fell from the beast and landed in a dusty heap.

The rider was down for now but the beast was still coming. Its long face was contorted with hate as it readied to trample both creatures.

"Dre!" Faye shouted at the pine marten. He had an arrow prepped awkwardly in his bow. He had tears in his eyes as he stared up at the giant demon coming to kill him.

"AAAHHH!" the pine marten yelled as he fired an arrow with his eyes closed. It sailed harmlessly past.

"Duck!" Faye jumped onto the pine marten and flattened him to the ground. Four hooves studded into the ground around them, but the creatures were unharmed. The beast spat in anger. It galloped away before turning around and facing them again.

"Shoot it, Dre! Shoot it!" Faye shouted as she helped her friend up. "It's too big for my pebbles!"

The beast began trotting towards them.

"I can't!"

"Yes, you can!" Faye grabbed one of Drefan's arrows out of his quiver.

It was sprinting now.

"Take it!" Faye screamed, offering him the arrow.

Drefan was crying as he loaded his bow.

The beast was above them, it reared up onto its back hooves and made to crush them with its front two.

"FIRE!" Faye roared.

Dre closed his eyes again and unleashed an arrow directly upwards, straight into the long face of the beast. The beast whinnied as the arrow popped its right eye. It staggered around in agony and Faye and Drefan ducked and weaved out of the way of its flailing hooves. The soldier Faye had shot was stirring too.

The hedgehog retreated into the cover of the smoking village with Drefan hot on her tail.

"You did it, Dre," Faye said to him when they were sure they weren't being followed.

"Yeah," Drefan panted. Only his eyes could be seen amidst his soot-covered fur. "What was it?"

"I think it was a horse."

"I think it was a demon."

"Maybe it was both."

"They're not Vikings, that's for sure."

"No," said Faye.

If the Normans had horses as big as those, then no wonder father had never returned. Had he been trampled like I nearly was?

"Meet back here in ten then?" Drefan wheezed.

"Huh? Yes, yes. My family, I need to find my family." Her mind was like a plate of her mother's famous scrambled egg. "Good luck."

"Good luck," said Drefan awkwardly. They hugged before the pine marten darted away. As unconvincing as Drefan was as a soldier, Faye felt vulnerable and alone as he disappeared out of sight. She took a deep breath to steady herself before running in the opposite direction.

As she headed deeper into the village her heart broke at the carnage. She passed the burning houses of friends and saw families calling out for each other. Creatures she had known since birth were sprawled along the floor, killed either by the point of a blade or else suffocated by the smoke. Three times she saw swarms of horses and their armoured riders chasing helpless villagers down. She aimed pebbles when she could. The Norman soldiers howled and fell from their steeds, looking around angrily, but Faye never stopped long enough to be seen.

Even amongst the dense black smoke it didn't take long for Faye to find home. Amidst the darkness her house was the brightest star. Flames cackled through the windows and the walls whined and creaked, warning passersby of its imminent collapse.

"No," Faye whispered, looking up at the only home she had ever known ablaze in almost savage beauty. She was so caught up with the scene that she didn't at first notice the hedgehog curled up in front of it.

"Hugo!" Faye shouted. She gave her brother a fierce hug. The little hoglet looked blankly at her, his face a picture of fear and shock. "Where's Benedict? And Ma?"

Hugo pointed a tiny paw towards their burning home. At the same time Faye heard a cry from inside. Faye didn't pause to think. She charged into the house, ordering Hugo to stay where he was.

The heat inside was unbearable. Faye staggered through, feeling as if her spikes were sure to catch fire at any moment. The centre of the ceiling had already collapsed. Daylight fell through the chasm like an angelic beam, illuminating the fire and smoke. Faye's mother and brother were at the centre of hell, cowering from the flames that surrounded them. Worse still, two large Norman creatures were advancing upon them, laughing and swinging their swords tauntingly.

"Get back!" Eleanor roared at the Normans. She was shielding her hoglet with one paw and swung a large pan at the invaders with the other. Faye had been on the receiving end of that pan many times and knew it could be lethal.

The Normans, however, were not perturbed.

"*Tu es mort!*" they laughed in their foreign tongue. Faye stepped behind them, the roaring of the flames hiding the sound of her approach. She reached inside for her largest stone and aimed it at the soldiers' backs. The heat was so much that it was hard to concentrate. Her body was screaming at her to get out and away from the fire. She ignored this voice; one of the soldiers had his sword raised.

Eleanor was the only one to see her daughter. Her eyes widened with surprise just as Faye unleashed the jagged rock. It crashed into the back of the creature's head, and he fell snout first onto the floor, instantly unconscious. The other soldier looked confused at first before spinning around in outrage. Faye flung a pebble his way. It smacked him in the eye and he trampled around in agony. Unfortunately for the soldier he stumbled straight into the path of Eleanor, who duly thumped him across the skull with her pan. With both soldiers down Faye led them out to the open air where Hugo was still waiting.

"That was a good shot," Eleanor said stiffly to Faye as the twins hugged each other.

"Thank God I practised, huh?"

"Don't blaspheme, Faye," snapped her mother. Faye was used to such impatient treatment but something softened in Eleanor's face. She seemed to have regretted what she said. She pulled the twins closer to her and looked at Faye. "Where shall we go now?"

Faye was startled. Her mother was looking to her for answers. She loaded another pebble for good measure.

"Follow me."

The four hedgehogs ran. Faye led them with her slingshot armed. She peered around corners, fired pebbles and loitered in the shadows when horses passed by. Eleanor was puffing hard but followed Faye without comment. She had the twins on either side of her and wouldn't let them out of reach of her grasp.

More and more soldiers were pouring into the town. The sounds of screams began to dim as creatures escaped or else were silenced by steel. A trio of rabbits sprinted past the slow-moving hedgehogs and were trampled by horses right in front of them. The beasts galloped away and left the rabbits to crawl away, their bones shattered.

Faye felt sick as she led her family past the rabbits. The hidey hole by Stony Creek could only take so many and she had already promised Drefan he could join them. She had no idea how long it had been since she had parted with the pine marten. When they reached the place where they had arranged to meet it was deserted. Should she wait for him? Or had he already been here? Was he already on his way to Stony Creek?

"Where now?" Eleanor whispered. The twins coughed and wheezed but seemed adamant to try and appear brave.

Faye spun around three times. There was no sign of Drefan. Could she risk calling his name?

"Drefan?" Faye hissed. "Drefan?"

"We can't wait here," Eleanor said quickly.

"Drefan?"

"C'mon, dear, let's get moving."

Faye bit her lip, and then threw caution to the wind.

"DREFAN!" she shouted. There was silence for just a moment before the sounds of jeers and onrushing hooves erupted from somewhere nearby. The Normans had heard. They were coming.

"Suivez-moi! Suivez-moi!"

"SHHHH!" Eleanor screamed, quite as loud as her daughter had been.

"Faye! Faye!" a distant voice called out.

"DRE! WE'RE HERE!" Faye shouted back.

Out of the smoke came Drefan, blanketed in black ash with his loaded bow in his paws. His two sisters were running alongside of him, each bearing signs of painful burns and singed fur.

"Dre!" Faye called, waving him over. "Here!"

The pine marten caught her eye and stopped running. He shoved his sisters towards Faye and turned around with an arrow pointing into the smoke he had just emerged from. The sounds of hooves continued to grow.

"Take them," Faye whispered to her mother as Drefan's sisters reached them. "Head to Stony Creek, all of you. By the Old Oak tree there's a burrow, just downstream. Find it. I have to help Dre."

"Don't be ridiculous," Eleanor snapped, now surrounded with her hoglets and the pine marten sisters. "You're coming too!"

"I will, now GO!" Faye shouted. Three giant horses with riders were appearing from the smoke and converging on Drefan. As Eleanor rushed the young ones to the safety of Stony Creek, Faye ran to Drefan's side, arming her slingshot as she went.

Drefan unleashed his first arrow at the same time Faye shot her stone. His arrow hit the horse on the right and her stone struck the rider on the left. They loaded three more times each and fired with speed and precision. The horse Drefan shot slumped down, its body riddled with arrows. Faye's stones had knocked one soldier down and sent its horse galloping off course. Only one horse remained a threat, the one in the centre. Faye reached for a stone but her paws grasped nothing but empty air.

"I'm out!" she cried.

Drefan took a deep breath as he placed his last arrow in his bow. There was a burning ferocity in his eye and he suddenly looked a lot older than he had done when they had practised in the wood that morning. His paw was steady, and Faye knew he would not miss. The arrow thudded into the chest of a weasel rider.

"Yes!" Faye yelled.

The Norman weasel did not yell out in pain. He swayed on the back of the horse and began to tip over the side just as they rode in between Faye and Drefan. Faye leaped out of the way of the onrushing beast.

"Move!" Faye shouted to Drefan. The pine marten darted out of the horse's path but the weasel rider, who was midway through tumbling off the enormous beast, swung his blade at the pine marten as he fell. The blade sliced open Drefan's bare fur. When the weasel hit the ground the arrow in his chest was pushed further inside. It died instantly.

"Dre?" said Faye as the horse bolted away from the scene. "You ok?"

There was a nasty, bloody gash spreading on the pine marten's chocolate-coloured chest.

"I think so," Drefan smiled at her lopsidedly before he fell sideways with a crash.

"No!" Faye tried to run over but felt pain in her leg. She must have hurt it when jumping out of the way of the horse. She gritted her teeth against the pain and made it to Drefan. She shook his body. "Get up, Drefan."

"I'm fine," he said airily. "Really, I'm..."

She watched as the life left his golden eyes. His snout gave one last innocent twitch, and then his head rolled back.

Faye's whole body shook as tears sprang from her eyes. She grabbed his paw in hers and squeezed it. She nuzzled her pointy-nosed face into his chest but came away covered in his blood. She recoiled and cried even harder.

"I'm sorry, Dre," she whispered. "I have to go..."

Faye wobbled as she stepped away from him, her left hind paw was still in agony. She took one more step before freezing on the spot. The dooming drum of hooves was approaching yet again. Two horses approached. One of them was all white and enormous. She had always wondered what kind of creature God might be, and could only assume this would be it. Tall and terrifying, she stared at it in wonder. She would never be able to slingshot this beast down with a million stones, not that she had any left. As the two horses clunked nearer, Faye knew there was only one thing for it; she slumped down beside Drefan and played dead.

The riders on the two horses were speaking calmly in French to one another. Faye could not understand what they were saying but listened intently all the same.

"Harold will not allow such destruction in his beloved south," said Duke William. "He will not resist meeting me in open battle."

"He would be wise to wait until after winter," said Bishop Odo.

"If he possessed any wisdom he would have ceded England to me a long time ago."

Faye risked sneaking a look at the Normans as she heard them leap down from their horses. There was a rope dangling down from the smaller of the horses. It was tied around a small spiky creature that seemed to have been dragged behind it in a sack. The hedgehog was bruised and bloody, with many broken spikes. It was crying.

"What are you snivelling at?" Odo barked at it.

"I'm surprised it has lived this long." said William. "It has a will to live. Admirable."

The broken hedgehog could understand them as little as Faye could. He staggered to his paws and looked around at the destruction.

Fire glinted from the midst of dense smoke, any houses in sight were either burning or reduced to smouldering ash, and creatures he had known since birth were dead on the floor. Drefan the pine marten was there, and by him another creature he knew...

"Faye?" said Alfie.

Faye blinked at her father. Her jaw slid open.

"Shut up," snarled Odo from above, and then carried on speaking to William. He had not seen Alfie's recognition of his daughter.

"Pa?" Faye mouthed at her father, tears coming to her eyes once more.

Alfie's heartbroken face split into a hopeful grin for less than a second. It became hard and focused, and he mouthed one word back.

"Run."

Alfie looked up at his tall captors, talking together. His spikes had ripped holes in the fabric of the sack he was caged in. He wriggles and squirmed, cutting open a hole large enough to squeeze through. Edging free, he suddenly roared and rolled all over their paws. They yelped and hopped in pain as he spiked them.

"Ouch!"

"You little-"

Alfie began running off and Faye darted off in the opposite direction. The pain in her paw flared up but she managed to push through. She could hear Alfie being beaten by the two Normans, but she didn't dare look back.

It took just under an hour to hobble to Stony Creek and Old Monty's hidey hole. She had been putting provisions down there for months, as her father had suggested. Eleanor, the twins and Drefan's sisters were all waiting for her. They were shaken up but safe.

"Darling!" Eleanor cried, giving her daughter a painful hug. She hugged her mother back. Tears broke free at once as she mourned the loss of Drefan, agonised over her father's fate, and wondered if the village she had once resented would ever go back to being home again.

AUTUMN

The Messenger

As the north of England licked its wounds from the chaos and bloodshed of September, the south was subject to its own wave of desolation in the month of October. William's forces reconvened at Hastings as planned, leaving an almighty trail of destruction in their wake. William's knights cruised through and butchered the towns and villages of Hooe, Ashburnham, Hailsham, Ninfield, and Catsfield. His infantry soldiers, who had travelled across the bogs on paw, also laid waste to towns such as Bexhill, Crowhurst and Wilting.

A temporary fort was assembled in Hastings which provided a more secure base for the lynx to organise his conquest. After a few days William received intelligence on what exactly had been happening in his English kingdom whilst storms had kept him in Normandy. He heard of the great victory Harold had won against the last of the great Viking kings, Harald Hardrada. Some of William's lieutenants thought this boded ill for their chances, but William saw it as a positive.

"The fox and his creatures will be tired and vulnerable," the lynx assured them. "We must fight him now."

The news that Harold had slain his own brother in the battle was another boost. William let the information slip to his creatures, and it soon became common knowledge around the camp that the false king had beheaded his own kin and had paraded the head in the streets of York. There was outrage at Harold's supposed villainy and William delighted as the rumours continued to grow.

Other than pigeon stories about the "Battle of Stamford Bridge", William knew very little about what Harold was doing now. A week passed at Hastings with no more information. William sent more forces to destroy villages known to be under the protection of Harold himself in an attempt to tempt the fox into action. Many of the lynx's soldiers had been promised plunder and William did not renege. Food was also taken by force. His army needed to be fed - so what if peasant families went hungry over the winter?

You have driven me to this, Harold, William thought with good conscience. *Their lives are on you, not me.*

Morale was high in these opening days. All the creatures had waited many months for their invasion and were eager to get started. As the days wore on, however, the autumn weather brought with it an unpleasant chill. The cold seemed to be a warning; even with Hastings as a base they could not winter here. There was not enough food and supplies around to last them through the dark months: they would simply starve. William had to engineer a battle, one that would be decisive in victory or defeat. If he could not, then they would be forced to go home and the lynx's failure would be discussed in every street corner of Europe.

It took until the second week of October before a long-necked stranger appeared in the Norman camp. William was consulting with Odo and Eustace in a cramped room in their Hastings fort at the time. The three creatures were in a fierce debate on how best to proceed. Alfie the hedgehog, the English spy who had so audaciously spiked the duke in Hooe, was also there. He was wrapped in chains and had become the lynx's personal slave.

"More," William growled, snapping his paws. Alfie knew the signal and shuffled over to pour more wine into the lynx's goblet. Odo had wanted the spy killed immediately but William again let him live. The lynx could not help but marvel at the tiny creature's strength of character.

Eustace was in the middle of reporting on the various raids William had sent to the neighbouring villages when the door creaked open. A creature of pure, startling white walked graciously into the room. Its bill was a bright orange and its neck was shaped like a long, cursive number two. Two of William's rat servants were either side of its webbed feet.

"A messenger from Harold, sir," they said together nervously.

"Which of you is Duke William?" said the swan in an extremely deep and sombre tone. It spoke in fluent French though William detected an aristocratic English accent.

"I am," said William, dropping his voice a few octaves to match the swan's. "Leave us," he told the rats.

The swan ruffled its feathers and cleared its long throat pompously. It spoke in the same droning voice and with a certain preciseness that suggested he was reciting his king's words exactly.

"Duke William, it is with regret that events have led to this. I do indeed recall that King Edward first appointed you his heir. But I also know that the badger bestowed on me the kingdom of England as he died in my paws. It has been the unbroken custom of the English to treat a deathbed request as inviolable. I therefore implore you to honour Edward's wishes, and to turn back to your country with your followers. If you do not, I will be forced to sever all friendship with you. The polar bear, Harald Hardrada, had already felt the full wrath of England. Go home William; do not make the same mistakes as that fallen giant. You cannot hope to survive this. The choice between life and death, I leave entirely to you. Your friend, King Harold."

William grinned sourly as he listened to the swan's dull recital. He knew the message was mostly posturing from the fox; surely Harold knew William would never turn back now. The fox was trying to intimidate him.

It would take a lot more than that to scare me, "my friend", the lynx thought savagely.

"You can tell Harold this," William started brusquely.

"William," Eustace blustered. "Surely we should discuss-"

"Tell him," William continued forcefully. "The choice between life and death is not mine, and nor is it his. That responsibility lies only in the paws of God, and He has already made His choice."

The swan did not react as William brandished his paw in his face. The lynx waggled the ring which the owl pope had given him under his orange bill. The swan only blinked slowly, almost bored.

"The pope has given me his support. You have been deemed to steal the crown, which is rightfully mine! You have been excommunicated by the church, and we are here as forces of God's justice. We are not invaders - we are *crusaders*. The light of God shines upon me. Meet me in battle, and let us see who God truly favours. Let God decide who should be king, once and for all."

The swan blinked a few more times in the silence that followed.

"Is there anything else?" said the swan.

William growled, annoyed at the creature's apparent lack of fear.

"Yes," said the lynx. "Take the hedgehog with you."

A flicker of surprise crossed the swan's face before it slid back into its deadpan gaze.

"What?" stammered Odo. "The spy?"

"That's right, release him."

"Are you-"

"Do it," William snapped and Odo dropped his head. He unchained the hedgehog who was looking around mightily confused at the whole event. Odo shoved him towards the swan.

"Wha's 'appenin?" Alfie asked aloud. The swan turned its bill up at the dirty, beaten hedgehog.

"This is a gift to *my friend* Harold; a gesture of my good will."

"Very kind," said the swan stiffly.

"One last thing," said William. He held out the ring to the two English creatures. "Kiss it."

The swan breathed impatiently before prodding the ring awkwardly. It gave the hedgehog a nudge with its great neck and the hedgehog kissed the ring too.

"Good," said William. "Now get out of my sight."

The two creatures left, the hedgehog stealing one last stunned glance back at William as he did.

"You should have consulted us. We could have formed a response together," said Odo quietly.

"I am quite capable without you," William spat back. "Now Harold knows. He knows that the pope and God are with me."

"If he knows this he will never meet us in open battle!" cried Eustace.

"He will," said William. "Only by beating me can he prove he is meant to be king."

"And what about the spy?" scowled Odo.

"That hedgehog saw us demolish every southern village we came through," William explained impatiently. "I want Harold to know what I've done to his land. He will seek revenge on the battlefield."

Odo and Eustace looked uncertain. William did not much care.

"Now I suggest we rest," he said brutishly. "And wait."

AUTUMN

The Decision

Eight days after King Harold had heard of the lynx landing at Pevensey, the fox and his brothers were in London. The northern creatures that had rallied to join the fight against the Viking threat stayed behind. The foxes had marched only with the professional housecarls. Though the Battle of Stamford Bridge had taken the lives of many English creatures, the army was still a couple of thousand strong.

The hares, Earl Edwin and Earl Morcar, did not immediately follow them. They promised to come south a couple of days later once they had gathered their strength. Harold was more than happy not to have them amongst his camp and did not argue the matter. Only after William had been dealt with would he turn his focus on what to do with his northern earls.

Exile them both, he fantasised.

When Harold reached London he once again returned to Westminster. He sent a message to William through a slightly indifferent swan that could be trusted to reproduce his words accurately. The next two days passed slowly and painfully as he waited for the lynx's response. He barely left Edward's abbey for a moment. On the second night he was joined in prayer by his sister Edith. They sat together in silence for a while.

"I tried," Harold said eventually. Edith looked at him. "I offered Tostig all of Northumbria. All he had to do was step out of the Viking army."

"But he chose to fight?"

"Yes."

"He was a fool."

"Yes."

They shared a weak smile.

"And now the Norman is here?"

"He is."

"You are going to fight him too?"

Harold took a deep breath. "I will do what I have to."

"We're proud of you," Edith squeezed his paw with her own.

"You're a great king, Your Majesty," another voice squeaked.

"Mabel!" Harold said in surprise, noticing the diminutive mouse on Edith's head for the first time. "Thank you. Thank you both."

Edith and Mabel left him. The hours dragged on and still the swan had not returned. Harold drifted off to sleep in the abbey picturing the many disasters that may have befallen his messenger. He woke in the dead of night, a lucid dream of the lynx feasting on the swan's flamboyant neck fresh in his mind.

"Hello, Your Majesty," said a painfully deep voice.

Harold started and actually yelled out. That same white neck was right in front of him. Moonlight pierced the Westminster glass and illuminated the swan as it blinked blandly at him.

"Good gracious," Harold spluttered. "You frightened me."

"I have returned," said the swan.

"Quite right," Harold said, rubbing his racing heart.

"With a message...and a 'gift'," the swan bent its head low to the ground. Harold saw the hedgehog and cried out again.

"Alfie!"

"'ello, Yer Majesty!" said the hedgehog.

"You're alive! How...I don't believe it..." Harold twisted his whiskers. Even after a year of never-ending surprises, the return of Alfie might have been the most shocking of all. Harold had long considered him dead and it appeared as if he had nearly been right. The hedgehog looked awful. He was missing countless spikes and his little face was covered in dried blood.

"Not sure I believe it meself, ser!" Alfie said. "They 'ad me for a long while!"

"And you escaped?" said Harold, incredulous.

"Set free," the hedgehog shrugged. "Lord knows why."

"What about the beaver?" Harold said quickly.

Alfie's face scrunched together. "That thing, that monster...took Tata's paws."

"William."

"Aye."

"Tell me everything, Alfie."

The hedgehog did. He described in detail what he and Tata had first found in Normandy before their capture and the subsequent murder of the beaver. He spoke about the horror of being the Normans' prisoner and the ongoing storms before the eventual voyage across the English Channel.

"How many creatures does he have, Alfie?"

"Thousands! Maybe ten thousand? They've got creatures I ain't ever seen before. Ginormous things, four-legged monsters with long faces and swishy tails. I think they migh' 'ave been 'orses."

"Impossible," Harold gasped. "How could he get them over the Channel?"

The fox did not hear the hedgehog's response. It was a devastating blow. Harold had always stayed clear of horses, as his mother had taught him. He had known of the Normans' fighting skills on horseback, but had never considered for a moment they might be able to shepherd the wild beasts across the sea.

"What happened when you landed?"

Alfie then described the devastation of countless southern towns and villages; how his home had been reduced to nothing but ash and rubble. At this moment Harold tugged so hard on his whiskers that several of them came away in his paw. The king had sworn to defend England's peaceful inhabitants and its idyllic hills and forests with his life. Now the green fields were burning, and where had Harold been?

Off fighting some other battle, winning glory, he thought miserably. *Even in victory I fail.*

The hedgehog bit back tears as he described causing a distraction to allow his daughter to escape. He spoke about the Norman forces taking total control of Hastings and the fear that gripped the coastal town.

"That's enough," Harold said shortly as Alfie described the deaths of a family of squirrels at William's own paw.

"Oh, righ', sorry," Alfie winced, noticing what distress he was putting his king under.

Harold's tail began to choke his leg. He understood why William had sent the hedgehog back. The lynx was trying to torment Harold and, so far, he was succeeding.

"I though' I'd never get out o' there, ser," said Alfie. His eyes looked sunken and white and Harold knew he could never truly understand the poor hedgehog's pain. "I was his slave. Then this swan came, and he just...lemme go."

"Just like that?"

"Uh-huh," said Alfie. "I didn't much understand anythin' that were 'appenin'. I 'ad to kiss that ring o' 'is, then we was on our way. 'ad to ride on the back of the swan, wasn't at all comfortab-"

"Ring? What ring?"

Alfie opened his mouth wordlessly and gave another shrug. Harold looked to the swan who had been watching them both with a vacant expression.

"There was a ring, yes," droned the swan.

"Well?" demanded Harold.

"It was from the pope. The owl has granted William his favour. You have been excommunicated."

Harold's tail went limp. So did the rest of his body. He fell to the floor.

"Yer Majesty!" cried Alfie. "Yer alrigh'? What's 'excomnicated'?"

"Excommunicated," corrected the swan pedantically. "Harold can no longer count on God as an ally."

Harold felt like he was going to be sick. He listened as the swan told him exactly what William had told him, how the pope agreed that Harold "had stolen the crown".

Was I truly wrong to become king? Should I have stepped aside and let William take it? Or has the pope been hoodwinked by the lynx? Should I not have at least been able to state my case before the church abandons me?

"Thank you both," Harold eventually gasped, not looking at either creature. "Please leave me now."

The swan and hedgehog began to leave the abbey.

"Alfie."

"Yes, Yer Majesty?"

"Find the vixen, Edith, and the mouse, Mabel. Tell them I sent you. They will see you are taken care of."

"Righ', thanks sir!"

Harold stayed in a heap on the floor for a further hour, his mind spinning. He only had one thought with clarity.

I cannot let this get out. If my creatures know God is with the lynx they might be tempted to abandon me too. William must be defeated before anyone else knows. It must be now.

He left the abbey as the night sky was beginning to grey. He strode across the courtyard, imbued with panicked energy. He needed to find his brothers. He needed to march his forces to Hastings immediately.

He went to Gyrth's room in the palace first. He knocked loudly on the door to wake his brother up. The door swung open almost instantly and Harold was surprised to find Gyrth fully dressed and wide awake.

"The messenger returned?" Gyrth's slanted eyes were hard slits.

"Yes."

"Come in."

Harold followed Gyrth into his bed chamber. It was similar to the one King Edward had died in but was only two thirds of the size. The four poster bed looked like it hadn't been slept in.

"We must march to Hastings immediately," said Harold.

"I see," said Gyrth quietly. "What exactly did the messenger say?"

Harold hesitated.

God stands against us.

The king turned away from his brother. He couldn't say it.

"He spoke of the destruction of so many towns and villages," Harold told the wall. "William will rampage for as long as he needs. We must stop him."

"He is trying to draw you out to battle," said Gyrth simply. "You know this."

"What else would you have me do?" demanded Harold, spinning around. "I beat the polar bear, why shouldn't I be able to beat the lynx?"

"I have another solution."

"Of course you do," Harold sighed. "Let's hear it."

"Let me go instead."

"What?"

"I will fight William," Gyrth's jaw was so tight Harold could hear his teeth grinding. The fox looked tense and determined.

"I don't understand," said Harold truthfully.

"There are a multitude of reasons," said Gyrth. "Firstly, yes, Hardrada was defeated, but the battle and marches have stolen your energy."

"I hardly think-"

"You are not at your best, Harold, that is a fact. If you die in battle England is lost. If I should fight the lynx and die, the war continues. You can raise further armies to avenge me, and England will be safe."

Harold considered his brother. Gyrth could always be trusted to find the most efficient response to just about any problem. Harold expected cleverness from his brother but what he was suggesting required something else: *bravery*.

"Whilst I fight the lynx you will not be idle," Gyrth continued. "You must empty the fields and villages that have not been touched by the lynx's forces. Move the creatures north to safety... and then burn the towns."

"Burn the-"

"Yes. Destroy all the food, ruin all the roads. If William beats me he will be stranded in a country with no creatures, no towns, no roads, and no food. His armies will starve and die in the winter."

Harold twisted his whiskers once more. Could he let his brother do this? Could he hide behind Gyrth as he put his life on the line? Did honour really matter? Tostig had honoured Hardrada and Tostig had died.

"It is the only way," urged Gyrth. "But I am not king. It is your decision to make."

Harold thought about what William had told the swan.

"Meet me in battle, and let us see who God truly favours. Let God decide who should be king, once and for all."

William had the support of the pope, but was God really on his side? Harold had waited for the lynx all summer but winds had kept him in Normandy. As soon as the fox left to fight the Norwegian threat the weather had turned in William's favour. Was there such a thing as coincidence? Or was it only God's will?

I have to know, thought Harold with grave finality. *There is only one way to know.*

"The decision isn't mine, brother," sighed Harold. "We march today; together. *I* must meet William on the field. Then we will know the answer."

"The answer to what question?" frowned Gyrth.

"Who is the rightful king of England?"

AUTUMN

Taillefer's Taunt

The London fyrd had been summoned. Brave and timid creatures alike answered the call. More and more were cascading in from the countryside all the time but Harold was determined to march at once.

"At least let us wait for the hares," Leofwine said on the morning they were due to leave. Both he and Edith had sided with Gyrth. They agreed that Harold should stay in London. The king ignored their advice.

"Open your eyes, brother," said Harold shortly. "Edwin and Morcar aren't coming to help us."

"But- but they have to," Leofwine gasped. "They said they would-"

"Prepare your creatures," said Harold, walking away.

The King's Wolves and Gyrth and Leofwine's surviving housecarls led the procession south. The common creatures of the fyrd followed the columns of organised housecarls in a shapeless, hectic crowd. They brought with them whatever weapons they could muster. Some came without anything but the ambition to defend England. Harold found Alfie the hedgehog amongst them as they set off.

"You have done enough," Harold told him. "You don't have to do this."

"They destroyed me 'ome, I..." Alfie looked for the right words. He didn't need to. Harold understood.

The great host of creatures marched across the London Bridge and many Londoners came to see the army off. Songs were sung and tears were shed as families watched their sons, husbands and brothers shrink into the distance.

It was a two-day march to Hastings. They took an old, straight Roman road that was sheltered by dense forests on either side. Rows of dark and naked trees shivered in a persistent breeze. Leaves of brown, red and yellow created a wet, soft carpet for the thousands of heavy paws coming through.

Woodland creatures appeared on the edges of the forest as they went. Herds of stags that refused to fight in England's wars watched them with vacant expressions. Owls eyed them sleepily, wondering what all the fuss was about. Other rural families of rabbits and squirrels that preferred forests to society's walls looked on with sad, pitying expressions. A dozen or so rabbits began handing flowers to passing soldiers with the grim silence of a funeral. Some crossed their hearts with a paw in prayer.

"You're all doomed!" one voice cried out. Harold scanned the edge of the forest for the culprit. The creatures he saw looked away from his gaze. They must have already heard the news of William's destruction of the south if they hadn't seen it with their own eyes.

"Turn back! Save yourselves!" the voice continued.

"Up there," Gyrth pointed to a trail of gossiping birds that were following the army's march.

"Ignore them!" Harold barked to his nearest soldiers.

The atmosphere amongst Harold's camp was contemplative and quiet. Much of the army had fought against the Vikings at Stamford Bridge. The King's Wolves, now led by Ceej after the death of Wulfric at Hardrada's paw, were subdued as they mourned their fallen friends.

At dusk on the second day a pink and orange sky lit an ancient apple tree that stood at the top of a long and overgrown hill. Thousands of creatures of varying sizes stood beneath its stooping branches. Harold had sent more wings ahead for the fyrds of Kent and Sussex to prepare for battle. The king addressed them as night fell.

"England is under attack!" he shouted. He heard his words echoed by other creatures as his words were passed on down the vast crowds.

"The only thing that stands in between the destruction of everything we hold dear...is us! The Normans are eager for battle...let's not disappoint them! Tomorrow morning we will fight! Tomorrow morning our fate will be decided! Tomorrow everything ends!"

The English creatures, who had at first been cheering their king's words, looked at each other anxiously at the last line. Harold heard "tomorrow everything ends!" repeated through the ranks. He swallowed a dry throat.

"That is to say, we will defend England with everything, our lives if we have to," there were a few muted cheers. Harold raised his voice to a bellow. "This is England! This is our home! Whilst they fight for treasures and glory we fight for honour and family! We will fight harder, faster and for longer! The lynx shall regret the day he ever stepped paw on our beautiful sand!"

This seemed to get his creatures back on track. They roared their support for him. Harold caught snatches of their words through the tumultuous shouting.

"They don't stand a chance!"

"Bring 'em on!"

The Kentish and Sussex creatures joined Harold's forces as they marched the rest of the way. They continued through more forests before coming out at the top of a grassy ridge. This was the place where Harold and his brothers had agreed to make their stand. It was five miles outside Hastings and was strategically ideal for the oncoming battle. Firstly, it cut off the only road out of Hastings so if William wanted to head north he would be forced to cross the hills. Second, the ridge was a perfect assembly point for all his creatures. They could form a shield wall here a thousand strong and eight creatures deep. Thirdly, there was a gradual but steep incline of more than fifty feet beneath them. William's army would have to march up the hill to reach them, and the power of their horses would be stifled.

"The high ground gives us the advantage," Leofwine said with a brave face that night. His eyes twinkled in the golden blend of the white moonlight and the red embers from their crudely assembled fire.

"Perhaps William will not come tomorrow. Perhaps he'll wait for a better opportunity."

"No," said Harold simply. "He's waited long enough. He will come."

There was much laughter from a nearby fire. Harold saw Alfie joking around with a guffawing otter and smiled. Creatures were drinking well into the night, knowing that it may well be the last night of their lives under the stars.

Tomorrow they might be amongst them rather than below, thought Harold.

"Eight thousand, more or less," Gyrth said. "That's how many we have."

"Will it be enough?" asked Leofwine.

"I don't know," said Gyrth.

"Harold?" Leofwine looked at his oldest brother.

Does it matter how many we have? Or has God already decided?

"It'll be enough, Leo," Harold smiled. He gripped Leofwine's paw with his right. He offered his left to Gyrth who took it quietly. "We can do this, brothers. Just think - we can't leave Edith with just Stigand to speak to. You know how much the mole gets under her whiskers."

"I think she'd kill him," laughed Leofwine.

"Exactly," said Harold. "What kind of brothers would we be to leave her all alone in this world?"

The smiles on the three foxes' faces slid slowly.

"Terrible ones," Leofwine said.

"Then we add her to the list of the things we are fighting for," growled Harold. He felt pain in his paws as both Gyrth and Leofwine's claws tightened in his fur. "We beat Hardrada. We can beat this cat too."

William combed Leroy's mane as the great horse rested on a mattress of fresh hay. He plucked out tangled thorns and berries with his claws.

"Not long now," the lynx whispered. The horse turned away from him moodily. William sighed.

"My lord?" a voice called from outside the stable.

"Come," William barked.

Bishop Odo entered with dignified excitement.

"Four scouts have returned and reported the same thing. A great host draws near."

Leroy's head perked up.

"Banners?"

"The Dragon of Wessex and the Fighting Fox," said Odo.

"Then Harold is with them," William grinned.

Leroy scrambled up. He flared his dark nostrils and began pounding his hooves excitedly.

"We shouldn't keep them waiting," William smiled. He stroked Leroy's side as the horse thrashed around and sent hay all over him. "How many creatures were seen?"

"Scouts differ on their numbers; at least as many as our seven thousand."

"Thousands of pawns but no knights," William said. "Our horses give us the advantage."

Leroy whinnied again.

"Or perhaps our bishop will win us the match?" William placed a paw on his brother.

"To checkmate England we have to go after the king."

"Harold will die," William nodded. "And we shall have peace."

The Norman army was ready for war by first light as demanded. William at first put his chainmail on the wrong way round but banished the ill omen with a booming laugh. His creatures marched out of the fort they had assembled in Hastings in an immensely long and thin column. The only path to the hill the English had gathered on was so narrow that it took many hours to cross the five mile distance. The creatures at the front of the army had almost arrived by the time those at the back set off.

The duke rode up and down the army making grand speeches. To the honourable he spoke of how they were God's disciples and crusaders, bringing down the treacherous fox in God's name. To his barons he reminded them of the lands and households that he had promised, and to the many mercenaries he spoke of the riches and glory that awaited them after victory.

"What can you offer *me*, sweet duke?" said Taillefer as the lynx passed. The albino polecat's pink eyes twinkled impishly.

"What is it you seek?"

"I told you once before, the night before we found the great horse you sit on right now."

William thought back to that fateful day in the Forêt d'Écouves.

"You wanted your name to be remembered," the lynx said. "You fight well today and there's every chance."

The polecat laughed and shook his head.

"What?" said William, amused.

"You'll see."

It was coming up to noon when the full Norman army was fully convened at the bottom of the large heath. The English army stood at the top of the ridge looking down on their foes in a great shield wall: the last barrier of England, the final defence of Harold's nation. The Dragon of Wessex and the Fighting Fox banners fluttered in the wind above the English. Banners displaying the Lynx of Normandy and the Owl Pope were waved above the legions of invaders.

William organised his troops into three divisions. He and Odo would take command of the centre. These creatures were the Normans; the ones most loyal to the lynx himself. Eustace the chamois was given command of the right flank. These were made up mostly of French and Flemish creatures. The left flank was led by Alan the Red, a stoic boar of oddly ginger complexion that could be trusted to lead the creatures of Maine, Anjou and Brittany with honour.

Each of the three divisions were organised in the same way. At the front stood the unarmoured archers, mostly made up of ferrets, minks and weasels. Next came the larger creatures such as boars and great horned ibex that made up the infantry. These were heavily clad in chainmail and carried swords or pikes. Beyond them were the horses and their riders. These were the elite rank of William's army and they carried iron maces and lances. The horses snorted and reared in their agitation to begin the battle. William himself was nearly thrown from the almighty Leroy as the horse prepared to charge.

"Easy, boy," said William as he examined the English defences. The first line of the shield wall was almost entirely covered by wolves. He knew this must be the infamous King's Wolves; the housecarls that were feared all across Europe.

One day you'll fight for me, the lynx thought. *If any of you survive.*

Behind the wolves came ranks of strong beavers, badgers and otters. He could not see the fox king or any of his orange brothers from this angle.

"Hiding behind your wall, are we Harold?" William said aloud. "Come on, come out and play."

Over in the English ranks their king was marching between the creatures of the fyrd at the back and the rows of housecarls at the front. The shield wall was so tightly formed that little of the Norman army could be seen. Harold could not see Gyrth or Leofwine either; the former was taking command of the left flank of the army and the latter the right.

Harold's creatures cheered after him as he passed up and down, his signature red cloak brushing over their paws. He raised his sword and yelled encouragement to the fyrd who needed it most. His face was grim and set in a permanent frown as his insides squirmed in fear. The English mistook his grizzly expression for savage determination and roared some more.

"My friends!" the king bellowed. "The devil approaches!"

The creatures responded with jeering and boos.

"Those creatures over there have come for one reason; to destroy everything we hold dear! They cannot be allowed beyond this ridge, WE WILL NOT ALLOW THEM BEYOND THIS RIDGE!"

Harold passed Alfie amongst the cheering fyrd. He had sourced a slingshot from somewhere. The hedgehog roared as loud as any bear with his shrunken face contorted with rage.

"This wall cannot break! This wall will not break! We will not move; we will not budge! I am depending on you; your families are depending on you, ENGLAND IS DEPENDING ON *YOU!*"

Any soldier with a shield beat it with their weapons and the army became an orchestra of war drums.

"They're coming!" a wolf yelled from the front.

"PREPARE FOR ARROWS!" Harold thundered.

"Wait!" said the same wolf. "No, it's just one!"

The wolf was right. One singular invader was striding up the hill.

The Normans were quite as surprised as the English.

"Taillefer! Get back here!" Bishop Odo shouted after the polecat.

"Let him be," William said, trotting his horse over to Odo.

"Remember me, sweet duke!" Taillefer called back as he went past the Norman archers. He scampered up the hill on all fours and came to a halt just in front of the centre of the shield wall. The English creatures looked at it with confusion as the polecat drew two swords.

"What's he doing?" Odo muttered.

"Making a name for himself," William smiled.

The polecat pointed both swords at the English with an exaggerated flourish. He jumped up and did a backflip, landing perfectly balanced on one paw. Then he threw his first sword. Not at the English, but up. Then he threw the second. Soon he was juggling both swords and had tossed in a third, smaller blade for good measure. He flipped around like a creature possessed, executing remarkable catches and throws. As the Norman creatures began to laugh at their performing comrade the polecat added one further insult to the English; he began to sing.

"L'épée au poing, fier et sanglant,
Il crie aussi le bon Roland
Il court dans la bataille!"

Harold couldn't see the jongleur. He could only see the three blades flying through the air. He barged his way through creatures to get nearer the front. He called to the new leader of the King's Wolves.

"Ceej! What's happening?"

"Polecat!" the wolf said with disdain. "I'll kill him."

"No! Don't break lines! Keep the wall intact! It could be a trap!"

Ceej looked resentful as Norman laughter grew. The English wolves shouted abuse at Taillefer as he flipped and sang and danced. Eventually, one wolf could take it no longer. He broke free of the shield wall and ran at the albino polecat.

"No!" Harold winced.

Taillefer had his head craned to the sky as he juggled his three blades. Out of the corner of his pink eyes he saw the white grey blur of the English wolf coming to rush him. He tossed the blades way above his head and jumped upwards. The wolf swung his sword across fresh air as the polecat soared. Taillefer flipped mid-air, caught the lowest sword he had thrown, and landed back on the wolf's shoulders. The weight of the polecat forced the wolf to the ground. It winded the larger creature and he struggled to get up. Taillefer brought his sword down into the wolf's back, killing it instantly. The polecat then leaped off again, caught the other two swords that were still falling, and continued to juggle.

The two watching armies erupted in respective delight and disgust. William's laughter boomed the loudest amongst the Normans. Harold scowled and looked away. The fox knew how important it was to keep a good morale amongst his ranks and the polecat was making a mockery of him.

"Enough of this," he told Ceej. "Kill it."

Ceej nodded, but before he could react, another two of his wolves had taken matters into their own paws. They bent down low and used their hind legs to propel themselves at the polecat. Taillefer dodged both their advances, leaving his three blades to land harmlessly in the grass. The wolves swung and missed over and over as he ducked and weaved beneath them and hopped and flipped above them. At one point the two wolves struck each other's swords in their haste to kill the arrogant pest. This gave Taillefer just enough time to grab the smallest blade out of the floor. A moment later, two fresh gashes had been opened up across the wolves' necks. The two English creatures fell down dead, and the Normans cheered.

"TAILLEFER! TAILLEFER! TAILLEFER!"

The polecat grinned and bowed dramatically to his audience. His work was done. He placed the short, bloody blade between his teeth and picked up the other two swords. More wolves were preparing to take on the challenge, but Taillefer was not about to wait. He sprinted at the shield wall and leaped right over it. He landed atop a wailing beaver and killed it instantly. The polecat wriggled free of creatures, slicing all that came near him. He must have wounded another half dozen creatures before he was finally overwhelmed.

Harold stepped over to the dead polecat with Ceej.

"Let's send a message of our own," said the fox.

The Duke of Normandy watched agape from Leroy's stirrups.

"Incredible," William remarked to Odo.

"Stupid," he retorted.

"You think so?" William gestured to his army. They were still roaring Taillefer's name even after the polecat disappeared behind the English shields.

"TAILLEFER! TAILLEFER! Taillefer! Taillefer..." the chants broke off as an orange creature in a red cloak stepped out of the shield wall. In one paw he held the polecat's severed head. He flung it onto the heath that separated the two armies and quickly withdrew behind the shields once more. The invaders watched as the head bumpily rolled down towards them.

William growled along with his army. He drew his sword. Eustace the chamois and the boar Alan the Red did the same at the tips of the left and right flanks.

"Archers!" the lynx bellowed.

The weasels and ferrets stomped forwards and drew back their strings.

The thuds of the English shields overlapping once more echoed across the heath.

"LOOSE!"

The birds that watched the scene from above flew to safety as the sky was filled with whizzing shafts.

A hailstorm of pointed steel crashed into the English shields. The first death rattles of the day were heard as tenacious arrows slipped through the most minute of cracks.

The Battle of Hastings had begun.

AUTUMN

Battle of Hastings

It took the average weasel, mink or ferret six seconds to select an arrow, load it into their bow, take aim, and fire. William had one thousand archers meaning that with every minute that passed, ten thousand arrows fell out of the sky atop the English. The first two rows of the shield wall were so tightly packed that few arrows were able to make it through. If, however, William's archers could fire beyond this initial layer of protection, then there was nothing an English creature could do but keep a watchful eye and pray.

William observed the scene with his ranks of mounted knights. The horses were snorting and trampling the ground agitatedly. The lynx could feel Leroy's muscles constricting beneath him. He kept one paw firmly on his neck and the horse settled down. Other creatures looked to the bond William had with his steed enviously as their own refused to heel. Even Odo was struggling to control his bucking horse.

"Get a grip," William told his brother. "No return fire; they don't have archers."

"Let's see," said Odo, wincing as his horse recoiled.

Behind the rows of kneeling archers were the legions of infantry soldiers. Many creatures were so pumped full of adrenaline that they couldn't bear to wait much longer. The creatures led by Eustace on the right flank charged past their archers and up the hill. The mercenaries on the left flank, led by Alan the Red, saw the infantry on the left surge forward and duly followed. Only the infantry at the centre of William's army, led by the duke himself, stayed where it was.

"Fools," the lynx scowled. He had wanted to barrage the English line with arrows for longer before he sent in soldiers on paw.

"Shall I call them back?" asked Odo.

The time for that had already passed. The two swarms of creatures were nearly upon the English line.

"No," William said before raising his voice. "INFANTRY! IN!"

His creatures did as they were told. They roared and raced ahead of one another to catch up with those who had attacked prematurely. As the soldiers collided with the English shield wall the archers stopped their firing. They flexed their tired muscles and gloated about their finer shots to one another (although it had been quite impossible to know which arrow came from whom at this distance).

William could feel his heart twitch uncomfortably in his chest as he watched the bulk of his army engage with the enemy. He'd rather be in the thick of the fighting than a safe spectator. The horses pounded the ground ever more impatiently. Leroy was shaking.

"Soon," he said. He twisted his goatee of fur and closed his eyes, drinking in the delicious, distant shouts of triumph and despair that could only be war.

The dull thudding of arrows in wood, ground and flesh came to a halt. Harold looked around. There had been a few near misses and a hare in the fyrd had died nearby. The fox had not moved as the arrows came; he knew any display of fear from him would spread like a disease through his ranks.

The king was still situated several rows of creatures deep into his army. He heard the first close combat engagements ahead of him.

"INFANTRY!" roared Ceej, who was right at the front. The King's Wolves fought shoulder to shoulder, protecting one another with their overlapping shields. The enemy flung themselves at the defenders with reckless abandon, swinging blades blindly. This initial wave threatened to swarm over the English wall but they forced the tide back with shouts of "OUT! OUT!"

Ceej pushed his shield out with such vigour that he sent a horned ibex sprawling in the mud. He lifted his shield for just a second and buried his battle axe in the creature's neck. He pulled the axe free and slipped back into the shield wall. All along the line the wolves of England did the same. They absorbed the pressure with their shields and only broke free to deliver swift, fatal blows before retreating back into safety.

Harold marched in between his creatures. He cupped two paws to his mouth and roared, "MISSILES!"

Those creatures with a good throw flung spears and stones over the heads of those in front. Harold saw Alfie the hedgehog fire his slingshot blindly to the sky. He knelt down beside him and stopped the hedgehog from reaching for another stone.

"I'd save them if I were you," said Harold. "Things might get up close and personal before long."

"Oh, righ' yer are, yer Majesty," he nodded.

William kissed his ring and hummed a string of prayers under his breath. His infantry were struggling. They battered the English line of shields with their bodies and their steel but were repelled every time. Tossed spears, axes and stones rained upon them from above.

Duck! William willed as he watched an English wolf break lines to attack a Norman boar. *Parry! Parry! Thrust!*

The boar was not so skilled. The wolf slit him open and then slipped back behind his shield.

William scowled and leaned over the side of his horse. So much saliva had built up in his mouth he had to spit it out. Leroy turned its neck to face the lynx. Its eyes were pleading.

William nodded.

"Knights! Prepare to join!"

The horses and their riders snorted and cheered. William shoved his helmet low over his face.

"The infantry have barely made a dent!" Odo whined. The plan had been for those on the ground to make far more headway into the shield wall.

William ignored his brother and waved his sword above his head, alerting Eustace and Alan the Red to prepare their knights for the charge.

"Oughtn't we wait?" said Odo.

Some of the riders heard the bishop's words and looked uncertain. William directed the throbbing Leroy over to his brother. He gripped Odo around the neck and dug his claws into the fur.

"I'm not waiting any longer," the lynx hissed with such venom that Odo nearly fell out of his stirrups. Odo ducked his head in deference to his brother. William rode away and stared up at the ridge just as the sun pierced the lurking clouds. The battle was cast in golden light.

Destiny calls me.

The lynx didn't need to direct his steed; Leroy knew it was time. The horse bolted up the heath and William ducked low against the wind. His knights followed him but they were not half as fast as the duke. The infantry soldiers who had been attacking the shield wall without success cheered as they saw their leader join the fray. William saw terror in the eyes of the English wolves as Leroy kicked at their shields, and he swung his great sword down upon their heads.

Harold felt the sun prickle the back of his neck and wondered if God was at last showing signs that He supported the fox as king. The Norman infantry soldiers were making little progress on the English shield wall. His housecarls could match any soldier across Europe and Ceej was such a lethal wolf that they were hardly missing the likes of Wulfric and Dunstan who had fallen at Stamford Bridge. Harold crossed along the back of the ridge as much as he could, making sure as many creatures as possible heard his words and saw the flash of his red cloak. He left the flanks unattended, however, leaving its defences to Gyrth and Leofwine.

"Out! Out!" Harold called in time with his wolves. "Out! Out..."

The shield wall suddenly stopped chanting, and the king's voice tailed off with them. There were desperate cries and a chaotic panic flared up in an instant. Creatures were pushing over one another to back away from the front lines. Harold was too far from the fighting to see what was happening at first. Then, as a pawful of creatures tried to flee, the king glimpsed what those at the front had already seen.

A giant white beast was upon them. It was more elegant in stature than Hardrada, yet the glint in its eye signified it shared the same lust for bloodshed. The figure riding it was covered in shining steel. Beneath the helmet Harold caught a glimpse of two yellow eyes and a light red fur halfway through the process of turning winter white.

It was William.

The king stood rooted to the spot. For a moment he felt lost for words as he watched the great lynx ride his magnificent beast headlong into the shield wall. William slashed with his sword and creatures around him crumpled.

"That's 'im!" cried Alfie, hastily loading his slingshot and firing a stone harmlessly through the sky.

More and more mounted knights were arriving. The Norman infantry backed away to give the horses free reign to attack. Harold had witnessed William mount a stallion once before, but he never expected so many riders. He marvelled at how the Normans had managed the voyage across the Channel despite himself. Many of the English had never seen a horse, and those that had had certainly not seen them ridden into battle. Their courage failed them, and those that looked to Harold saw their own panic reflected back at them.

"Get back here you cravens!" Ceej roared. He forced a wolf who had been looking ready to bolt back into position. "Hold the line!"

William and the white horse disappeared from view as Ceej reorganised his troops. Harold blinked out of his stupor.

"Hold the line! Hold! Hold!" the king called. "England is counting on you!"

For the next hour many lives were lost. The terror the horses spread amongst the English was nearly enough to destroy the hearts of the defenders in one fell swoop. They held the shield wall together as tight as they could, but the strength of the horses was too much. Any gap in the shields was quickly filled with a Norman sword. Hundreds of wolves fell and their places were filled by the rows behind. Soon beavers and otters occupied the front line as much as the wolves, and Harold found himself getting closer and closer to the fighting as creatures died around him.

It was Ceej who stemmed the English suffering just in time. He was the first to bravely step out from underneath his shield. Again he swung his axe, this time directly at the legs of the horses that terrorised them.

"They bleed like any other creature!" he shouted as he retreated into the wall. "Chop the legs!"

Emboldened by the wolf's bravery, English creatures began to shift the balance from defence to attack. They broke free of their shields and hacked at the horses' legs with bloodcurdling ferocity. The wailing of horses now became the dominant song in the chorus of violence, and the self-belief of the invaders staggered for the first time.

A wolf ran screaming at Leroy, swinging its battle axe at his legs. The horse spat in indignation. He rose onto his hind legs and smacked the wolf with his front hooves. The wolf went flying backwards, his ribs splintered into tiny fragments.

William grunted in satisfaction. Another two wolves came at them, but this time William's sword brought the creatures to their end.

Resilient little vermin, he thought. The lynx was panting hard. The attack from his knights had started promisingly but had now begun to falter. No matter how hard they fought, the rows of English defenders seemed endless and indefatigable. In an open field his knights would cut through the English like butter, but their compact defence upon the ridge seemed unbreakable. What's more, chaos had now spread within his own attack. Horses and their riders attacked without formation or process. Dead and dying horses were heaped on the floor, sometimes crushing their riders underneath them and blocking the path to the shield wall. Even worse were the horses who had lost their riders. They charged around recklessly without instruction and

William remembered why some creatures stayed well clear of the mercurial beasts.

The sunlight that had briefly basked the battle in glorious splendour had long since passed. The day was bitterly grey and cold, and the fighting was even more brutal. Neither side wielded the strength to bring a swift ending to the conflict. William knew he had to keep manoeuvring his chess pieces across the board. Stamina and patience would be the key to winning a long endgame against Harold.

Despite the tribulations of battle, William could not help but enjoy himself. The year had been too long, too arduous, and quite frankly too *boring* for a creature who longed to be at war. Sitting atop Leroy, the lynx felt invincible. Even as horses collapsed under battle axes around him William knew he would not fall. Together, William and Leroy slaughtered dozens of English creatures. The lynx was so distracted with killing that he had wandered far from Odo and the centre of the Norman attack. Rumour began to spread that the duke had been killed and there was a wave of horror among the invaders. William allayed their fear by casting off his helmet and riding circles around his forces.

"I am alive!" he cried. "God is with us! Victory beckons!"

His words inspired fresh impetus in his forces. They gathered together and prepared for a united lunge into the heart of the English wall.

"With me!" William roared at the centre of a group of forty or fifty knights.

"Brother!" Odo rode over to him. His club was a bloody mess.

"Join our attack, Odo!" William bellowed.

Odo shook his head and pointed to the left flank, the one that had been led by Alan the Red. "Look."

The invaders on the left had been beaten back. Great numbers of horses were dead. The attackers were retreating back down the hill, and the English were following them.

Unlike his brother the king, Earl Leofwine had decided to fight amongst the shield wall. He led the defence of the English right flank, standing beside his own housecarls. An arrow from the first volley had split his ear in two.

"Are you alright, sir?" a creature had asked him tentatively.

"Say that again, I can't hear you!" he had responded loudly. A couple of seconds later he erupted into laughter, and everyone joined him. All the creatures that served Leofwine admired him, which is perhaps why they fought so well.

The young fox hacked at horses' legs and duelled with fallen riders with the same gusto as the warriors that surrounded him. They forced the invaders away from the ridge and down the hill. Leofwine yelled out in triumph and was one of the first to sprint after them.

The English roar echoed across the length of the heath so clearly that Harold understood what had happened before Ceej reported it back to him.

"Your Majesty," the wolf barged his way through creatures to reach the king. "Earl Leofwine is pushing them down. What shall we do?"

Harold twisted his whiskers.

Our advantage is the ridge. We must hold the line.

"Do nothing. The shield wall must not falter."

Ceej's black nose twitched. His eyes shifted confusedly.

"Your Majesty, we have them on the run-"

"Do nothing!" Harold snapped. "We need you back on the front lines, Ceej."

The wolf dropped his head and nodded before disappearing back to the front of the shield wall. Harold turned away and took a deep breath.

Come back, Leo, he thought. *Come back.*

Earl Leofwine had no intentions of doing any such thing. He holstered his sword and crouched down on to all fours as he pursued the fleeing enemy. The horses barged back through the Norman infantry and archers in their desperation to escape. Many bolted entirely from the battleground, while others collapsed into ditches at the bottom of the valley. Thousands of English creatures converged upon them, led by an orange flash.

"We can end it here, lads!" Leofwine shouted.

Friends and foes were everywhere. The fox cut down three fallen riders in the space of a minute but nearly beheaded an English badger in the confusion.

"Watch it!" the badger shrieked.

"Sorry, chap!" Leofwine grinned. The badger laughed too before launching into an attack on a nearby enemy boar. The fox was about to join him when he noticed something that made his sword arm falter and his smile slip.

The rest of the English army had not moved an inch off the ridge. Both Harold's and Gyrth's creatures weren't following.

"Come on," he whispered with a frown. "What are you waiting for?"

The rest of the Norman army, unpursued by Harold and Gyrth, were free to back away from the shield wall and come and help the broken wing of their army.

"Oh, God," said Leofwine. "We need to get back. RETREAT!"

The order was already too late. The knights and infantry led by William and Odo had already cut off the path for Leofwine's creatures to return. They had broken too far from the protection of the shield wall and were now surrounded. The time for Harold to order a charge had passed, and Leofwine now faced enormous numbers without any protection. The Norman knights began slicing down this group of English creatures with ease.

"RETREAT! RETREAT!" Leofwine roared. He turned to the badger he had spoken to the moment before but found the boar had been victorious. The boar began chasing Leofwine down and the fox ran. A beaver stepped in to fight the boar as the young earl began scrambling back up the hill.

"RETREAT! Retreat..." A panic the fox had not felt before began to burn his skin. He couldn't breathe. He tore off his helmet and gasped for air.

"Are you hurt, sir?" An otter who had served Leofwine for many years came to help him.

"Up the hill, lads! Back up..." the fox's voice tailed off. He could no longer see the ridge and Harold's unmoving creatures. The way was blocked with rampaging horses. The rider leading them had also taken off his helmet. It could only be William.

Leofwine found his breathing calmed upon seeing the lynx. If death seemed a certainty, at least he could take the duke down with him.

"Come on then!" he shouted, wheeling his sword above his head. He locked eyes with the lynx upon his great horse. William was almost upon him when Leofwine heard the trampling of hooves from behind. He turned and looked up. Another horse ridden by another lynx was upon him. This one carried a bloody club. The rider swung the club with deadly precision as he passed. It cracked Leofwine's skull in two and the fox crumpled down on impact, dead long before he hit the floor.

William watched as Odo clubbed the fox dead with a single stroke.

"That was my kill!" he shouted. "Was it Harold?"

"No," said Odo, peering down over the side of his horse. "One of the brothers, I think."

"Hmph," William grunted before riding off. It did not take long to kill the English who had foolishly left their position atop the ridge. William and Odo's knights encircled them and picked them off one by one. It was nothing short of a slaughter.

"We were lucky," William said to Odo an hour later, once all the stranded English had been killed. As the lynx had pulled all his forces away from the shield wall, he ordered another attack from his archers. Whilst the Normans could catch their breath after the hours of fighting, the English still had to cower from arrows. "If our creatures had not run away, the English would never have moved."

"It's much easier to kill them when they're not behind that damned shield wall," Odo scowled.

"Harold does not want to leave the ridge," William mused. "So, we need to tempt them out."

"What do you suggest?"

William smiled as the memory came to him. It was less than a year ago, but it felt like it belonged to another creature entirely.

"You remember when we heard King Edward had died? We were playing chess."

"You won," Odo nodded.

"I did. But how?"

Odo's eyes glistened as he remembered.

"A feigned retreat. You pulled your knight back."

"Yes, and you took the bait."

"Can it work again?"

"Time will tell. Go tell Eustace, he can be the one to do it."

Odo rode away to tell the chamois the plan. William signalled for his archers to stop. He stroked Leroy's neck again.

"Ready?"

Leroy stamped the ground.

"Let's go then."

Leofwine's wing attack had been a disaster for Harold. The king watched as his brother and his creatures were surrounded and routed. Stragglers managed to break free and return to the safety of the shield wall, but most were not so lucky. Harold sent creatures to go and search the survivors for Leofwine. They returned shaking their heads, and the king was forced to accept he had lost another brother in the space of a few weeks.

"We must plug the gap," Harold ordered, delaying mourning for after the battle. The fox sent a mixture of King's Wolves and members of the fyrd to refill the wing Leofwine had led to disaster.

"I'll go, sir," said Alfie. The hedgehog had been doing his best to stay with Harold all day.

"Good," said the fox offhandedly, still thinking about Leofwine.

The Norman archers were battering the English once more as Alfie made his way to the right flank of the army. Alfie was too small to carry a shield but he headed to the front lines nonetheless. He crept between a beaver's legs and prepared his slingshot.

Eventually the arrows stopped and the enemy soldiers returned.

"Here cometh the infantry!" the beaver above him shouted.

"And the knights!" another creature called.

Alfie took a deep, steadying breath as horses, ibexes, boars and chamois charged. He drew back his slingshot and sought a target amongst the chaotic swinging of claws, horns and swords. Any one of them could have been there at the destruction of Hooe, his hometown. He'd seen Faye run away but who knew if she had made it to safety? And what about Eleanor and the twins, Hugo and Benedict? Alfie thought of them all as he fired and when he knocked a rider off his horse he screamed a guttural war cry.

"What a thot!" the beaver above him cried.

"Ta'," he smiled, drawing back another stone. This time he thought of Tata as he struck another rider through the visor of its helmet. It fell, unconscious, and slipped off the side of its horse. Its paws were caught in the horse's stirrups, and it dangled precariously as the horse galloped away.

"You're good at thith," said the beaver.

"Thanks- LOOK OUT!" Alfie screamed as a horse aimed a fierce kick with its front hooves at the beaver. The sound of breaking wood rend the air as his shield shattered. The beaver, either dead or knocked out, fell back and pinned Alfie to the floor. Alfie wheezed and pushed feebly against its weight.

"'elp! 'elp!" Alfie called. He could see the horse readying itself to trample him. "Aaaah!"

A wolf intervened. It swung a battle axe and cut right through the horse's bony shins. It swiftly killed its rider too before helping Alfie free.

"This is no place for a 'hog," he grunted.

Alfie was half of a mind to agree. All he wanted was to go home, to find his family and hug them all near to death. But what kind of life would they all be living if they let William be king?

"I can still figh'," Alfie said shakily. He loaded his slingshot and searched for another target.

Far to the left of the battle, Gyrth was fighting resolutely on the front line. From his viewpoint he hadn't seen Leofwine's attack. Word had come that they had suffered heavy losses but he still wasn't aware of his younger brother's death. If he had, he might have behaved differently when the creatures he had been fighting began to flee.

"They're retreating!" one of his housecarls cheered, pointing his favourite spear into the sky. It was a young fox who had always been very taken with Gyrth. The earl saw him as something like a son.

"But why?" Gyrth asked rhetorically. They had been struggling and losing many creatures against the power of the horses. Why were the enemy suddenly retreating down the hill, screaming as if it was they who were on the backpaw?

"Should we attack?" asked the young fox.

Gyrth scanned the battlefield with his sharp, slanted eyes. Some of his creatures had already set off after the enemy, not waiting for the order. The earl felt uneasy, but more and more of his creatures were breaking free of the shield wall in pursuit. He had to make a decision quickly: to follow or to stay?

"I..." said Gyrth. If only there was time to get word to Harold. Quick communication on such a large battlefield was near impossible.

Harold will not want to leave the high ground where we have our advantage, Gyrth thought. He looked up at the clouds, searching for the bright spot. The sun was already low in the sky. They had been fighting for hours and, if they did not act, they would be fighting for many more. He sighed as he came to his final evaluation.

We cannot beat them from here.

"Sir?" asked the young fox.

If we stay here, the battle will rage for hours. Slowly but surely, the horses will grind us down. We have to attack.

"We go," said Gyrth.

"We go?"

"Yes," he nodded, then roared to his creatures. "AFTER THEM!"

The left flank roared in approval and began chasing down the retreating enemy.

Follow me, Harold, Gyrth thought gravely. *It's the only way.*

Gyrth ran with the young fox right behind him. The earl ran his sword through the back of a running Norman polecat. The English killed many of the enemy infantry who were fleeing on paw, but the horses were too quick. They gathered at the bottom of the valley with the archers before turning back around to face the English.

Gyrth growled as he watched the horses regroup. They did not appear to be running scared at all. He saw now that their retreat had been organised to tempt them out. It didn't matter. If Harold was bold enough, they could still force the Normans on the defensive for the first time.

Trust me, brother, he thought. He stole a glance back at Harold's centre forces and felt a rush of cold dread slide down his spine. The Normans led by William were coming to assist their flank, but Harold was again refusing to move off his ridge.

Trust me.

"Your Majesty, we *must* help them!" Ceej implored.

"We must keep the shield wall intact," Harold muttered, barely audible. His eyes were glazed and his mind fuzzy. "The horses are too...the ridge, I told him to stay on the ridge..."

"But all our creatures – they're going to be surrounded, just like Leofwine and the others!" Ceej had lost all decorum in his desperation. He looked ready to shake the king with both paws.

"I told him to stay on the ridge..." Harold said, turning around. He moved away from Ceej with his head down. "I told him to stay."

William had watched carefully as Eustace's creatures retreated as planned. The lynx grinned mischievously as the English chased after them. He and Odo called for their knights to join them as they wheeled around to attack the outstretched left arm of the English army. Harold, just as he predicted, was too scared to act.

Just as with Leofwine, William and his creatures swiftly encircled the overreaching English. They kept their backs to Harold, confident that the fox would not attempt an attack. The fighting here reached a crescendo in its brutality. Gyrth managed to keep his creatures tight together so they were therefore harder to pick off for the duke and his knights.

William rode laps around the English, thrusting his sword down into any creature that was tempted out by the potential glory of killing the duke. One young fox attempted to stab Leroy with a spear, but the horse kicked out with its hind legs, knocking the fox unconscious into the dirt. The fox was too common-looking to be related to Harold, and William rode off dismissively.

"WILLIAM!" roared a booming voice. The lynx pulled on Leroy's neck and the horse spun around.

Another fox was standing over the one who lay unconscious. This one was tall with a regal, emerald cloak that matched the colour of his eyes.

The other brother, William grinned. *Leroy, charge.*

Gyrth did not move as the lynx and his great horse began hurtling towards him. His eyes flitted from the beast to the ground beneath him. Very calmly, he stowed his sword back into its holster. The young fox who had been like a son to Gyrth lay passed out in the grass, his spear limp in his paw. Gyrth flicked the spear into the air with his leg and caught it. He stepped forward and aimed it like a javelin directly at the lynx's exposed head. It whistled as it flew through the air. The lynx yelled out as the spear connected with flesh.

"Aaah!" William was thrown backwards off Leroy's back. The spear had been intended for the lynx, but the great horse had reared its neck and taken the blow. Leroy collapsed, with the javelin still embedded just below its jaw, and William landed in a painful heap.

"Leroy?" William crawled to his horse. He pulled at the spear, but Leroy whinnied helplessly. Blood was gushing from the wound and oozing in congealed lumps from his mouth. "No."

Gyrth readied his sword as the lynx cared for his horse. He took several rapid steps forward and swung his blade high above his head. He was nearly upon the lynx, but the horse saw him and widened its eyes. William turned, baring his awful fangs. It was enough to drive fear into the hearts of the bravest of creatures. One second of hesitation in the fox was enough to doom him. William leapt from the floor at Gyrth like a snarling lion. He tore at the fox's limbs and ripped fur and flesh with his claws.

It took a long time for Gyrth to die. The fox was forced to watch as the lynx tore him to shreds. Eventually, his death came as a mercy.

"That's enough, he's gone," Odo said when he found him.

William stayed on the ground. He wiped blood from his fur goatee as he looked around. Without Gyrth, the English were falling in their droves. Many tried to run back to Harold and were cut down in the attempt.

"The retreat worked perfectly!" cried Eustace the chamois, appearing next to Odo atop his horse. "I hope to be paid my worth for all this! Say, why are you on the ground? Where's Leroy?"

William stood. He could not bear to cast an eye at Leroy, whom he knew would be dead. The rage at losing such a wonderful weapon was devastating. He walked over to Eustace.

"Give me your horse."

"What?"

"Now!" he jumped up and pushed the chamois off. His fury was so great that the horse did not protest as the lynx clambered on. He rode towards Harold's centre. "Time to finish this."

It was impossible to know for sure in the heat of battle, but after the destruction of Gyrth and Leofwine's flanks, the king figured he had lost something close to three thousand creatures. The momentum of the battle had swung towards William and Harold did not know how he would begin to bring it back.

The Norman archers once more took to battering the English. With so many creatures lost, the gaps between shields were only getting larger. The shield wall was cracking, and William did not give the English a second to consolidate. His infantry and knights attacked together whilst the archers headed further up the heath and looped arrows over their heads.

Fighting now ensued on three fronts. With Gyrth and Leofwine gone, William's flanks swarmed the English from all sides. Creatures in the front lines had been fighting for hours and were ready to collapse from exhaustion before any blade reached them. King Harold had now drawn his own sword and was engaged in combat for the first time in the day.

The fox collected a shield from a fallen wolf and used it to block the powerful kick of a horse. He recoiled from impact but kept to his paws. The horse raised its hooves again and Harold stuck his sword in its neck. The fox grunted in satisfaction at his first kill of the battle. His devastation at the loss of his brothers was transformed into rage with a sword in his paw. He struck down many creatures and threw caution to the wind. The King's Wolves were emboldened by finally having their king beside them. Harold and Ceej combined repeatedly to bring down horses and their riders.

"What are we to do, sir?" Ceej asked in a brief moment of calm. A volley of arrows came their way and the fox and wolf protected one another with their shields. "We're surrounded on the left and right. If we are to retreat, now is the time."

Harold considered this as an arrow slammed into his shield and poked its point through the wood. Behind the ridge was a dense forest that could be used for an escape. That was in part why Harold had chosen this spot to make his stand.

"Your Majesty?" prodded Ceej as the fox disappeared into one of his long silences.

"There's still a chance," said the king. Ceej frowned. "If we can kill William, their confidence will crumble."

The wolf nodded, almost managing to hide his disapproval.

"Hunt him down, Ceej," said Harold.

"Yes, sir."

The wolf ran away, collecting a few of his trusted wolves.

I have to know, Harold closed his eyes, hoping to hear word from God. *Am I supposed to be king?*

William rode Eustace's horse directly into the heart of what little remained of the shield wall. The horse screamed in its ancient tongue as it was struck by four consecutive spear tips. William kicked the horse harder and forced it deeper into the enemy lines. Eventually, the steed collapsed, and the lynx leapt off its back. The duke clawed and stabbed every creature in sight as his creatures followed him inside the shield wall defences. Few of the true guardians of England, the housecarls that were spoken about across Europe, were still alive so late in the day. William and his knights now found themselves fighting the creatures of the English fyrd, those creatures that were conscripted to fight despite having no battle experience. They fought with weapons they had brought from home, sometimes using equipment that would be better at ploughing fields than taking lives.

"As the waning wood falls to the stroke of the axe, so the forest of English is brought to nothing," William remarked at the devastation.

Having lost Eustace's horse, the duke quickly ordered another creature to give up his own. He strutted around the bedlam of the battlefield, not even bothering to kill the commoners. Instead he hunted for a glimpse of orange fur or a splash of red cloth. He did not know where Odo was, but Eustace, who had also sourced another horse from a lower-ranking creature, helped him in his search for the false king.

It was the chamois who saw Harold first. Eustace pointed at the battling fox who was surrounded by English and Normans alike. The king was carrying a shield and a bloody sword as red as his cloak. He was roaring instructions and duelling so fiercely that spit was frothing around his mouth.

William watched him for some time, enraptured by finally seeing his enemy in the flesh. All the sounds of battle had dimmed. Arrows flew through the air without a sound. Swords struck each other with nought but a dull thud. Dying creatures screamed for mercy in silence.

"This is my destiny," said the lynx, and his voice felt like it belonged to another creature.

"We're behind you," said Eustace excitedly. He called for two helmeted weasel mercenaries nearby.

"I don't need your help," said William. He nudged his new horse and it plodded forward clumsily, unused to his touch. "God is with me."

Harold was fifty feet from the lynx. The fox hadn't seen William at all. The duke slapped his horse with the flat side of his blade and forced it onwards. The lynx stretched out his sword arm ahead of him. His eyes narrowed on his target with cold concentration. The fox still had not seen him, and now had turned his back.

"Harold!" William yelled as he rode.

I will not stab you in the back. Let this duel decide once and for all who is the greater creature.

"Harold!" William roared again, louder this time. The fox turned and looked around. His eyes passed over where the lynx was charging but didn't focus. "Here!"

The fox looked up and finally found him. There was a brief moment of recognition and an intake of steely calm breath. There was no fear there, only readiness.

William knew only a king could give such a look. He brought his horse to a halt and made to step down so he could fight the fox as an equal.

He never got the chance. One paw was halfway out of his stirrups when something happened that made the lynx gasp and his sword slip loose.

"No."

Harold saw the lynx approach at breakneck speed, his armour glittering. It felt like a moment out of a dream. He found he had already lived this moment many times at night, and knew that no matter the outcome, certainty would at last arrive for both creatures. One creature would die, and one would walk away a king.

As the lynx began to dismount, the fox's ears twitched towards a single sound amongst the chaos. He heard the gleeful whiz of the arrow a second before it connected. Somehow, he found the time sufficient to think of so many things. He thought of his brothers, Gyrth and Leofwine, dead somewhere in a tangle of grass and bodies. He thought of Tostig, and the duck who had been his friend, searching a field of bones for his master. He thought of Edith, quietly praying for his safe return in Westminster Abbey. He thought of King Edward offering him a sickly paw and telling him he would be "a great king".

Was I?

He was surprised when another voice deep inside answered.

Yes.

The arrow that he had sensed zeroing in on him struck true. It landed directly in his right eye socket and drove deep into his skull.

Harold fell to the ground. There was no real pain. He tried to open his left eye but found he could not see anything at all. He decided this was a shame, as it would have pleased him to look upon the earth one last time.

I tried, he thought with peaceful resignation. *History was not my tale to write.*

He sensed creatures surrounding him. It did not matter whether they were friends or foes.

God had made His decision.

I am not meant to be king.

William stood over the kneeling fox. Harold did not offer so much as a whimper. He knelt there in silence, an arrow protruding out of his right eye, his whiskers still smiling.

William pointed his sword at the fox as Eustace and the weasel mercenaries came by his side.

Goodbye, Harold.

The lynx plunged his sword into the fox's heart, killing him instantly. It wasn't the moment of triumph he had wanted and expected. The world had been deprived of a legendary duel by a stray arrow, delivered by a creature who never knew he had killed the king of England.

The fox slumped back in death but did not entirely topple over. William closed his eyes and muttered a prayer. Eustace and the other two knights showed no such dignity. They hacked at Harold's body with their blades and ran off carrying separate limbs high above their heads.

The lynx would have them punished for such insolence, but that would come later. The word that King Harold was dead soon spread amongst the English creatures and any lingering hopes of victory died with him. Hundreds of survivors made for the protection of the forest behind. All that stayed were slowly cut down.

The battle was over.

England had been lost.

And won.

AUTUMN

The Waning Wood

Alfie was surrounded. The shield wall had collapsed. The Normans were on the ridge and killing every creature in sight.

"C'mon, lads!" the hedgehog shouted. He couldn't hear his own voice over the sounds of swords and screams. "We can't give in..."

Alfie continued to fire stones from his slingshot. He struck a fat boar in the neck. It turned around, wrinkling its ugly face in annoyance. Alfie ducked under a shield to hide, but a moment later it was being wrenched away from above him. The boar glared at him, and he sent another stone into its slimy black snout. It made to stab him with the grinning horns that peered out of its lower lip. Before it could, it roared and spat blood all over Alfie. For the second time in the battle a wolf had come to the hedgehog's aid. Alfie recognised him as the new leader of the King's Wolves as it pulled its axe free of the boar's back.

"Get up, little one," said Ceej. "Into the forest, now!"

"Wha'?" Alfie gasped. "We can't give in - coward!"

Ceej looked furious. "The king is dead. We have to go."

"'arold," Alfie whispered. The fox couldn't be dead, he just couldn't be. The hedgehog had never met a creature as wise, as noble and true.

And William, his blood boiled at the thought. *Yer 'alf the creature 'arold was.*

"RETREAT! RETREAT!" Ceej was calling to the remnants of English survivors. He looked back down at Alfie, who at this point was close to tears. "Are you coming?"

"I..." Alfie tailed off as he saw a horse galloping towards them. Ceej heard and spun to meet it. He raised his battle axe but never needed to use it. A volley of Norman arrows landed around them, accidentally killing the horse and its rider. Alfie and Ceej looked at each other, both miraculously untouched by the flurry of arrows.

"Retreat," Alfie nodded.

Ceej bent low on all four legs. "Get on."

Alfie clambered up onto the wolf's back. He gripped Ceej's fur as tight as he could as the wolf bolted into the forest behind the ridge. Even with the hedgehog clinging on, the wolf raced in between trees faster than most. He weaved between creatures of the fyrd as they were all pursued by Norman paws and hooves. The slowest creatures were cut down as they ran. Some turned and organised defensive standpoints to keep the enemy at bay. Ceej was inclined to join them but knew he had to stay alive. All the foxes were dead. He needed to get to safety; he needed to be able to fight for the next king the Witan would elect. He would never submit to William.

The hedgehog closed his eyes as Ceej ran, wanting to shut out all the pain and all the loss. He couldn't see any more death. He could hear horses and laughing knights behind them and gripped Ceej more tightly.

Please get me 'ome, he prayed. *Get me 'ome, get me 'ome, get me 'ome.*

Ceej was panting hard and the sound of hooves was growing ever louder. Alfie risked an eyelid open.

"AHHH!" Alfie shouted at the same time as the Norman knight leapt from his horse and landed atop the wolf and hedgehog. The horse skidded to a halt as the three creatures wrestled in the mud. The knight, a Norman weasel, yelped as its unsuspecting paws were pricked by the hedgehog's spikes. Alfie himself was nearly crushed by the two larger creatures as they stabbed each other with blade, claw and tooth. The hedgehog cowered in the mud and only came up a minute later, spewing autumn leaves out of his mouth and looking for the wolf.

"Ceej?" he asked tentatively.

"Here," winced Ceej, who was limping away from the weasel's dead body.

"Are yer...did 'e get yer?"

"I'm fine, just my damned leg." The fur on Ceej's right leg was dark and dripping.

Alfie stared, not at the wound, but at what was approaching from behind Ceej.

"Don't move," said the hedgehog.

Ceej froze. "What is it?"

The horse that the Norman weasel had ridden was approaching. It was blacker than night and moved with quiet grace. It sniffed the weasel's corpse and gave a disdainful snort. It began moving towards Ceej.

"Shhh," Alfie whispered.

Ceej gripped his battle axe tight and took a deep breath. The horse was right behind him.

"Wait," said Alfie, noticing something different in the horse's demeanour.

"Wait?" Ceej repeated incredulously. The horse's great head bent down towards Ceej. It nudged his leg and began licking the wound. Ceej grimaced as it did so but he didn't strike the beast. Eventually he lowered his axe and stroked the horse's head, who whinnied happily in response.

"Think yer've got yerself a new pal," Alfie said, and laughed. It sounded like a foreign noise coming out of his mouth and his smile soon passed.

"Guess so," said Ceej, who looked as confused as he did pleased.

"*Là-bas!*"

Alfie, Ceej and their new friend turned to face the shout. A half dozen horses and knights had spotted them. The riders whooped and hollered as they directed their horses through the maze of trees towards them.

"There's too many," Ceej scowled.

"Run?" said Alfie.

"My leg, I can't," Ceej shook his head.

"Then what?"

The wolf and hedgehog looked into each other's eyes desperately for a moment. At the same time, both sets of eyes expanded with sudden inspiration. Ceej bent low to allow Alfie to climb on his back once more, and then the wolf stood and leapt atop the black horse whose allegiance he had won. The beast stomped around but did not throw them off. The Normans were closing in, and their horse wasn't moving.

"Go, dammit! GO!" Alfie cried.

"How?" Ceej yelled, nearly losing his balance. Alfie twisted his head to see the horses pounding towards them.

"*Allez! Allez! Allez!*" the knights were shouting.

Alfie shrugged and followed suit. "Allay!"

The horse shot forward at once. Ceej and Alfie screamed as they were propelled forward. The wolf had to cling on to the straps around the horse's neck and Alfie in turn nearly pulled clumps out of Ceej's fur as he held on as tight as he could.

"Well done!" Ceej bellowed.

"Dunno 'ow to stop it, mind!" Alfie shouted back.

The wolf and hedgehog drew curious looks from other escaping English creatures. They panicked at the sight of the black horse stampeding towards them but when Ceej or Alfie yelled "LOOK OUT!" they lowered their weapons and let the horse tear by. Of course, there was little time to be amused as the creatures also had to avoid the train of knights that were in hot pursuit. The original half dozen hunters called for others and soon there were nearly fifty horses chasing after the hedgehog, wolf and stolen horse.

"They're gainin'!" Alfie shouted against the rushing wind. Whilst their horse was as fast as any in the Norman army, the chasing knights were far superior riders. They manoeuvred the ditches, rocks, bushes and trees expertly. Ceej and Alfie knew how to direct their steed forward but little else. Their horse ran in out-of-control zig zags and soon two horses were on either side of them.

"Hold on!" Ceej roared as he swung his axe at the horse on their right. He missed by inches and the Norman knight laughed. As it raised his mace and aimed at their horse Alfie fumbled for a stone in his pouch. There was only one left. He aimed at the knight but changed his mind at the last moment. He instead aimed it at the horse and fired the stone into its eye. It screeched and spun off running in the other direction.

"I'm out of stones!"

The horse on their left was right beside them. The rider reached for his sword and Alfie looked on helplessly.

"*Arrêtez!*" the rider suddenly cried. The horse came to an immediate halt, leaving them to ride on unchallenged.

"Why'd they stop?" Alfie said. He looked over Ceej's head and saw where they were going. He knew at once.

"Stop!" Alfie and Ceej said together. The horse didn't understand them and continued to run. It scrambled over a pile of jagged grey stones before treading on thin air. They tumbled off the edge of a thirty-foot drop, all three creatures crashing into the mounds of rock that had gathered at the bottom of the dark forest ravine.

Alfie knew he must have been knocked out for a while because when he woke the sun had disappeared and the air was freezing cold. He stumbled around, only seeing what rare shafts of moonlight would allow.

"Ceej? Ceej?"

"Over here," came a hoarse whisper.

"Yer alrigh'?"

"Fine," said the wolf, poorly masking a wet cough. "Thought you were dead."

"Not yet. What about that 'orse?"

"Disappeared before I woke," said Ceej. "Seems he's a hard creature to impress," the wolf laughed before breaking down into painful coughing.

"Yer sure yer alrigh'?"

"Yes," said the wolf dismissively. "I nicked myself on the axe when we fell, nothing to worry about."

"Oh, righ'," said Alfie, who very much thought that sounded like something to worry about. "What's the plan, then?"

"We stay here tonight."

"'ere? I don't wanna stay in no forest at nigh'. There be demons and ghosts around me village, y'know?"

"Are there?" Ceej said, not really listening.

"So Old Monty used to say..." Alfie sighed. He wondered again if Faye and the others had made it to the rabbit's hidey hole. "Maybe I'll get a fire goin'."

"No," Cee said immediately. He coughed some more before croaking, "They might see."

Alfie nodded in the dark. Who knew if the Normans were still hunting?

"Come to me," said Ceej. "Follow my voice. We need to stick together to stay warm."

"Don't think yer wan' me spikes diggin' in to ya all nigh', chap."

"Right, right," said Ceej weakly. "Then let's just be quiet and rest then."

"Ok," said Alfie. It took him a while to find a comfortable spot. He curled into a ball to generate as much warmth as he could and tried to sleep as Ceej's ragged breathing became fainter and fainter.

Alfie woke the next morning with a start as hot breath rolled over him in waves. He jumped up and reached for his slingshot but he had lost it in the fall. He scrambled away from the breath and backed up against a cool, flat boulder. The creature that had been standing over him wasn't a horse or a Norman of any kind. It was a stag.

"Stay back," said Alfie, sounding braver than he felt. He knew stags were native to most forests in England. He also knew they weren't to be trusted.

The stag watched with him curious black eyes and a pair of glorious antlers that sprouted off its small, pointed face.

"Your friend is dead," it said with painful simplicity.

Alfie looked around. The morning sky now illuminated Ceej. The wolf was sprawled on the ground with his eyes open. The pool of blood that came from a nasty gash on his side was already dry.

The stag trod over to the wolf to examine the body.

"Stay away from 'im," Alfie warned, his voice quivering.

"I'm not going to hurt you," said the stag. He looked down at the wolf. "And I don't think I could hurt him if I tried."

Alfie couldn't argue with that. He grimaced at the sight of Ceej; another fine young creature to lose his life. He knew he would never have managed to escape the battlefield without him and made a silent promise to honour the wolf if he ever made it home.

"What happened?" said the stag, looking up to where they had plummeted off the day before.

"We fell," said Alfie, keeping one eye on the stag's antlers.

"No," said the stag. "What happened at the battle? You fought the lynx?"

"Yes."

"And?"

"What do it look like?"

"Hmm," he did not sound happy or sad. "Things are going to change." He thought about this for a moment before deciding, "I don't like change."

"You could 'ave 'elped us. England could 'ave done with your 'elp."

"It is not our place to help."

Alfie shook his head. "William will be king now, and he won't let yeh keep these forests for yerselves. Nothin' will be the same ever again."

"Perhaps, perhaps not. Fate is a funny thing." Without another word the stag began to walk away.

"'ey! Please 'elp me, I need to get 'ome."

"It is not my place to help."

"Please? Do yer know 'ooe? 'ow do I get there?"

The stag gave a stern look. Very reluctantly, he pointed his antler back up to where they had fallen from. "Back that way, I know that."

"Thank you," said Alfie.

"Hmm," said the stag again as he left Alfie alone.

The hedgehog closed Ceej's eyes before he left. He had no idea where he was or how long it would take to find home. He had no idea how many English had survived or how many Normans were still in the area. He only knew he would have to stay low and out of trouble if he could make it to Stony Creek and find his family.

Finally, he thought. *It migh' just pay to be a little 'edgehog this time.*

AUTUMN

Surrender at Berkhamsted

In the days that followed the Battle of Hastings the Normans cleared the stinking fields of corpses. They buried their friends in mass graves but left the broken bodies of Harold's army to rot. William only demanded that the fox's remains be salvaged. He had Harold's body taken to a nearby clifftop and marked the spot with a stone slab that read;

> *By command of the Duke, you rest here a King, O Harold,*
> *That you may be guardian still of the shore and the sea.*

William stood by the grave alone as an aggressive wind whipped up around him. His creatures didn't understand his impulse to bury the fox. Harold, after all, had been the dishonourable one; the fox had stolen the kingdom away from William and deserved what he had got. The lynx didn't disagree, but felt a twisted kinship to the dead king. The fox's past was now his future.

"I hereby shed the name of duke," William told Odo when he rejoined his army at the base of the cliff. "Burying Harold was my last act under that title. In England, I will now be only referred to as king."

Once the battleground had been cleared (William swore he would build an abbey on the site as penance for the lives he had taken there), the Normans continued with their conquest. William had half expected an early surrender from whichever nobles were still out there, but the English forests lay dormant, shrouded in mist. It was so spooky that some creatures did not want to pass through. They claimed that the souls of the damned English were trapped inside. William scoffed in the face of these cravens, but he led the march rather hastily through the misty woods all the same.

The Normans went first to Romney and left it a pile of smouldering embers. Next they headed to Dover which was well defended by its peninsula and rocky terrain. The creatures that had gathered there in resistance lost hope on seeing William's forces and took flight before any fighting took place. The surrounding lands were burnt and any food or treasures seized.

William next set his sights on London, the heart of the English. As his army trooped through the south of England many representatives of towns and cities came to meet him. Word had spread of the Battle of Hastings and the destruction of Romney and Dover. Creatures came offering peace and allegiance. Food and wine were gratefully accepted by the invaders who had only been living off what they could plunder. The most notable creature to appear was a small mole dressed in exuberant, colourful fabrics.

"My name is Stigand, Your Majesty, Archbishop of Canterbury. I welcome you to England," said the fuzzy mole. William could detect the sycophancy before his translator had repeated his words into French. The mole wanted to remain archbishop and William airily agreed in order to get him to be quiet. The lynx had already promised the role to the red squirrel Lanfranc who had garnered the pope's support for his invasion. He would find a way to get rid of Stigand later.

Despite many submissions from many creatures, no representative from London came forward, and William knew there may still be some flickers of rebellion yet.

Indeed, he found London was ready for him. Armed defenders protected the city from the Normans in the name of their new leader: the young badger, King Edgar. Edgar was of the old English line of kings and great nephew to the late King Edward. He was but a cub and William did not fear him half as much as he did Harold. The lynx knew he could crush Edgar and the creatures of London by force if necessary, but was keen to avoid a slaughter. He did not want to reduce London to cinders; he wanted it intact and prospering for when he was fully in command of the nation. William took his creatures west and instead laid waste to the surrounding areas. The lynx let his creatures do whatever they desired to the villages and their creatures. They had earned it.

William then moved north and east, circling London with distant smoke. Halfway through his lap of destruction William paused in the small town of Berkhamsted. He ordered the construction of a motte and bailey castle that would serve as a strong outpost should the London resistance persevere through the dark, lengthening nights.

In the end, it did not take long for the gentle flame of Edgar's courage to flicker out in the winter cold. It was early December when London yielded. A party of English nobles made the thirty mile trek through the snow to Berkhamsted.

William, Odo and a party of fifty soldiers met the English outside the primitive timber frame of what would become Berkhamsted Castle. There wasn't a drop of red in William's fur at this time of year. He was all white and his black spots looked all the more formidable. The sun had already gone down when the English arrived, but the white snow was enough to light every one of their terrified faces.

The translator for the English, a small duck that William recognised from somewhere, announced who had come before the lynx.

"Greetings, Lord William. Before you stand, Archbishop Ealdred of York," Copsi pointed to a stern-looking beaver in an all-white cloak; "Earl Edwin of Mercia, and Earl Morcar of Northumbria," he pointed to two hares; the tall one was shivering whilst the ugly one stared at the ground; and "Earl Waltheof of Huntingdon," a baby-faced otter who also couldn't meet William's eye.

Scandalous bunch of cowards, William thought. *This will have to change.*

"And," the duck said lastly. "Ki..." the duck coughed embarrassedly. "Edgar."

The badger was no king; William knew that from the moment he saw him. He was almost entirely wrapped up in cloaks, but from what little William could see, he seemed to lack the strength of colour in his black stripes.

"Why are you here?" William asked them.

"We have come to surrender," said the duck.

"Do it then," the lynx grinned. "One by one."

Copsi looked shocked, then meekly told the nobles. First up was the otter, Earl Waltheof.

"I surrender to your will, Your Majesty," the otter knelt in the snow.

"I don't even know who you are," William yawned, and Odo laughed harshly beside him.

The hares, Edwin and Morcar, knelt next.

"Y-Your M-M-Majesty," Edwin's teeth were chattering.

"My little birds tell me that you two fought Hardrada - that you were killed? Were my reports wrong?"

"We fought him," Morcar growled.

"With Harold?" said William.

"No," said Morcar.

"Then before? What happened? Did you run away?"

Edwin and Morcar stared at the ground together. William looked away with contempt. He was ready to scold the hares, but Odo whispered in his ear.

"They're the House of Leofric. Old family, best keep them on side for now."

Archbishop Ealdred surrendered next.

"You are a calmer creature than the archbishop I already have," said William, thinking of Stigand. "The mole is an abomination. I will need to be crowned; I would have you perform the ceremony."

"It would be an honour," Ealdred said, looking relieved to be let off so lightly.

"Did you crown this one?" William pointed at Edgar.

"No," said Ealdred. "He wath never...no."

William turned to Edgar with a savage grin.

"So, this is the best you could find?" William asked the assembled nobles. "After I killed Harold, you thought this cub would save you?"

The young badger was trembling, but not from the cold.

"Do I have to worry about you Edgar?"

The badger shook his head.

"I can't hear you."

"I am here to serve, Your Majesty."

The duck translated as usual, but William wasn't listening; he knew the sounds of an English surrender well enough by now. The kingdom was his at last.

"Leave me," William announced. "I give you license to return to London."

The English nobles shared wide-eyed anxious looks.

"Should we not offer them a place to stay?" whispered Odo. "The night is very cold."

"No," said William happily. "Safe travels to you all."

William waited with a beaming smile. Eventually, after much muttering and scowling, the English creatures turned around and started making the long trip back to London. Odo and the soldiers headed back to their temporary holdings for warmth, leaving William standing alone in the snow. He closed his eyes, feeling completely at one with his surroundings.

England.

My England.

William waited until the gentle crunch of paws on snow faded and the English were out of sight before retiring inside.

WINTER

Conquered

Christmas was drawing near. Days upon days of blizzard had abated and the sun now shone unopposed. Its warmth kissed the frozen stream that wove between Hooe and the surrounding fields like a dragon's tongue. The ice began to thaw and the trickling sounds of liberated water grew as the day reached noon.

At the place that locals called "Stony Creek", a great oak tree stood shivering and snow slipped off its knobbly branches. Beneath it, a black button snout poked its way through the white slush and sniffed clean air for the first time in months.

"I'm through! I'm through!" Faye cheered.

The hedgehog scrambled out of the snow-covered burrow and collapsed outside the entrance. She gazed into the depths of the clear blue sky as other creatures began to emerge. Her brothers, the twins Hugo and Benedict, came together. They whooped as they popped out of the burrow and immediately began dancing around. Next came Drefan's sisters, the two young pine martens. They looked around nervously, suspicious that Normans might still be in the area.

Last to appear from the earth was Eleanor, Faye's mother. She was a plump creature and needed a helping paw from the others to make it to the surface. She panted heavily and gave a dignified "Ta," in thanks.

"It's good to be out," Faye smiled, taking another lungful of air.

"Hmm," Eleanor pursed her lips pointedly. She was very wary to be leaving the safety of Old Monty's burrow and had only agreed to it because of their severely dwindling food resources. "Where are those berries, Faye?"

Faye drew out six red berries from her stone pouch and gave one to each of the creatures. The twins gobbled theirs up immediately. Faye placed hers delicately on her tongue and held it there a while before chewing. Its juices splashed against the sides of her dry mouth. She savoured the moment before the flavour faded. She ached for another but there was only a pawful left.

"I want another one," Hugo whined.

"Well, that's what we've got to look for, isn't it?" Eleanor snapped.

"There's nothing 'round here," said Faye. "Why don't we check the orchard?"

"Hmm," Eleanor brooded again. She knew Faye was desperate to see home again and was quite as keen to stop her. It had been many weeks since the Normans had attacked the village, but who could say if they were still there?

"C'mon, Hugo's hungry," Faye said innocently.

"Ok," Eleanor huffed. "We go to the orchard, but if we see any strangers, we're coming *straight home!*"

Faye hoped Eleanor was being facetious in calling Old Monty's burrow 'home'. The tunnel had only been dug large enough to host one superstitious rabbit who clearly hadn't intended on having any dinner guests. Heavy snowfall over the entrance had stolen what little light made it down there and the place had started to feel more of a prison than a sanctuary.

The hedgehogs and pine martens went unopposed as they followed the stream back towards Hooe. The hog twins and the pine marten girls were relishing the outside air. They created a game where they had to hop between rays of sunlight and avoid any shadow. Eleanor had to keep hushing their laughter, but Faye was heartened to see them happy. There had been no laughter in the burrow.

Faye often replayed Drefan's death in her mind. She examined the memory from every angle, hunting for something she could have done differently, something she could have done to keep him alive. It hadn't been easy to tell his sisters that their brother was dead. They had spent weeks not talking and barely eating. Faye was glad they at least had each other and silently promised Drefan that she would continue to look out for them.

As much as her friend's death stuck with her, Faye was more often drawn to the memory of her father. No matter how often she thought about it she couldn't find a single rational explanation as to why he might have been the Normans' prisoner. Alfie had rolled over the big creatures' paws and studded them with his spikes, allowing her to escape. She had been sure he was dead before and was even surer now. She hadn't even told her family about seeing him; it was just too painful.

The joyful atmosphere of the small band of creatures diminished as they reached the outskirts of the village. They glimpsed the scorched wood of burned huts, left abandoned. Lively gusts kicked up idle ash and covered the snow with a layer of dark powder. The creatures gathered together to pray for their fallen friends and neighbours before heading on to the orchard on the other side of town. They still hadn't seen another soul, but they took the long way around Hooe to be sure.

Faye found the orchard to be mostly untouched. Rows upon rows of fruit trees had not suffered the taste of the Norman flames. She could see the dents in the snow where plums had fallen to the ground, but no plums themselves. It seemed a creature had been here to collect them.

"Maybe I should go alone," said Faye.

"No," said Eleanor. "Let's just be quick about it."

All the creatures hurried through the orchard, searching the ground for fallen fruit. At every tree they found signs that the fruit had already been taken. Eleanor huffed nervously whilst Faye drew her slingshot. She had gathered a pawful of stones from the stream on the journey over. She loaded one now and had it primed to fire. There was a pair of wide prints in the snow weaving from tree to tree. Faye scurried after them.

"Faye!" Eleanor hissed. "Don't wander!"

Faye ignored her. The prints were as fresh as her own. She rounded a tree and nearly cried out in shock. A furry beaver was bent over the ground, collecting a series of ripe plums from the snow. She made to put one in her basket and saw the hedgehog standing there. At first the beaver stared blankly at the slingshot. Faye could see the exact moment recognition dawned on its chubby face.

"Faye!" the beaver yelled.

"Mopps!" said Faye. She had known the beaver for as long as she could remember. Mopps was wife to Tata, one of the creatures that had gone to fight for King Harold with her father.

"My dear, I don't believe it!" the beaver hurried over and hugged Faye. "Ouch!" the beaver backed away from her spikes.

"Sorry."

"My dear, don't apologithe! I'm tho happy to thee you alive!"

"It's good to see-"

"Thith ith unbelievable – and after – but you don't know yet – oh, I've got thomething to tell you – or maybe I thould juth thow you?"

"Calm down, Mopps," Faye smiled.

"How did you thurvive?"

"We hid in-"

"We?"

"Yeah, Ma and the 'hogs are here too! Look!" Faye pointed as her mother and the others shuffled over.

"Mopps?" Eleanor panted.

"Oh! How fantathtic!" screamed Mopps.

"Hullo," waved Benedict.

"I don't believe it! Thith ith -"

"Qu'est-ce qui se passe?"

Faye froze. The deep, foreign voice came from two or three trees behind her. Mopps' eyes widened as she saw the creature first.

"Thtay cloth to me," Mopps whispered. Faye sprang beside the beaver and turned around, keeping her slingshot behind her back and out of sight. Eleanor pulled her hogs closer and Drefan's sisters clung to one another.

A creature with a shaggy brown coat was approaching. It had a pitiful tuft of fur under its chin and lazy, arrogant eyes. It strolled across the snow confidently, no doubt emboldened by the two immense horns that curled out of his head.

"*Qui es-tu?*" asked the Norman ibex. "What is...? *Non*...who arr you?"

"They're here to help," Mopps pushed a plum into Faye's paws. "Thee?"

"*Je ne comprends pas*," the ibex squinted at Faye. "I don't know who you arr."

"I..." Faye stammered.

"Where arr you from?" the ibex frowned.

If I can just get one good shot in...

"Ansser me!"

Faye made to bring the slingshot out from behind her back, but Mopps's fat tail covertly slapped it out of her grip.

"Pleath, Faye ith with me," Mopps pleaded to the Norman. "They all are!"

"I am not talkeen to you!" barked the ibex. "Who arr-"

The Norman was interrupted by the whine of a distant horn. He spun around and looked for the source of it.

Let it be the king, Faye prayed. *Come and save us.*

The horn blared again and to Faye's dismay, the ibex smiled.

"He is 'ere."

"Who?" Faye couldn't resist asking.

"Shoosh!" the ibex snapped. "Follow me! All off you!"

The ibex began marching out of the orchard and towards the village centre. Faye turned to her mother.

Do we run? Eleanor mouthed.

No, Mopps interjected silently. *There are more.* The beaver nodded to where a host of Norman soldiers were waiting at the orchard's edge.

The twins began to cry, but Faye grabbed their paws.

I'll get us out of this.

They sniffled and nodded. Faye gathered her slingshot from the snow. Together with Mopps they began to follow the ibex. It led them out of the orchard and into the war-torn village square. There were more creatures that Faye knew here, maybe fifty or so survivors from the attack. All of them looked ragged and many sported injuries from fire or blade. Directing them all into the square were Norman soldiers, at least three to every English creature. They corralled the villagers into a huddle and stood around them, holding their weapons and growling menacingly.

"What's happening?" Faye whispered to Mopps.

"I don't know, love," the beaver replied. "They've had control of the village for weekth. No creatureth are allowed to leave. If you try they...well, they get quite nathty. But they've never got uth all together like thith before."

"No talkeen!" the ibex shouted at them. "He iz almost 'ere."

"Thtick cloth to me, Faye," Mopps whispered, holding her back.

"Shoosh!" the ibex shouted again, and the huddle fell silent.

Silence prevailed over the next few minutes, save for the horn that blared intermittently, getting louder every time.

A team of six horses rode into the square. Weasels rode five of the horses, but the sixth was commanded by a lone creature which Faye recognised at once. It was the one that had been dragging her father behind his horse. Faye immediately searched for sign of a bedraggled hedgehog nearby but there was nothing.

What did they do to you, Pa?

The riders halted in front of the rabble of English. The villagers instinctively backed away, whilst the Normans that had occupied Hooe bowed their heads in respect.

Could it be...him?

The lynx surveyed the cowering English. He seemed to have something caught in his teeth the way he scowled uncomfortably at them.

After a nod from the lynx one of the weasels hopped down from his horse. He grinned at them and cleared his throat.

"*Bonjour.*" The corners of his mouth twitched and he looked ready to burst into laughter at any moment. "My master cannot yet speak your language. Perhaps in time he will learn *Engleesh*, or perhaps it will be easier if you learn *Français!*"

The English shared uncertain looks. Surely he wasn't serious?

"Therefore," the smirking weasel continued. "Imagine my next words coming from that scary mouth up there."

Faye could see the lynx's fangs peeking out from under his upper lip. She could feel her mother quivering next to her.

"My name iz Bishop Odo," said the weasel for his master. "I am brother to King William. He iz in London, and will be crowned on Christmas Day."

Chatter broke out at once amongst the villagers. The weasel rolled his eyes but Odo reached for the club at his side and the English resumed their silence.

"If you arr not already aware, King Harold is dead. Your previous earl, Leofwine, is also dead. I, and that is to say, *him,*" the weasel pointed at the lynx. "Am now the earl of this village and everywhere nearby. I own this land, and whoever's paws touch my grass now belongs to me. I expect this village to grow into a prosperous marketplace. Much work needs to be done."

Faye bristled at the last line.

Perhaps if you hadn't burned half the village...

"We are here to improve this nation...not destroy."

Ha.

"Our success will be your success, and your success will be...mine."

Odo puffed out his cheeks and stifled a yawn as the weasel spoke.

"Who iz leader 'ere? The creature your people call 'thane'?" said the weasel, his little eyes flitting over the trembling English.

Faye looked around as well. Her father had been the thane here but there had never been talk of who would replace him if he died.

"I am," said a voice in the midst of the English.

Faye's eyes bulged. Creatures rushed out of the way as a hedgehog strode boldly out into the open.

Pa!

"Oh my Christ!" Eleanor gasped and went limp. She crumpled to the floor and the twins, who hadn't seen their father, became distracted trying to help her up. Faye barely noticed. She couldn't take her eyes off her father. Alfie didn't look well. There were gaps in his spikes and he had scars lining his furry white face. Nevertheless, the hedgehog stood in front of the lynx and weasel with open disdain.

"You," Odo spat, looking almost as shocked as Faye felt.

"Odo," Alfie stared the lynx down. He hadn't seen his family. Faye was desperate to call for him but found her tongue had turned to lead.

The club-wielding lynx dismounted his horse and stood over Alfie and jabbered in French.

"He knows you," said the weasel. "He says he ought to kill you."

Alfie shuffled forwards.

"Tell 'im I 'ave nothin' left to lose," Alfie sneered. "There's nothin' 'e can do to me now."

We're alive! We're alive! Faye screamed but somehow the words would not come out.

"If you are happy to die..." Odo laughed when he heard the translation.

"Papa?" whispered Hugo. "Is that Papa?"

"Don't look!" cried Mopps.

Odo raised his club.

"Faye! Do something!" Eleanor wheezed from the floor.

Alfie closed his eyes.

Faye unfroze.

"No!"

The young hedgehog leaped through the air. She landed on her father and pushed him to the side. The club grazed her, snapping the tips of her spikes. The two hedgehogs rolled in the mud, eventually coming to a halt still locked together.

"Faye?" Alfie blinked at her.

"Hi, Pa."

"Is this real?" he whispered.

Faye frowned. "Sure, I think so…"

The hedgehogs staggered to their paws. Odo was striding towards them, pointing his club at them both. Faye stood in front of her father and shook her head.

"No!" She spoke with such authority that Odo actually paused. Before he could do anything else, Mopps had raced out. She stood beside Faye, protecting Alfie.

"No," she quivered. "Not like my Tata."

A rabbit hopped to join them, then a mole, then a family of mice. Hugo and Benedict came rushing next.

"Boys?" Alfie laughed.

"Hiya!"

"Papa!"

Soon the fifty strong rabble of English survivors reorganised themselves around Alfie. A pawful of squirrels dragged the still faint Eleanor over. All the creatures of Hooe told Odo together.

"No."

Odo looked amused. He came closer and the English gathered around Alfie even tighter.

Faye revealed her slingshot. She aimed it at Odo's head.

"You won't hurt my father," she said.

All of the weasels that had ridden in with Odo were laughing. The creatures that had already occupied Hooe, such as the arrogant ibex, looked ready for a fight. There was only one winner of that battle if it took place. Faye knew they could all be slaughtered in an instant. It did not matter. The Normans could not kill them all if they wanted a "prosperous marketplace".

Odo knelt down to Faye and Alfie. The slingshot did not waver.

"Hedgehogs." He shook his head and turned away, barking French to his weasel translator.

"My master has other towns to see. He will return here in one month and will expect to see results."

The English didn't move. Odo barked something else, and the weasel smiled.

"He says you can relax. Killing you would not be worth the time it would take to clean his club."

Odo rode away with his weasels. The Normans that had occupied the village remained and they immediately set about putting the villagers back to work. The family of hedgehogs only had moments. The twins nearly tackled their father to the floor with the excitement of their embrace. Eleanor and Alfie brushed noses and soaked each other's cheeks with tears.

Faye hung back from the reunion at first. Only when the ibex began ushering them back towards the orchard to pick more plums did she and her father speak.

"'ello, Spike," said Alfie.

"Alright?"

"Yer saved me, Faye, I don't believe it."

"You saved me first," Faye smiled. "You spiked those creatures!"

"That was William, y'know!" Alfie laughed.

"What?" Faye squealed.

"I've got so much to tell yer!"

"Me too."

"I was lookin' for yer all at the Creek. I couldn't find the entrance - damned snow. Everyone 'ere told me all o' yer were dead."

"I got them there, Pa. I packed the burrow with provisions, just like you said. The Normans had Ma and Benedict, but I fought 'em off."

"My little soldier!"

"What happened to you?"

"I only got back a week ago."

"Got back from where?"

"The battlefield."

Faye's mouth dropped open.

"All in good time," Alfie smiled sadly.

"What next? Where shall we go? Where's the fight?"

"There is no figh', Faye."

"What do you mean?"

"It's over. 'arold is dead."

"There must be-"

"No, we 'ave a new ruler now."

"We can't give in!"

"We must."

"Pa-"

"'Tis 'ow it 'as to be for now. I 'ave met him. *William.* Can't deny he scared me. But 'e wants to rule us, not kill us...I think. What matters most is that we're all together, eh?"

Faye was silent for the rest of the walk towards the orchard, thinking on her father's words. Eleanor and the twins were still ecstatic. They laughed as they collected fallen plums under the watchful eyes of Norman soldiers.

Out of nowhere Faye suddenly felt tears begin to spill.

"What's wrong?" said Alfie.

"We're not going back to Monty's burrow, are we?"

"No," said Alfie. "We 'ave to rebuild our life 'ere."

"But – but –"

"There's nowhere to go, my darling. They are everywhere. We lost. This is our life now."

They watched the twins wrestle in the snow as they both reached for the same plum.

Now Alfie began to cry. "God, 'ow I've missed you all."

"Don't blaspheme," Faye said in her best impression of her mother.

"Sorry, dear," Alfie winked.

"Pa?"

"Yes?" he turned.

"Nothing will ever be the same, will it?"

"No, darling," Alfie sighed and looked around. The ibex was shouting for the twins to get off each other. They ran to Eleanor and hid behind her spikes. "This is England now."

CHRISTMAS DAY

William was never prone to sentiment. He found anger and revenge to be useful enough emotions, but any sort of melancholy was strictly forbidden. It had been so long since he had felt anything of the kind that at first he didn't understand what was happening to him when he looked up at Westminster Abbey. He found his mouth was dry and his stomach unsettled. He stroked his fur goatee and frowned at his own body.

The abbey was linked to both of England's previous kings. It had taken Edward twenty years to create, and his successor Harold had been enthroned here. Now the doors opened for William, less than a year after the badger had died and the fox had been crowned.

Hundreds of creatures filled the courtyard as the lynx crossed and faced the abbey doors. Cheers and jeers mingled into an undefinable uproar. Londoners had made the trek to Thorney Island in their droves to see their new king, but whether to offer support or to disrupt affairs it was unclear. They were being carefully watched by William's armed guard. Any creature with a bright idea of rushing the king-to-be would be met with a dozen blades before they ever got near.

Standing in the archway entrance to the abbey was one solemn-looking creature with a black lace veil covering her face. William paused as he reached her. He squinted at the face behind the veil.

"Lady Edith?" he asked. William had met her many years before when he had visited Edward's court.

The vixen uncovered her face. Her eyes lasered into William's.

"I am sorry for your loss," William said. "Edward always spoke very highly of you."

"Funny," sneered Edith, and William was surprised that her French was perfect. "He never spoke of you once."

A CLASH OF CLAWS

William's lip curled. The last of the Godwin foxes was no less fierce than the others. The lynx gave her a curt nod before heading on.

"I hope your reign goes as well as you deserve," she called after him.

Inside the grand abbey Norman barons and English nobles occupied the pews. William paced down the centre aisle, his strides empowered by the feel of every eye being fastened upon him. He wished his family could have arrived from Normandy in time but the waves of the Channel would not permit it. Even his brother Odo wasn't there to witness his crowning as he was already dealing with matters as William's newly appointed Earl of Kent.

Archbishop Ealdred was waiting for him at the end of the altar beside the royal throne. The beaver was swamped in sparkling fabrics which gave him the rare luxury of warmth in the otherwise stagnantly cold abbey. Stigand the mole stood nearby, grumpily staring off centre. William nodded to the beaver and the ceremony began.

The hum of chatter in the abbey dissolved at once, but the loud commoners outside its walls continued to holler. Ealdred was forced to shout to be heard over the tumult.

"Will you honour our great nation by ruling with the thame grace and thtrength as the best of the kingth that have come before you?" the beaver asked at the end of a winding speech.

"I will," said William in rehearsed English. Every creature in the abbey cheered as was custom.

"VIVAT! VIVAT!"

As the noise rose inside, so did the shouting from outside. The atmosphere in the courtyard had become so turbulent that nervous muttering began to ripple through the abbey. William scowled and was about to tell Ealdred to continue when his nose twitched. He spun around. Smoke was pouring in through the cracks in the abbey doors.

"What's happening?" William barked. Creatures flinched at his booming voice. Eustace the chamois was one of the creatures that rushed to the doors to examine. His eyes bulged when he opened the door, and he soon ran back to William.

"Your Majesty," he bowed.

"What's going on out there?" William snapped. "Are the English revolting?"

"I- I don't know," Eustace blustered. "It's hard to say. There are a few...bodies... on the floor. Our creatures have started...burning things."

William glared down at the chamois, his nostrils flaring. "Get it under control-"

The lynx was cut off by a shriek from some unknown creature. The doors to the abbey were still open and smoke continued to pour in. The English and Normans were getting to their paws and going to investigate. The highest-ranking creatures were being escorted out to safety by their servants.

William shook his head and called them back. Nobody heard him as the chaotic, violent scenes outside took precedence. Eustace ran off to try to establish some order. The lynx turned to Ealdred and waved for him to continue.

"Are you thure?" said the beaver. "Thould we wait?"

William's glare was enough. Ealdred hurried to finish the ceremony.

"I bleth you with holy oil." Ealdred dipped a paw in an inky substance and ran it over William's forehead.

Smashing glass could be heard outside.

"Take your throne now, the theat of kingth." The beaver steered William into the golden chair.

Multiple screams. A creature caught in the smoke coughed and cried for air.

"It doesn't mean anything," said William in French.

Ealdred looked at him blankly.

"All this," William pointed at the fleeing creatures and the swirling smoke. "It's just coincidence. My reign will be pure."

Ealdred guessed the right time to nod. He waddled over to the side and returned holding the crown.

"I hereby name you king," said Ealdred. His paws shook as he placed the crown on the lynx's white and black spotted fur. "Long may you reign, Your Majethty."

Those still left in the abbey barely noticed that the coronation was complete. He rose to his paws, and was met with pockets of sparse clapping.

"There is much work to be done," said the lynx, and with that, he strode away from Ealdred and the throne and marched out into the smoke.

The wings circling Westminster waited for William to appear with the crown before flying to spread the news to every corner of England. The lynx of Normandy had a new name. The less inventive birds called him "William the First, King of England". It was the pigeons who first gave him the title that every creature across Europe would soon use.

"William the Conqueror."

A note from the author...

What I'm about to tell you may come as a shock, but I find honesty to be the best policy. The real King Harold wasn't a fox, mice weren't in charge of healthcare in the realm in 1066, and poor little Copsi actually had real hands.

Despite this sinister skulduggery of mine, I have endeavoured to make the events told here as accurate to their real world parallels as I humbly can. We are approaching the one thousand year anniversary of this pivotal year in English history, so, naturally, the precise details can be a little foggy at times. Whether or not King Edward did in fact promise the kingdom to William before Harold can be debated by historians (yawn), however, like so much of this time, we will never fully know for absolute certainty. I consider my job to be that of the sacrificial lamb, trawling through texts to piece the story together so you don't have to (you're welcome).

So, let's start with whose names we actually see appear in the history books and who I have made up. Faye, Alfie, and their little clan from Hooe are creations, intended to show the common folk of England. As are the English military leaders, Wulfric, Dunstan, and Ceej, and our mouse friend Mabel. Outside of this, the main characters are all names taken from various sources, including Odo, Gyrth and Leofwine, Lanfranc, Eystein Orre, and Stigand.

I am sorry to have written such a horrible end for the fictional beaver, Tata, but I did need a way to show William's brutality. The real William is indeed said to have chopped the hands and feet of people as punishment. As King of England, he also perpetrated one of the worst war crimes in English history. After Edwin and Morcar led a northern rebellion against him in the wake of the events of 1066, William laid waste to villages, lands, and crops. This dark moment is now known to us as the "Harrying of the North", where it is thought that as many as 100,000 people starved to death as a result.

In Tostig's story, we see the fox visit Normandy to petition for William's support. This is believed to be true, though it is doubtful they really did have a duel in the streets of Caen. The comet that appeared overhead was in fact recorded, however. Modern historians believe this to be Halley's Comet, though it was interpreted as a sign from God at the time. After William, Tostig would also visit Scotland before Norway as he sought the help of King Malcom III.

Copsi is the true name of a lieutenant of Tostig, though any information on his personality has been lost to time. I'm somewhat loath to tell you what happened to the real Copsi, because I love that little duck so much. King William made him his Earl of Northumbria, which seemed like a perfect end. Unfortunately, Copsi's rule is believed to have only lasted five weeks before he was murdered by a rival. If it wasn't already clear, the 11th century was a brutal time to be alive.

King Harald Sigurdsson, whose epithet "Hardrada" is believed to translate to "Hard Ruler", is one of the period's most colourful characters. The poems and stories you find in this book have often been lifted from the work of Snorri Sturluson, an Icelandic historian writing in the 13th century. With Snorri writing well over a hundred years after 1066, the line between fact and myth is blurred. However, we do know that Hardrada led a remarkable life and an even bloodier career, fighting numerous wars and serving the Varangian Guard in the Byzantine Empire, and is well worth reading more about if you're interested.

I came across numerous fun stories that have echoed through the ages and have tried to keep them in as much as possible. Kit Iron Jaw, whilst a fictional name, is my representation of a Viking who is said to have solely held the line at Stamford Bridge. This berserker warrior supposedly killed dozens of Englishmen, and was only bested after being speared from below. The Norman jongleur, Taillefer, is said to have sung the *Chanson de Roland* at the Battle of Hastings, juggling and taunting the English before attacking the shield wall alone. Harald Hardrada's banner was a black raven, called Landøyðan or Land Waster, which became a literal character in the book.

As for Harold, the last Anglo-Saxon king, I'm sorry it couldn't have been a better ending for him. He is one of history's most tragic figures; a great strategist and ruler, who was undone by the sheer misfortune of having two invading armies arrive nigh on the same time. The infamous myth of Harold dying from an arrow in the eye originates from the Bayeux Tapestry. The Tapestry is a sort of medieval film played out on an enormous, 230ft scroll, with a number of images displaying the Norman Conquest embroidered into the cloth. It's somewhat biased, as it was made by the Normans themselves shortly after 1066. In it, Harold is the vile enemy, and William the conquering hero. In the image displaying Harold's death, it (kind of) looks like he has been killed with an arrow to the eye. Historians will say this is inaccurate, but I wanted it in the book anyway because why do we always have to take the fun out of things?

Work has begun on the next book in the series, which this time will follow the life and wars of Alfred the Great, the Anglo-Saxon badger who was faced with the largest invading force of Vikings the land had ever seen...

I hope you enjoyed A Clash of Claws: *1066!* If you did, please consider leaving a review on Amazon, so that more people can join us on our tour of history's greatest stories...

A Clash of Claws: *Alfred the Great*

COMING SOON

Keep up to date with developments by visiting
https://aclashofclaws.com/

A Clash of Claws

@a.clashofclaws